# Lickety-Split Meals

## FOR HEALTH CONSCIOUS
### PEOPLE ON THE GO!

**3 Books in 1**

**Recipes, Grocery Guide, Health & Fitness Tips**

by Nutrition Expert
## ZONYA FOCO, RD

ZHI Publishing

*Lickety-Split Meals*

# © Copyright

***Direct reproduction requests in writing to:***

ZHI Publishing
P.O. Box 275
Walled Lake, Michigan 48390-0275
Fax: (248) 960-8157
Email: zonya@tir.com
Website: www.zonya.com

***To order additional copies, see order form in the back or call:***

ZHI Publishing **toll free** at:

1-(888) 884-LEAN

ISBN 1-890926-01-9

This book is intended as a reference to healthy eating and exercise. It is not intended as a substitute for any treatment prescribed by your doctor. It is recommended that everyone receives regular checkups from a medical doctor and inquires specifically about nutrition and exercise recommendations. If you suspect that you have a medical problem, by all means, see your doctor.

The food and exercise tips discussed here are designed to help individuals in general live a healthier and more active life.

# Dedication

## Dedicated to —

**All families and individuals seeking healthy meals and regular exercise, despite limited time.**

**May this book help you, once and for all**

*Make your good intentions come true!*

# Early Praise

**Donna Wielgus Lilley**
**Interior Designer**

"This book is great. The tone of the tips is so positive-I carry it around like a novel. It's better than Richard Simmons talking! I've been on my treadmill ever since! What cookbook does that? And, my teenagers are eating everything & loving it."

**Chuck Bobeldyk**
**VP of Sales and Marketing**

"I love this food. I love eating healthy! And that's really saying something since I was a burger & fries junkie! I liked the book so much, I gave copies to my parents and best friend for Christmas. And now they're losing weight too. 20 pounds collectively, and still counting!"

**Gail Posner, RD, MS**
**Registered Dietitian**

"No kitchen should be without this book. I recommend it to ALL my clients who even slightly cook."

**Trisha Klassa**
**Registered Nurse**

"For a busy mother of two, this book is perfect!"

**Linda Orbach**
**Motivational Speaker**
**and Weight Watchers® Leader**

"I love this book because it reinforces what I teach my Weight Watchers members in every meeting: how to live healthy." I wish this book was around when I went off to college, so I could easily learn how to eat healthy and take care of myself, and avoided years of roller coaster dieting."

**Michele Kranick**
**Executive Assistant**

"I have now lost 21 pounds in just 7 weeks of using your book! I cannot thank you enough for the motivation to start eating healthy and exercising. I'm even finding it easy to keep up with the new lifestyle!"

**Alena Root**
**Opti-Copy Puncher**

"This book is *much* more than a cookbook. I lost 17 pounds in 8 weeks simply from reading *the tips!*"

**Cindy Lucarotti**
**Registered Nurse**

"This book is *SO FUN* to read. You just can't put it down! It truly makes me *not* want fast food now that I know I can get something healthier and more quickly at home!"

**Frances Omanowski**
**Retiree**

"There are so many fast and easy recipes in here! I just love the book. It's well worth the money."

### Jan Hutto
**Bookkeeper**

*"I love the layout and ease of the recipes. After a full day of work, it makes cooking for my family super easy."*

### Jackie Kelly
**Full-time Mom**

*"My husband and I have **each** lost 7 pounds in just 4 weeks of cooking from this book. We love the recipes and all the tips. The book never leaves our countertop!"*

### Robert F. Tacy
**Retiree**

*"I find this book perfect for me, now that I have taken up cooking for the first time in 40 years of marriage. Fast, healthy and easy to follow, this is a book I can use!"*

### Char Brooks
**Busy mother of teenagers**

*"Wow!! What a user-friendly book!!! It is the first time that I can remember making 17 recipes out of a cookbook and all them coming out scrumptious. This book is a treasure!"*

### Barbara Christenson
**Agent**

*"I have made nearly every recipe in the book by now, and have loved everything. This book is the best!"*

### Tess Kirby
**Speaker, Author Consultant**

*"I have always hated cooking and now feel "saved" by this book! I especially appreciate the 1 minute mini-meals."*

### Carol Poulos
**Mother of two**

*"Over 90% of this book are recipes we make on a regular basis, which makes this book so unique. It's just perfect for getting a meal on the table for my family every night!"*

### Sheila Feigelson
**Professional Speaker & Humor Consultant**

*"This is not just a cookbook! It's loaded with so much valuable health information. People just have to get this book!"*

### Tom Holden
**Retired English Teacher and Heart Patient**

*"This book is the perfect extension from everything I learned in my 'healthy heart' classes. In addition to the easy and delicious recipes, I especially enjoy the grocery list. By taking the time to go through the list before I shop, it saves me all kinds of time in the store. Out of all our cookbooks, THIS is the one we use!"*

### Denise Shelle
**Extremely Busy Mom**

*"This book is a dream come true! It is most definitely saving me time! I am really pleased to own it and will continue to recommend it to others."*

### Barb Pursifull
**Home Economics Teacher**

*"As a single professional woman, I love your book! I actually look forward to making dinner now, thanks to you! As a home economics teacher, my teaching is even being affected as the low-fat cooking emphasis is spilling over into class."*

# Acknowledgements

**an•gel** (ān'jəl)
n. 1. One of the immortal beings attendant upon God. 2. A kind and lovable person.

While I've had the idea for this book since I was 16 years old, it would still be just that, an idea, if it weren't for so many talented, encouraging and sharing "angels" along the way:

◄◄◄◄◄◄ My parents, **Grace & Don Edwards**, who, along with everything else, provided me with fine formal and informal educations. Without your love, emotional & financial support, I never would have acquired the expertise for this passion, which truly fulfills me.

◄◄◄◄◄◄ My former colleagues at NutriCare of St. Joseph Mercy Health System, who helped me over nine years to "apply book knowledge" to successful weight and cholesterol control. I'm indebted to you for practical application of lifestyle change, for client counseling, and for helping me with my own weight control issues. My thanks to: **Toni DeMilde, RD; Lynne DeMoore, MS, RD; Diana Dyer, MS, RD; CNSD; Arlene Erickson, MS, RD; Dennis Gordon, RD, CDE, M. Ed; Jennie Hahn, RD; Lori Hunt, RD; Ann Jones, MS, RD; Cheryl Simon-Bell, RD; and Linn Storch, MS, RD.**

◄◄◄◄◄◄ All the delightful clients (you know who you are), who have taught me for over ten years about the obstacles to weight loss. From you, I've learned what is needed to make "good intentions come true," and exactly what was needed to make this book work.

◄◄◄◄◄◄ **Janine Konkel,** who enthusiastically responded to my "thinking out loud" by volunteering to create the initial unique recipe design and typeset the first 80 recipes. Your talent, patience and support getting me over this first hurdle was immeasurable. Thank you, Janine!

◄◄◄◄◄◄ **Dan Gauthier,** who patiently typeset the remaining recipes, working well into the night, and helping me with tough decisions along the way.

*Lickety-Split Meals*

Of course, my graphic designer, (I call her *Princess*) **Vicki Grucz,** whose beautiful and efficient design surpasses the layout I dreamed of. If you have any graphic design needs, give my princess a call at (248) 446-0304.

Then there's the recipe contributors and testers: **Connie & Rich Bloom, Mini Burgess, Tom & Jean Cellantani, Barbara Christenson, Suzy Crossley, Gloria Edwards, Grace Edwards, Jo Edwards, Barb Filler, Trista Foco, Karen Hettel, Lori Hunt, Jay Johnson, Deb Norbotten, Karen Pender, Virginia Pender, Diane Petersen, Lori Poi, Stacy Rafalko, Eric & Ann Tooley, and Elizabeth Wagner.** Yes, Barbara, you won the award for testing the most!

Also, there are the editors, to whom I owe so much, **Barbara Christenson, Pat Materka, Diane Petersen, Becky Walden,** and most importantly, **Katie Enders.** Superb work Katie! If you have editing needs, give Katie a call at (812) 234-8602.

**Holly Noble, RD,** for her professional advice and fine work on the computerized nutrition analysis. Great job, Holly!

Fine photographer, **Murray Goldenberg,** for capturing a front cover photo I'm proud of. (This is not an easy job!) If you have a photo challenge for Murray, give him a call at (248) 350-2420 in Southfield, Michigan.

Professional mentors who've helped me in so many ways: **Carol Brickenden, Barbara Christenson, Cynthia D'mour, Sheila Feigelson, PhD, Lou Anne Flanagan,** and **Rob Pasick, PhD.**

My brothers **Cliff** and **Mark Edwards,** who helped teach me the value of fitness at an early age.

**Caroline Smoyer,** who has never stopped being the best friend in the whole wide world. I love our annual goal-writing sessions. (Hey, this year, I finally get to check this goal off!)

My husband and soul-mate, **Scott Foco,** who *forever* encourages me in my work and everything I do. Those of you who know him know what a very, very lucky wife I am!

**Diane Petersen,** who completely rescued me. It's hard to say which of your talents helped most: editor, counselor, encourager, decision maker, recipe tester, or successful homemaker and mother of three. But together, they've made everything in this book "work." Thank you, Diane, for all your dedication, talents, and hard work!

Last but not least, **all the people who pre-ordered my book!** I know you waited patiently and I hope that it is everything and more than you expected.

*Zonya*

# Table of Contents

*Lickety-Split Meals*

# Introduction

## Lickety-Split Meals:
## How the seed was planted

### Life Lessons 101

I will never forget the summer I was 16 years old. I was working 40 hours a week at one of the nearby tourist attractions for $1.85 per hour. Every dime I made went to support my new (to me) pride and joy, a Datsun 280z. I was thoroughly enjoying my independence and steps toward adulthood.

Like most 16-year-olds' parents, Mom and Dad still saw to it that I had house chores to do. "In addition to working 40 hours a week?" I moaned.

"Welcome to adulthood," they said.

One night while I was begrudgingly doing the dishes, Mom offered a deal that I could not believe.

"You want to get out of doing dishes?" she asked.

"Well yeah," I muttered.

"Since you have your own car now, why don't you get the groceries and make the meals?" Hungry for more grown-up independence, I liked the sound of this.

"I'll make arrangements at the bank and the IGA store so you can sign my checks,"

Mom explained. "You can buy however many groceries you think we need, no limits. Plan the meals, cook them, and I'll do the dishes."

"You'll do the dishes?" Well, this idea sounded really good to me. Cooking was definitely more fun than doing dishes. Then her deal got even better.

"I'll also pay you for it," she said.

"Pay me?" I'd been trying to get them to pay me for doing chores for some time.

"Yes, how does $40 a week sound?"

I did not need to think about this one!

I knew it took me 25 hours to bring home that much money from my other job. Had Mom lost her mind? I knew I'd better jump on this before she came to her senses. I made her shake on it, right then and there.

## The first week

Fortunately, Mom agreed to help me my first week. We glanced through her Betty Crocker cookbook and her trusty recipe box. I already knew how to make 5 dinners, we decided. We agreed that for my first week I could make those 5 dinners, and we would have soup and sandwiches for the other 2 nights. No need to learn new meals the first week. "Why is she being so nice?" I wondered.

Then it was off to the grocery store. She quickly taught me her "no list" method of shopping. You walk up and down the aisles, glancing at everything. If you think we might need it, buy it. And always include a 4-pack of toilet paper. "That's all you need to know," she said.

I was trained and ready. This was going to be a piece of cake. $40 a week, and no dishes. I couldn't wait!

The first week of grocery shopping, I arrived home with $120 worth of groceries.

Mom would have only spent $80. Did she say anything? No. She did not want to discourage me. She knew better than to throw in the economics lesson, just yet. That could come later.

Needless to say, a lot of food spoiled (yes, I overbought). Again, no criticism from Mom and Dad. One night, while making dinner, I discovered that the can of tomatoes I had was 14 ounces and the recipe called for 28 ounces. The store was 15 minutes away. That's OK, I loved to drive my car. It's a good thing Mom never said that dinner *had* to be *on time*.

## The second week

I managed to spend less this week (only $75), but my cooking got worse. All new recipes! I really struggled getting a whole meal on the table at the same time. **Why is it, that after slaving through a recipe, I would read, "serve with hot cooked noodles and a tossed salad??" So when *were you* supposed to boil those *darn* noodles and make that tossed salad?**

I turned to books for help. Shouldn't there be a book out there that instructs people on how to put an entire meal on the table? The only one I found was too gourmet and definitely over my head. I wanted simple, everyday meals that my family would eat. I wanted recipes that were fast and easy to follow. I also needed a list of groceries to buy. **Did I have to make that list each week? Mom never did!**

And thus, the seed for *Lickety-Split Meals* was planted. After 6 years of college, 9 years of marriage, and hundreds of ideas from clients, the seed has blossomed. The fast, easy-to-follow recipes, including how to get a whole meal on the table, and a **complete grocery list, are all right here!**

Then I got to thinking…what about all the helpful tips I've collected from and for clients along the way? All the simple nuggets of wisdom to help win the battle with weight, cholesterol, and finding time to exercise? …**They, too, are included for you.** You will appreciate these inspiring tips about nutrition, exercise, time management, and positive living, sprinkled page by page throughout the book.

**It is my sincerest wish for this book to help you, once and for all, make your good intentions come true!**

# Why *Lickety-Split Meals* is Unique

## Categorized EXACTLY to your time limits

With your demanding schedule, how much time do you have? 1 minute, 5 minutes, 15 minutes, or 30 minutes? Or, would you like to put something in the oven, exercise, and then eat? Is it pasta, stir-fry, or pizza tonight? Or is it breakfast time? Simply flip to the section that fits your needs.

## Easy to read layout for recipes

Just glance at a recipe and you'll see how easy it is to get an entire meal on the table. Great for Busy Moms, Mr. Moms, and just plain Frazzled Moms! Excellent for high school students, college students, singles, and newlyweds.

## All recipes are health conscious

The recipes are designed for today's health-minded family. It seems everyone wants to have more energy, ward off aging and raise healthy children with positive eating habits. In addition to these goals, this book is helpful for people trying to:

♥ **Lose weight**

♥ **Lower cholesterol**

♥ **Control diabetes**

♥ **Reduce risk of cancer**

♥ **Increase energy level**

♥ **Perform well in sports**

♥ **Slow the aging process**

With so many important health recommendations making news headlines, you will be reassured to know that these recipes are designed to be:

♥ **Low in total fat**

♥ **Low in saturated fat**

♥ **Low in cholesterol**

♥ **Low in calories**

♥ **High in fiber**

♥ **Moderately low in sugar content**

♥ **Moderately low in sodium content**

♥ **High in phytochemicals (anti-cancer and anti-aging compounds)**

♥ **In accordance with the *preferred* American Institute for Cancer Research recommendations for eating 9-11 fruits and vegetables per day.**

## Complete nutrition facts for each recipe

### Are you trying to lose weight?

If so, you'll be glad to know that these recipes and menus are devised to be conducive for weight loss. You'll find information on total fat, percent of calories from fat, fiber, and calories helpful in your efforts. Be sure to follow the suggested serving sizes for both the entrée and accompaniments. If you are **not** trying to lose weight, simply take larger servings and/or enjoy extra bread with the meal.

### Are you a *Weight Watchers*® member?

If so, you will be glad to know that you can easily calculate the *Weight Watchers*® *Points*® from the calories, fat and fiber listed at the bottom of every recipe. Most recipes calculate to be low in points, for maximum success. If you prefer, the *Weight Watchers*® exchange values are also provided. *Lickety-Split Meals* is the perfect companion for any of the *Weight Watchers*® food plans!

### Are you a person with diabetes?

If so, you will enjoy knowing these recipes were designed with your health goals in mind. Whether you are following the exchange diet, counting grams of carbohydrate, protein, fat or fiber, the information is provided for you.

(Note: the fat listed in the "Exchange Values" refers to the number of servings from the fat group, not the grams of fat. You will find the number of grams of fat just below the exchanges.)

### Do you need to lower your cholesterol?

Then you are in luck! These low-fat and high fiber recipes and tips will help you to do exactly that. For your information, total fat, saturated fat, percent of calories from fat, and cholesterol are provided. For more information about lowering your blood cholesterol, see my tips on pages 146.

### Complete grocery list so you can make any recipe in the book is for you!

Whether you have health concerns or not, if you would like to eat smart in as little time as possible, then *Lickety-Split Meals* is for you!

Shop from the *Lickety-Split Meals* grocery list, and you'll ALWAYS have EVERY-THING you need. Check the items you run out of, and your next week's list will always be ready.

### Convenient Weekly Menu Solutions

When you hear that dreaded question, "What's for dinner?", there'll be no more floundering, as you will easily know the answer. By following the base "lickety-split" menu, you'll be able to save time on weekly menu planning while still maintaining plenty of variety. (See inside the front cover for details.)

### How to get the complete meal on the table

No more slaving over a recipe only to discover," serve with hot cooked noodles and a tossed salad." You will be instructed when to boil water, when to add the noodles, and when to make the salad, so everything is hot and ready when it's time to eat. When a helper is required to meet the time frame, simply look to the starbursts for what jobs to delegate.

### Recipes eliminate any unnecessary steps

Long gone are the days of boiling the noodles first when making Lasagna and Tuna Noodle Casserole. No more mixing things in separate bowls. You save time both in preparation and clean up!

### Tastes Great!

*Lickety-Split Meals* features tried and true family favorites. The menus are colorful, flavorful, and well balanced. You will find that for nearly all the menus, there is either a serving of fruit or a dessert suggested. By ending your meal with a hint of sweetness, you will feel completely satisfied, therefore ending any tendency to "roam" the kitchen all night!

# Getting Started with *Lickety-Split Meals*

## "Speedisize" Your Kitchen

Are you really ready to take this system to the max, and **save yourself up to 5 hours each week?** Then say *YES,* to investing the time you need to get your kitchen "speedisized"! Minutes spent now will save you hours in the future! (And how are you going to spend those 5 extra hours a week? **Exercising, of course!)**

Some people will have no problem at all turning out one of my 15-minute meals in 15 minutes. Others will swear it takes 40. The magic is in a properly equipped and organized kitchen!

## 1. Clean and organize your cupboards and cabinets.

Still looking for that can of tomatoes? Let me help. Group together canned fruits, vegetables, meats, tomato products, etc. Label your shelves, so that everyone putting groceries away can easily place items on their proper shelf. Hey, there's your tomatoes!

## 2. Clean and organize your refrigerator and freezer.

Say goodbye to wasting minutes searching for a green pepper on every shelf and in every drawer. Designate specific areas for your common items and don't forget a special shelf for leftovers. You will now be able to find things in seconds flat. Now, put on some gloves and tackle your freezer.

## 3. Inspect your spice rack.

How old are your herbs and spices? Did you get those as a wedding present? If so, and you've celebrated 3 or more anniversaries, then it's time to *spice* up your life. Throw those old spices out! But hang on to the containers. With your *Lickety-Split* spice list in hand, head out to your local bulk food store, health food store or co-op, where you can purchase spices *by the ounce.* (The staff will show you how.) You can purchase as little as 1 tablespoon, if that's all you want to try. Once you're back at home, it's time to alphabetize!

## 4. Utensil Drawer

You're only a spoon away from your completely "speedisized" kitchen! Now it's time to untangle that jammed utensil drawer. It should only take 2 seconds to grab just the right spatula, measuring spoon, measuring cup, or ladle, all without skewering yourself! (Unrecommendable acupuncture.) *HANG* in there! If you have the wall space, hang your frequently used utensils, *including your strainer.* You won't believe how much time this will save you!

## Getting Equipped

To achieve the *Lickety-Split* time requirements, you will need the following:

- **Microwave**
- **Food processor**
- **Electric can opener**
- **Slow-cooker or *Crock-Pot*® (see page 127 for buying suggestions)**
- **Silverstone® or T-Fal® coated cooking pans (cook with minimal fat and quick clean-up)**
- **Silverstone® or T-Fal® coated wok**
- **Plastic spatula and serving spoons (appropriate for nonstick cookware)**

# Recommended ingredients that pass the test of time, taste, and health

- **Sharp knifes (and I do mean sharp!)**
- **Sharp vegetable peeler (yes, there is such a thing)**
- **Hot air popcorn popper (optional, but recommended)**

## Crushed garlic in a jar

If you want to make things *Lickety-Split*, you won't have time to peel and crush fresh garlic cloves. Thus, welcome to the convenience of minced garlic in a jar. (Look in the produce section.) Garlic powder can also be quickly and conveniently substituted as well. Here's the conversion:

1 garlic clove = $1/2$ tsp crushed garlic = $1/4$ tsp garlic powder.

## Fresh ground pepper

I highly recommend using a fresh pepper mill. If you have one, you know why! If you don't, simply substitute "10 grinds of fresh ground pepper" with "10 dashes of pepper." And go shopping, ehh?

## Light cream cheese

I find that many people do not like the taste of fat-free cream cheese but love the taste of light cream cheese. To keep everything tasty and shopping simple, all recipes call for light cream cheese. I have carefully calculated and used the amounts that still allow the recipe to meet recommended guidelines.

## Light sour cream

My personal experience and that of my clients, is that some recipes taste fine using fat-free sour cream, while others do not. I therefore suggest buying light (instead of fat-free) and have analyzed the recipes accordingly. If you prefer to use fat-free, please do.

## Parmesan cheese

Parmesan cheese *is* high in fat; however, the amounts called for do not add unreasonable amounts of fat. I therefore suggest using regular Parmesan cheese and have calculated the recipes accordingly. If you would like to use fat-free instead, please do. (I have also had great results mixing regular and fat-free 50-50.)

## Miracle Whip® Light

While I'm aware that fat-free mayonnaise is available, I've found that for taste, many people prefer *Miracle Whip*® Light, which is, therefore, what I call for throughout the book. You are welcome to substitute fat-free if you wish, and you will save a few more fat grams if you do.

## Non-fat plain yogurt

This is a cooking and baking gem that I call for quite a bit. Yogurt is a nutrition dynamo, loaded with calcium, potassium, protein, and other great things. It works great on baked potatoes, in a cream sauce, or in baking. Quite often I will have you mix it 50-50 with *Miracle Whip*® Light, to keep calories and fat grams down, while simultaneously adding valuable nutrients. You can easily transform plain yogurt into any other flavors you desire. For instance:

Vanilla = 1 cup of plain yogurt with 1 tsp vanilla and $1 1/2$ T sugar

Lemon = 1 cup of plain yogurt with $1/2$ tsp lemon extract and $1 1/2$ T sugar

Fruited = 1 cup of plain yogurt with 2 to 3 T jam or preserves (use the flavor of your choice)

## Spaghetti Sauce

The goal is to find a sauce that is 5 grams or less of fat and 800 mg or less of sodium *per cup*. I have recommended *Healthy Choice®* in my recipes simply because it meets these recommendations, and is readily available. However, there are more sauces that meet and even exceed this criteria and I encourage you to shop around for the sauces you like best. Refer to page 178 for selection suggestions.

## Margarine

Margarine goes through a process called hydrogenation (which makes it thick and spreadable). This process creates "trans-fatty acids," which are now believed to be almost as artery-clogging as the saturated fat in butter. Instead of margarine, opt for small amounts of oil. Yes, oil. In almost every recipe, I've managed to use a moderate amount of oil instead of margarine. Do buy a small tub of light margarine (to store in the back of your refrigerator), and use it sparingly. (For more information about breaking the margarine habit, and whether or not butter is better, see my tip on page 151.)

## Canola oil, olive oil, sesame oil

There are many different types of vegetable oils on the market. For the best ratio of monounsaturated fat (the good fat), to saturated fat (the bad fat), the winners are canola oil and olive oil. I tend to use the canola in baked goods, and the olive in tomato-based dishes. If you prefer to stock just one oil, make it canola. It's the most versatile and can be substituted for the others. The sesame oil lends incredible flavor to oriental-flavored dishes, i.e. stir-fries. You'll only need a small bottle of this, and I promise, it's worth getting. Note: You will be using only small amounts of each oil.

## Oil vs. Pam cooking spray

You may be surprised to see that I call for 1 tablespoon of oil quite often in sautéing, while some nutritionists recommend using a cooking spray exclusively. 1 tablespoon of oil is perfectly acceptable for serving 4 people, if there is minimal other fat contributed. If you find that you need more oil because of sticking, buy a new nonstick pan!

## Oat bran

Uncooked oat bran (similar to a dry flour) is located in the cooked cereal section in a "cream of wheat" type box. You can also buy it by the pound in the bulk food section. It's a great way to add cholesterol-lowering soluble fiber to baked goods, etc.

## Whole-wheat pastry flour

This flour is a very nutritious "whole grain" flour, yet it is light and cakey in texture, similar to that of white flour. It can be used in equal amounts to replace white flour in any "non-yeast" recipe. (For more information about this flour, see my tip on page 154.)

Because it is considered specialty flour, it may be found among special brands like *Arrowhead Mills®* or *Bob's Red Mill®*. If not, request it from your grocer. I buy it in bulk quantities at natural food stores or co-ops. Until you find it, you can substitute:

For each cup of whole-wheat pastry flour:

$^{1}/_{2}$ cup all-purpose and
$^{1}/_{2}$ cup whole-wheat flour
(what you do find easily in the store)

OR (as a last resort)
use 1 cup of all-purpose flour

## Nuts

Nuts have many wonderful trace minerals along with fiber and the "good" kinds of fat. As long as nuts are consumed in moderation, they are a fine addition to a healthy diet. (Eating by the handfuls is not moderation! However, it is perfectly acceptable to use 1/2 cup of nuts in a recipe that serves 6.)

## Cheese (mix fat-free with reduced-fat for great tasting low-fat cheese!)

The ideal is to use fat-free cheese. But what about the taste? There are good tasting low-fat cheeses available, but they run 6-7 grams of fat per ounce, which is TOO MUCH. So, when it comes to shredded cheese, why not mix fat-free with the reduced-fat, for a great compromise?

I recommend *Sharp Reduced-Fat 2% Milk by Kraft®* and I mix it 50-50 with the fat-free cheese by *Kraft®* or *Healthy Choice®*. I do this with both shredded cheddar and mozzarella cheeses. This produces a wonderful, tasty, and evenly melting cheese for only 3 grams of fat per ounce. This is the "reduced-fat shredded cheddar and mozzarella cheeses" I refer to in all recipes. If you prefer to use the fat-free exclusively, please do!

# Lickety-Split Meals

## Handy Conversions

| | | |
|---|---|---|
| 3 tsp | = | 1 T |
| 2 T | = | 1/8 cup |
| 4 T | = | 1/4 cup |
| 5 1/3 T | = | 1/3 cup |
| 8 T | = | 1/2 cup |
| 16 T | = | 1 cup |
| 1 cup | = | 8 ozs |
| 1 pint | = | 2 cups |
| 1 quart | = | 4 cups |
| 1 gallon | = | 4 quarts |
| 1 cup of shredded cheese | = | 4 ozs |
| 1 skinless, boneless, chicken breast half | = | 4 ozs |

## Abbreviations

| | | |
|---|---|---|
| T | = | tablespoon |
| tsp | = | teaspoon |
| oz | = | ounce |
| lb | = | pound |
| g | = | gram |
| ml | = | milliliter |
| l | = | liter |
| bxs | = | boxes |
| pkg | = | package |
| qt | = | quart |
| pt | = | pint |
| sm | = | small |
| lg | = | large |
| opt | = | optional |
| 0-1 | = | some weeks you will buy 0, some weeks you will buy 1 (or 2 or 3 as stated) |
| 1+ | = | buy 1 or more, depending on your family's size & needs |

## Hello Canada & England!

| | | |
|---|---|---|
| 1 oz | = | 28 g |
| 1 lb (16 oz) | = | 453 g |
| 1 T | = | 15 ml or g |
| 1 cup | = | 237 ml or g |
| 1 quart | = | .946 liter (946 ml) |

### Nutrition analysis of recipes

Recipes were computer analyzed using *Nutritionist IV* software.

When two ingredient choices are given, the first one was used for the analysis.

Optional items are included unless otherwise noted.

<1 means "less than one."

# Breakfast

## "Breakfast is your most important meal of the day."

I know you've heard this a million times before (I even bet I know from *whom*!) I also balked at my mother's advice for the first 22 years of my life. But then in a college classroom, Mom's advice took on new appeal. A study found different rates of weight loss between two groups of people, although their calorie intakes were identical. The group who ate their calories across breakfast, lunch, and dinner lost more weight than the group eating their calories across lunch and dinner only. This shows how our gastrointestinal tract burns calories simply by digesting food. Starting that process early in the morning (when your metabolism is high) means a higher total calorie burn for the day.

I don't know how this sounds to you, but it sounds to me like breakfast is the most important meal of the day!

Try these great recipes to make your most important meal of the day, the most delicious meal of the day!

# Tip

## Great ideas from people like you!

*"The day I turned 65, something told me I would feel a lot younger if I lost weight. So with guidance from Zonya, I embarked step by step upon my new way of life. I did not follow a diet, just ate nutritious food and didn't deprive myself of anything. By the time I ate all the recommended fruits and vegetables, I was too full to eat junk foods. I felt then, as I do now, that I can eat so many tasty things, all without counting calories. I also began walking for 30 minutes over my lunch hour — raincoat, umbrella and all. Now that I'm retired, my husband and I walk 3 miles, 4 days a week. I absolutely love my new way of life!"*

—BETTY S., 67
maintaining a 60 pound
weight loss for 18 months
and counting

# Breakfast Casserole

Here's a special breakfast recipe that's not labor-intensive like pancakes or omelettes, yet is every bit as delicious. It's ideal to put in the oven before you head out to do your morning exercise. Be sure to keep this in mind for when you have overnight company—they'll love it!

4 OR 8

BREAKFAST CASSEROLE
ENGLISH MUFFINS
STRAWBERRIES, MELONS OR GRAPES

**Preheat oven to 375°.**
**Spray baking dish with nonstick spray.**
**(Be sure to coat the sides of the dish too.)**

Great as a morning
• Oven
Exercise •
Eat!

| For 4 | For 8 | |
|---|---|---|
| ½ bag | 1 bag | (24 oz) **frozen *Ore Ida*®** **O'Brien Potatoes** (hash browns with onions & peppers) |
| ½ c | 1 c | **reduced-fat shredded cheddar cheese** |
| 2 oz | 4 oz | **lean ham *or* Canadian bacon *or* lowfat smoked sausage** (*Healthy Choice*®) |

Use an 8" x 8" pan for 4 servings, a 9" x 13" pan for 8 servings.

Place the frozen potatoes in the bottom of the baking dish. Break up large chunks. Cut the meat into small chunks. Sprinkle the meat and cheese over the potatoes.

| | | |
|---|---|---|
| 2 | 4 | **whole eggs** |
| 4 | 8 | **egg whites** |
| 2 T | ¼ c | **skim milk** |

Whip lightly with a fork in a small bowl. Pour evenly over the potatoes.

| | | |
|---|---|---|
| 15 grinds | 30 grinds | **fresh ground pepper** |

Top casserole with pepper. Place in oven uncovered and set timer for 40 minutes (4 servings) or 45 minutes (8 servings). No, don't read the paper; how about using one of those aerobic videos you have?

Serve with English muffins and fresh fruit.

---

**EXCHANGE VALUES**

| 1 Starch | 2 Meat | — Veg. | — Fruit | — Milk | — Fat |
|---|---|---|---|---|---|

| Nutrition information for — 1 cup of casserole | | | Preparation Time —5 min. | Oven Time — 40 or 45 min. |
|---|---|---|---|---|
| Calories ............................. 165 | Fat ............................. 4.5 g | Fiber ............................. 2 g | Sodium ............................. 355 mg | Total Carbohydrate ............. 16 g |
| Calories from Fat ............... 26% | Saturated Fat ..................... 2 g | Cholesterol ..................... 117 mg | Protein ................................. 14 g | Sugars ................................... < 1 g |

# The Vegetarian Omelette: Friend or Foe?

**Tip**

Did you know that a "restaurant" vegetarian omelette, made with 3 eggs and cheese, served with buttered toast and hash browns, *racks up 50 grams of fat?* That's equivalent to ½ stick of butter!

Thank goodness, knowledge is power and you have choices! Next time you're at a restaurant for breakfast, try ordering my recommendation: vegetarian omelette, made with egg substitute or egg whites, hold the cheese, double the veggies (don't forget the spinach!), dry whole-wheat toast, with jam, jelly, or honey and fruit. If I'm exercising that day, I'll order the hash browns (11 grams of fat) and eat only ½ of the portion (5 grams of fat). Better yet, stay home and make *Scrambled Omelette.* Either way, you will have slashed 50 grams of fat down to 10, and you'll feel lighter and more alert all day!

## Super Time Saving Tip

Skip microwaving the potatoes and chopping the pepper and onion by using *2 cups of Ore Ida® Potatoes O'Brien* (a frozen hash brown product called for in previous recipe). It has no fat, just chopped potatoes, onions, and peppers, and saves you loads of time!

# Scrambled Omelette

Not patient enough to make an omelette, but crave the taste?
Here's the compromise — and they're healthy too!

**SERVES**

4

**MENU**

SCRAMBLED OMELETTE
TOAST
FRESH CANTALOUPE

*Delegate Someone to: Chop onion, green peppers and tomato Slice and peel cantaloupe Make toast*

| | |
|---|---|
| 2 med | potatoes* |

Scrub thoroughly and pierce each potato with a fork. Microwave on high for 7 minutes. (If you prefer your omelette without potatoes, then skip this step.)

| | |
|---|---|
| ½ | green pepper, chopped* |
| 1 sm | onion, chopped* |

Chop (or save time and use pre-prepped frozen!)

| | |
|---|---|
| 4 slices | Canadian bacon, chopped *or* |
| | 2 turkey sausage patties† (optional) |

Spray a nonstick skillet with nonstick spray. Sauté onion and pepper with sausage over medium high heat. Break sausage patty into chunks.

| | |
|---|---|
| 4 slices | whole-wheat bread *or* |
| | 4 English muffins |

Put in toaster.

When potatoes finish, chop and add to sauté.

| | |
|---|---|
| 4 | eggs |
| 6 | egg whites (yes, throw those yolks away!) |
| ¼ cup | skim milk |

Whip together with a fork in small bowl. Add to sauté and stir constantly.

| | |
|---|---|
| 1 | tomato, chopped |
| ½ cup | reduced-fat shredded cheddar cheese |
| 15 grinds | fresh ground pepper |

Fold in when eggs are almost completely done. Cover and let set 1 minute.

Top with fresh ground pepper. Serve with toast and fresh cantaloupe.

Note: If not using meat, you may wish to sprinkle on ¼ tsp. of salt.

---

**EXCHANGE VALUES**

| 2 Starch | 3 Meat | — Veg. | — Fruit | — Milk | — Fat |
|---|---|---|---|---|---|

\* See my Super Time Saving Tip above.
† See recipe on page 17.

---

**Nutrition information for — 1 cup omelette made with Homemade Turkey Sausage† and 1 slice of toast** | **Preparation Time —20 min.**

| Calories .................................. 300 | Fat ................................. 9 g | Fiber ....................................... 4 g | Sodium ........................... 540 mg | Total Carbohydrate ............. 29 g |
|---|---|---|---|---|
| Calories from Fat ............... 27% | Saturated Fat ................... 3.5 g | Cholesterol ..................... 236 mg | Protein .............................. 27 g | Sugars ..................................... 3 g |

**Tip**

If I eat breakfast, I'm hungry again mid-morning, again at lunch, and I seem to eat all day long...

It amazes me that people think this is bad. This is good! This is eating to match your metabolism. I promise that after a day of this, you'll find it's much easier to eat a light dinner with only a little evening snack.

# Scrumptious Swiss Oats 'n Fruit

SERVES | MENU

Think you don't like oatmeal 'cause it's gloppy? Have you tried uncooked oats, the Swiss way? You won't believe how absolutely delicious this dish is! Thanks to Elizabeth Wagner (culinary wizard, caterer and new-found friend) for this dish you'll be proud to serve your family. It saves time on the morning rush and is perfect for overnight guests. This also makes a great "dish to pass" for a morning meeting. Bye-bye doughnuts!

**4 OR 8**

SWISS OATS N' FRUIT
ENGLISH MUFFINS (OPTIONAL)

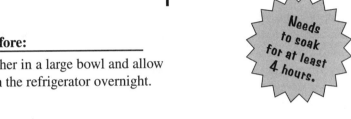

Needs to soak for at least 4 hours.

| For 4 | For 8 | |
|-------|-------|---|
| 1½ c | 3 c | dry oats (quick-cooking *or* old fashioned) |
| 1¼ c | 2½ c | skim, ½% milk *or* soy milk |
| 2 T | ¼ c | honey |
| ½ tsp | 1 tsp | cinnamon |
| 3 c | 6 c | any variety of fresh *or* dried fruit that you fancy: |
| | | • sliced banana |
| | | • sliced kiwi |
| | | • strawberries, cut in half |
| | | • blueberries |
| | | • raspberries |
| | | • bite-size chunks of apple |
| | | • raisins |
| | | • craisins (dried cranberries) |
| | | • dried cherries |
| | | • dried chopped apricots |
| ¼ c | ½ c | chopped walnuts, pecans *or* almonds |

**Night before:**

Stir together in a large bowl and allow to soak in the refrigerator overnight.

**In the morning:**

Add and gently mix together.

Serve in a large attractive bowl with matching small bowls. Include English muffins on the side if you wish.

---

**EXCHANGE VALUES**

| 1.5 Starch | 1 Meat | — Veg. | 2 Fruit | — Milk | 1 Fat |
|---|---|---|---|---|---|

**Nutrition information for — 1-1/2 cup serving**

**Preparation Time —p.m. 5 min. — a.m. 15 min.**

| Calories | 300 | Fat | 7 g | Fiber | 7 g | Sodium | 42 mg | Total Carbohydrate | 53 g |
|---|---|---|---|---|---|---|---|---|---|
| Calories from Fat | 21% | Saturated Fat | < 1 g | Cholesterol | 1 mg | Protein | 9 g | Sugars | 27 g |

## Don't have time for breakfast?

Trust me, breakfast doesn't have to be time-consuming. Here are 5 *fast breakfasts* you can count on:

- *The Eat While You Drive—*
  1 banana, 1 bagel or 3 *Breakfast in a Cookie* cookies, 1 juice box

- *The Eat at Your Desk While the Boss Isn't Looking—*
  8 oz light yogurt with ¼ cup of Grapenuts® mixed in and 1 *Breakfast in a Cookie* cookie

- *The 3-Minute Favorite—*
  Cereal & skim or soy milk and a piece of fresh fruit

- *The "Stick to Your Ribs" When You Know You Won't Be Getting Lunch Until Late—*
  Bagel with a thin spread of natural peanut butter, glass of skim or soy milk, or juice

- *The Quickie—*
  A glass of skim or soy milk, and a glass of orange juice. (Although this liquid breakfast may not seem ideal, it gives you 30% of your calcium needs, good carbohydrates and protein, and 160% of your vitamin C needs.)

**Throw in 3 *Breakfast in a Cookie* cookies and you really do have a meal!**

# Breakfast in a Cookie

Very low-fat cookies that are full of good nutrition — you can eat them for breakfast! This recipe makes a lot so you can freeze plenty for weeks of quick breakfasts, desserts and snacks.

SERVES

MAKES 5 DZ.
(THAT'S 60
COOKIES!)

MENU

3 BREAKFAST COOKIES
GLASS OF SKIM MILK
OR JUICE

**Preheat oven to 375°.**

| | |
|---|---|
| 1 cup | oatbran |
| ³/₄ cup | orange juice |

Mix together in a small bowl and set aside to soak for 10 minutes.

Make ahead for the freezer!

| | |
|---|---|
| 1 cup + 1 T | applesauce, unsweetened |
| 1 T | canola oil |
| 1 cup | honey |
| ¹/₃ cup | firmly packed brown sugar |
| 3 | eggs |
| 1¹/₂ T | vanilla |
| 1 T | grated orange rind |

Meanwhile… combine in a large bowl, using an electric mixer.

| | |
|---|---|
| 3 cups | whole-wheat pastry flour* |
| 1 T | baking powder |
| 1¹/₂ tsp | baking soda |

Measure into a sifter and sift into the large bowl.

| | |
|---|---|
| 1 cup | non-fat dry milk |
| 3 cups | dry oats (quick-cooking *or* old fashioned) |
| 1 cup | nuts |
| 1 cup | raisins |

Add the soaked oatbran and remaining ingredients to the large bowl and mix thoroughly with a strong wooden spoon.

Spray baking sheets with nonstick cooking spray.

Drop by slightly heaping tablespoons, a full 2" apart.

Bake for 12 to 14 minutes.

---

**EXCHANGE VALUES**

| 2 Starch | 0 Meat | — Veg. | 1 Fruit | — Milk | — Fat |
|---|---|---|---|---|---|

**\* If you don't have whole-wheat pastry flour, you can substitute with 1¹/₂ cups whole-wheat and 1¹/₂ cups all-purpose flour.**

| Nutrition information for — 3 cookies | | | Preparation Time — 30 min. | Oven Time — 30 min. |
|---|---|---|---|---|
| Calories ............................... 265 | Fat ............................................... 6 g | Fiber ........................................ 4 g | Sodium ............................ 200 mg | Total Carbohydrate ............. 46 g |
| Calories from Fat ............... 21% | Saturated Fat ........................ .6 g | Cholesterol ....................... 32 mg | Protein .................................... 8 g | Sugars ..................................... 23 g |

# Freezing Bananas

Do your bananas sometimes over-ripen before you can eat them all? Try this— peel them and slip them into a *Ziplock*® bag to freeze. Later, add the still frozen bananas to the *Smoothie* recipe for a frosty-fruity sensation.

You can also thaw and mash the bananas to use in *Nana' Bread/Cake or muffins* (pages 162 and 165).

P.S. A *Smoothie* is an ideal energy booster after a workout!

# Smoothies

These nutrition-packed drinks are very dessert-like. Kids and adults alike love them for breakfast
or a snack. *Smoothies* are especially good for an after exercise pick-me-up. Use blueberries instead
of strawberries for your kids and call them "Smurf" *Smoothies*. The smoothies can be made with
yogurt, skim milk, or soymilk, based on your personal nutrition goals.

4 | SMOOTHIE
BAGEL

| | |
|---|---|
| 1 cup | **skim milk, soy milk** *or* |
| | **non-fat plain yogurt** |
| 1 T | **sugar** |
| 2 cups | **frozen strawberries** |
| | (roughly ½ of a 20 oz. bag) |
| 1 | **banana** (a ripe frozen one is especially good) |
| 3 T | **wheat germ** (optional) |
| 3 | **ice cubes** (if your strawberries aren't frozen) |

Buzz together in a food processor or blender. This produces a thick,
frozen consistency, perfect for eating with a spoon.

| | |
|---|---|
| ½ - 1 cup | **orange juice** |

Add fruit juice to attain the desired consistency, perfect for sipping
through a straw.

Serve with a bagel or a *Breakfast in a Cookie* (page 15) for a complete
meal or snack.

**EXCHANGE VALUES**

— Starch     — Meat     — Veg.     1 Fruit     ½ Milk     — Fat

| Nutrition information for — 1-1/4 cup serving | | | Preparation Time — 3 min. | |
|---|---|---|---|---|
| Calories ................................... 125 | Fat ............................. < 1 g | Fiber ......................................... 3 g | Sodium ............................... 34 mg | Total Carbohydrate ............. 27 g |
| Calories from Fat .................. 6% | Saturated Fat ..................... < 1 g | Cholesterol .......................... 1 mg | Protein ..................................... 4 g | Sugars ..................................... 21 g |

# Why go to the effort to make Homemade Turkey Sausage?

| | | |
|---|---|---|
| **Regular Pork Sausage** | 20-24 grams of fat/serving | 75-84% of calories from fat |
| **Commercial Turkey Sausage** | 8-11 grams of fat/serving | 60-70% of calories from fat |
| *Homemade Turkey Sausage* | 1 gram of fat/serving | 7% of calories from fat |

### And it's more than just for breakfast…

This homemade turkey sausage is called for in the following recipes: *Scrambled Omelette, Herbed Italian Sausage over Pasta* and *Hot & Spicy Pizza with Sausage.* So make some up for the freezer today!

## Money saving tip!

Watch for turkey breast to go on sale. Skin, bone, and grind it yourself for delicious turkey sausage—the guilt-free way!

# Homemade Turkey Sausage

Since truly lowfat sausage is so hard to find, here's one you can make yourself. This sausage is rock bottom low in fat and is delicious. It's easy to make and you can enjoy it for months to come. The larger recipe makes enough to serve sausage every Sunday morning for a family of 4 for 3 months!

MAKES 16 OR 48 2-OUNCE PATTIES

HOMEMADE TURKEY SAUSAGE
SCRAMBLED EGGS
TOAST

| For 16 | For 48 | |
|---|---|---|
| 2 lbs | 6 lbs | extra lean ground turkey breast* |
| 1 tsp | 1 T | black pepper† |
| 1½ tsp | 1½ T | sage |
| 1½ tsp | 1½ T | thyme |
| 1½ tsp | 1½ T | rosemary |
| ¼ tsp | 1 tsp | red pepper flakes |
| ¼ tsp | 1 tsp | cayenne† |
| 10 grinds | 30 grinds | fresh black pepper† |
| ¾ tsp | 2 tsp | salt |
| ½ cup | 1 cup | applesauce, unsweetened |

*Make ahead for the freezer!*

Mix all ingredients together very thoroughly. Use your hands if necessary.

Stack up (16) or (48) 10" squares of freezer wrap or wax paper.

Divide the sausage into 4 equal quadrants in the bowl.

From each quadrant, make 4 (small batch) or 12 (large batch) 2" size balls. Place each ball in the center of the paper squares.

Fold the square up from the bottom, the sides, then the top. This will flatten the ball into a patty.

Put 4 to 8 patties each in a Ziplock® freezer bag and freeze.

## To cook:

Spray a nonstick skillet with cooking spray. Place skillet over medium high heat.

Unwrap frozen patties (no need to thaw) and place on skillet.

Cook patties 3 minutes on each side or until they are no longer pink.

Serve with scrambled eggs and toast.

\* If grinding turkey yourself, use either cutter for fine or coarse sausage, depending on which you like best.
† Three types of pepper are used to enhance flavor.

EXCHANGE VALUES
— Starch   1 Meat   — Veg.   — Fruit   — Milk   — Fat

| Nutrition information for — 1 turkey sausage | | | Preparation Time — 30 min. | |
|---|---|---|---|---|
| Calories ................................. 25 | Fat ........................................ < 1 g | Fiber ........................................ < 1 g | Sodium ............................. 110 mg | Total Carbohydrate ............ < 1 g |
| Calories from Fat .................. 7% | Saturated Fat ..................... < 1 g | Cholesterol .......................... 9 mg | Protein ................................. 4.5 g | Sugars ........................................ 0 g |

# Tip

**But I'm never hungry in the morning!**
**The mere thought of food makes me nauseous....**

As soon as I hear this from a client, I quickly ask about their nighttime nibbling. If you eat at night, very little digestion occurs during sleep. You wake up with a full stomach, so of course you are not going to feel hungry. When you start matching your eating to your metabolism and eat less at night, you will be hungry in the morning.

# Whole-Grain Pancakes

While you may think you love the white flour pancakes you grew up with, wait 'til you change over to whole grain. These offer texture without being too grainy. And talk about nutrition packed! A great way to start your day!

| SERVES | MENU |
|---|---|
| 6 | WHOLE-GRAIN PANCAKES |
| | APPLESAUCE |
| | FRESH FRUIT |

| | |
|---|---|
| 2 cups | whole-wheat pastry flour* |
| ½ cup | wheat germ (*or* just use more flour) |
| 2 tsp | baking powder |
| 1 T | sugar |

In a medium-size bowl, stir together until baking powder is well distributed.

| | |
|---|---|
| 1 | egg |
| 2 | egg whites |
| 2½ cups | skim milk *or* soy milk |

Add all at once to the flour and mix just until combined.

Heat griddle over medium-high heat. Spray with nonstick cooking spray. (It should be hot enough so that when you sprinkle drops of water on the surface, they dance.)

Use a ¼ cup measuring cup to measure and pour the cakes. Turn when bubbles come to the surface and pop, and the edges are slightly dry.

Serve with applesauce or light syrup and fresh fruit.

Makes approximately 18 pancakes. Left-over pancakes can be re-warmed in the microwave the next day, or frozen for another day.

---

**EXCHANGE VALUES**

| 2 Starch | 1 Meat | — Veg. | — Fruit | — Milk | — Fat |
|---|---|---|---|---|---|

\* If you don't have whole-wheat pastry flour, you can substitute with 1½ cups whole-wheat and 1½ cups all-purpose flour.

**Nutrition information for — 3 pancakes**

**Preparation Time — 40 min.**

| | | | | |
|---|---|---|---|---|
| Calories .................... 200 | Fat .................... 2.5 g | Fiber .................... 4 g | Sodium .................... 245 mg | Total Carbohydrate .................... 35 g |
| Calories from Fat ........ 10% | Saturated Fat ........ < 1 g | Cholesterol ........ 37 mg | Protein .................... 12 g | Sugars .................... 8 g |

## Changing Your Sweet Tooth

# Tip

*It is* possible for you to change your sweetness acuity. For instance, if you like to pour ¹/₂ cup of syrup on your pancakes, you can gradually reduce the amount. Soon, you are topping pancakes with only fruit.

Likewise, if you like 3 teaspoons of sugar on cereal or oatmeal, you can slowly cut back to 1. Sprinkling cinnamon, raisins, and other fruits on your cereal sweetens it while adding nutritional value.

Try these strategies for both yourself, and your kids!

# Banana-Oat Pancakes

SERVES | MENU

Since we are big fans of pancakes, I thought you'd like both of our favorite recipes. If we have bananas, we make these. If not, we make the previous *"Whole-Grain" Pancakes*. Enjoy!

**4**

**BANANA-OAT PANCAKES**

**FRESH CANTALOUPE AND BERRIES**

| | |
|---|---|
| ³/₄ cup | **dry oats** (quick-cooking *or* old fashioned) *or* **oatbran** |
| 2 cups | **skim milk** *or* **soy milk** |

Mix these together in a medium size bowl, and let them sit for 5 minutes to give them some extra "soaking" time.

| | |
|---|---|
| 1 cup | **whole-wheat pastry flour*** |
| 1 T | **baking powder** |

Mix together with a fork in another bowl. Be sure the baking soda is evenly distributed. Add to the soaking oats and stir.

| | |
|---|---|
| 1 | **egg** (*or* 2 egg whites) |

Gently mix in.

| | |
|---|---|
| 2 | **bananas** |
| ¹/₄ cup | **chopped walnuts** (optional) |

Slice bananas very thin. Fold with nuts into the batter.

Heat griddle over med-high heat, spray with cooking spray. (It should be hot enough so that when you sprinkle drops of water on the surface, they dance.)

Use ¹/₄ cup of batter for each pancake, cooking over medium heat. After spooning the batter onto the pan, give the pan a quick shake to spread the batter out slightly. Cook for about 2 minutes or until bubbles appear on the surface. Flip the pancakes and cook for another minute or so.

Serve with reduced calorie syrup, fruit spread, or applesauce on top, and fresh cantaloupe or berries on the side. Makes approximately 12 pancakes.

***** If you don't have whole-wheat pastry flour, you can substitute with 1¹/₂ cups whole-wheat and 1¹/₂ cups all-purpose flour.**

---

**EXCHANGE VALUES**

| 2 Starch | 1 Meat | — Veg. | 1 Fruit | — Milk | — Fat |
|---|---|---|---|---|---|

**Nutrition information for — 3 pancakes**

**Preparation Time — 45 min.**

| | | | | | |
|---|---|---|---|---|---|
| Calories ................. 295 | Fat ........................ 7.5 g | Fiber ..................... 5 g | Sodium ................. 445 mg | Total Carbohydrate ..... 48 g | |
| Calories from Fat ..... 22% | Saturated Fat ......... 1 g | Cholesterol ......... 55 mg | Protein ................. 13 g | Sugars ..................... 15 g | |

## Favorite Exercise Videos

**Tip**

Speaking of buns, one of my favorite exercise videos is "8-Minute Buns." These are very effective exercises for firming up. Also available are the "8-Minute Abs," "8-Minute Arms," and "8-Minute Legs," all of which are excellent and worthwhile. Call Collage Video at 1-800-433-6769 to order.

# Glazed Cinnamon Nut Buns

What a delicious holiday treat! You'll especially enjoy serving these for your overnight guests. Waking them up to this mouth watering aroma will make you a favorite host/hostess!

**SERVES**

9

(CAN BE
DOUBLED)

**MENU**

GLAZED CINNAMON NUT BUNS

FRESH FRUIT

YOGURT

*Set frozen dough out the night before to rise.*

| 1 | **frozen honey wheat bread dough** <br> **(1 lb.) (unbaked loaf)** |
|---|---|

### Night before (about 10:00 p.m.)

Remove dough from freezer and plastic bag. Place in a medium-size bowl. Cover with plastic wrap. Set out to thaw and rise overnight.

### In the morning (about 7:30 a.m.)

Prepare a clean work surface and dust with flour. *(I use the countertop or a cutting board.)* Punch down dough and roll out until it reaches a 10" x 12" rectangle.

| 3 T | **light corn syrup*** |
|---|---|

Evenly spread across dough.

Recipe continued on next page.

\* **1 T of light margarine can be substituted.**

# Tip

## What's your secret to fitness?

"As you might guess, as a mother of 3 (all under the age of 6), I have little time to myself. What works for me is to work-out before the kids wake up. Five mornings each week, I'm up at 6:30 a.m. and on my stepper by 6:40. At 7:00 I change to my treadmill. At 7:20 I cool down and do 100 sit-ups. At 7:30 I'm in the shower. (If any child wakes up early, my husband knows he's on duty.) I am both physically and mentally prepared for my children when my husband leaves for work and they wake up by 8:00."

—DIANE PETERSEN, 35
Attaining and maintaining her ideal weight (and flat stomach!) despite 3 C-sections. Wow!

| 3 T | sugar |
|---|---|
| 1½ tsp | cinnamon |
| ¼ cup | chopped almonds, pecans |
| | *or* **walnuts** (optional) |

Mix together in a 1 cup measuring cup and sprinkle across dough.

Begin rolling, starting on the long side, to form a long cylinder. Pinch the seams together to seal.

Spray an 8" x 8" baking dish with nonstick spray.

Cut roll into 9 equal slices and place in baking dish with spirals facing up and sides touching.

**Preheat oven to 350°.**

Cover the rolls and allow to sit on top of the stove for 45 minutes to 1 hour while the oven preheats to 350°. The warmth of the oven will help facilitate the 2nd rise. (*I use this time to grab a shower!*)

### About 8:45 or 9:00 a.m.

Place in oven to bake 15 to 17 minutes.

Meanwhile… slice fresh fruit, set out yogurt, juice & coffee.

Cool the rolls 5 minutes before removing them from the pan.

| ½ cup | powdered sugar |
|---|---|
| 2½ tsp | skim milk |
| ¼ tsp | vanilla |

Mix together the glaze in a small cup.

Transfer rolls to a serving platter. Drizzle with glaze.

### About 9:15 a.m.

Serve with yogurt and fresh fruit, and watch your guests' eyes pop!!

---

**EXCHANGE VALUES**

2.5 Starch — Meat — Veg. — Fruit — Milk — Fat

**Nutrition information for — 1 Cinnamon Nut Bun**  Preparation Time — 30 min.  Oven Time — 15-17 min.

| | | | |
|---|---|---|---|
| Calories ................................. 210 | Fat ........................................ 4 g | Fiber ................................. 2.5 g | Sodium ............................. 290 mg | Total Carbohydrate ............. 40 g |
| Calories from Fat ............... 16% | Saturated Fat ................... < 1 g | Cholesterol ..................... < 1 mg | Protein ................................. 7 g | Sugars ................................. 15 g |

# Tip

## This sleepy head's goof-proof method of getting up early to exercise:

1. The night before, I lay out exercise clothes in the bathroom (not beside the bed; that NEVER worked!), appropriate for both indoor and outdoor temperatures. (You know how plans may change, depending upon what the morning brings.)

2. I set my bedside alarm for 5:55 a.m., and a second alarm in the bathroom for 6:00 a.m. (The first alarm warns me before I actually have to get up.) The screaming bathroom alarm is my insurance to be up by 6:00 a.m. And there, lo and behold, are my exercise clothes, waiting for me!

3. While brushing my teeth, I focus on how good it feels to get my workout in before work, and how disappointed I would be if I didn't. (This is key— associating more pleasure with my new habit, and pain to my old.)

4. Once downstairs, I drink diluted juice to rehydrate and provide carbohydrates to get me going.

5. Music is my next saving grace. It does wonders for waking me up and energizing me. Out the door I go, or onto my exercise equipment.

While you may still feel groggy the first couple of days, your body will adjust. Be persistent! Before you know it, you'll be a die-hard morning exerciser too!

# Ambrosia Rice

The next time you find yourself with 2 cups of leftover plain rice, turn it into this! Not only does it make a delicious breakfast, but also a delight for the lunch box, picnic basket, or dessert table.

Great use for leftover cooked rice.

| | | |
|---|---|---|
| 2 cans | (8 oz each) **pineapple tidbits, in its own juice** | |
| 1 can | (15 oz) **Mandarin oranges** | |

Open cans and drain.

Reserve pineapple juice for another use.

| | |
|---|---|
| 2 cups | **cooked brown rice** (chilled) |
| ½ cup | **chopped pecans, walnuts** *or* **almonds** |
| ¼ cup | **oat bran** (dry, uncooked) |
| 2 cups | **seedless red grapes, washed well, patted dry** |
| ½ cup | **raisins** *or* **chopped dried apricots** |
| 1 container | ( 8 oz) **of strawberry yogurt*** |
| dash | **cinnamon and nutmeg** (optional) |

Add and mix gently.

Serve now or later. Will keep in fridge for 2 days.

---

**EXCHANGE VALUES**

| 1 Starch | — Meat | — Veg. | 2 Fruit | — Milk | 1 Fat |
|---|---|---|---|---|---|

\* If all you have is plain yogurt, simply stir in 2 T of strawberry jam or preserves to 1 cup of plain yogurt. Other flavors, like raspberry and peach, work great as well.

**Nutrition information for — 1 cup**

**Preparation Time — 10 min.**

| | | | |
|---|---|---|---|
| Calories ............................... 240 | Fat ...................................... 6 g | Fiber ..................................... 3 g | Sodium ............................... 20 mg | Total Carbohydrate ............. 44 g |
| Calories from Fat ............... 21% | Saturated Fat .................. < 1 g | Cholesterol ......................... 0 mg | Protein ................................. 4.5 g | Sugars .................................. 29 g |

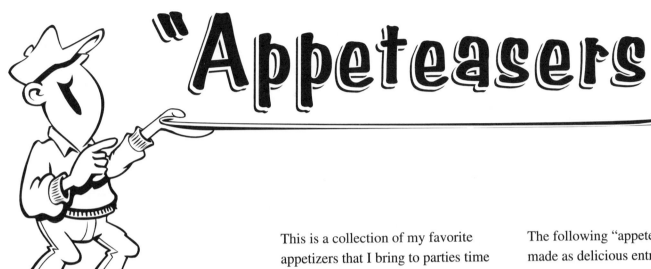

# "Appeteasers"

You're invited over to friends on Friday night. Great! You've been asked to bring an appetizer. Hmmm! What should you bring? The pressure to bring something everyone will like, and that you'll be proud of, can be quite nerve-racking. You want it to be attractive, delicious, unsuspectingly healthy, and above all, FAST. Wonder no more; it's all right here!

This is a collection of my favorite appetizers that I bring to parties time and time again. No more shuffling through mounds of recipes to find something tasty and easy, just thumb through these. *That's* a time saver in itself! And if you've used the *"Lickety-Split"* grocery list, you have all the ingredients you need.

Keep in mind these other recipes, which also make great "appeteasers."

- *Guiltless Nachos Supreme* (15-Minute Meals, page 51)
- *Shrimp Pizza* (Pizza page 109) or any of the pizzas

The following "appeteasers" can be made as delicious entrées.

- *Benito Bean Dip* (for burritos)
- *7-Layer Bean Dip*
- *Marinated Sesame Chicken Kabobs*
- *Simple Tofu Bites* (to stuff pitas or top salads)
- *Oklahoma Bean Dip* (to stuff pitas or top salads)
- *Herbed Salmon Spread* (to make sandwiches)

Enjoy these "appeteasers"; they are fast, fun and tasty!

## Food Processor Cleaning Tip

When processing dips, spreads, or cheese-cake batter that clings to the metal blade, try this cleaning tip:

1. Scrape most of the food out of the work-bowl with a rubber spatula, leaving the blade in place.

2. Put the bowl, with the blade, back in place on the base. Cover and process for about 2 seconds.

The excess food will spin off, leaving a clean blade!

# Benito Bean Dip

My husband makes this almost as soon as we run out. Also perfect for making *Benito Bean Burritos* and *Chicken and Bean Enchiladas*.

A favorite at parties!

| | |
|---|---|
| **3** | **green onions** (optional) |

| | |
|---|---|
| **1 jar** | **(48 oz) pinto beans, rinsed and drained** |
| **1 cup** | **salsa** |
| **¹/₂ tsp** | **cumin *or* chili powder** (optional) |

**5 minutes before serving:**

Chop in the food processor.

Add to processor and blend thoroughly.

Serve at room temperature or slightly chilled.

Serve with *Baked Tostitos®* or *Bagel Chips* (page 29).

---

**EXCHANGE VALUES**

2 Starch — Meat — Veg. — Fruit — Milk — Fat

**Nutrition information for — 1/3 cup dip with 10 baked corn chips**          **Preparation Time — 5 min.**

| | | | | |
|---|---|---|---|---|
| Calories .................................. 180 | Fat ............................................. 1 g | Fiber ...................................... 10 g | Sodium ............................. 500 mg | Total Carbohydrate ............. 37 g |
| Calories from Fat .................. 5% | Saturated Fat ........................ 0 g | Cholesterol ........................... 0 mg | Protein ..................................... 7 g | Sugars ........................................ 1 g |

**Party Survival Tip #1: Plan ahead**

Eat a low-fat breakfast and lunch to save-up a few extra fat grams to spend at the party. However, do NOT arrive at the party overly hungry either! In fact, eating a small snack before you go is a good idea.

# 7-Layer Bean Dip

Thanks to our neighbors, Dan & Karen Hettel, you can make this popular party appetizer which has been a hit at many of our get-togethers. It's both attractive and delicious!

Also makes a delicious, yet healthy, Friday night meal!

**20 minutes before serving:**

| | |
|---|---|
| 2 cups | *Benito Bean Dip* (see previous recipe) |

Spread this mixture all across a large decorative serving platter.

| | |
|---|---|
| 3 | green onions, chopped |
| 2 cups | shredded lettuce |
| 1 | green pepper, seeded and chopped |
| 2 | tomatoes, chopped |
| 4 oz | reduced-fat shredded cheddar cheese |
| 15 slices | black olives (optional) |

Layer on in the order listed.

| | |
|---|---|
| 1 large bag | baked tortilla chips (*Tostitos®*) |

Open chips, it's party time!

---

**EXCHANGE VALUES**

2 Starch — Meat — Veg. — Fruit — Milk — Fat

| Nutrition information for — approximately 1/4 cup of dip with 10 baked corn chips | | Preparation Time — 20 min. | |
|---|---|---|---|
| Calories ................................. 160 | Fat ........................................ 3 g | Fiber ........................................ 5 g | Sodium ............................. 365 mg |
| Calories from Fat ................ 14% | Saturated Fat ................... < 1 g | Cholesterol ......................... 5 mg | Protein ................................... 6 g |

| Total Carbohydrate ............. 30 g |
|---|
| Sugars ....................................... 1 g |

# Tip

## Party Survival Tip #2:
## Include exercise before you go

Let's face it, parties generally mean a few more calories than you usually eat. Overindulge on a day you don't exercise and your fat cells will grow all night long! To prevent this from happening, be sure to exercise before you go.

# Oklahoma Bean Dip

My thanks to Gloria Edwards for this tasty recipe that has become a regular at our family get-togethers. Great with *Baked Tostitos®*, rolled up in a flour tortilla or stuffed into a pita pocket for a quick sandwich. For a real change, try this served on top of tossed salad. You won't need dressing, since it's already in!

*Also makes a quick meal!*

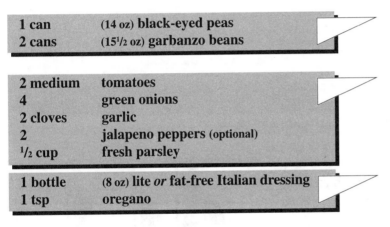

**2 or more hours before serving:**

Drain and rinse. Place in a medium size bowl.

| | |
|---|---|
| 1 can | (14 oz) **black-eyed peas** |
| 2 cans | (15½ oz) **garbanzo beans** |

Chop and place in bowl.

| | |
|---|---|
| 2 medium | **tomatoes** |
| 4 | **green onions** |
| 2 cloves | **garlic** |
| 2 | **jalapeno peppers** (optional) |
| ½ cup | **fresh parsley** |

Add to mix.

| | |
|---|---|
| 1 bottle | (8 oz) **lite *or* fat-free Italian dressing** |
| 1 tsp | **oregano** |

Mix all ingredients well.

Let stand for 2 hours or more before serving. This will keep for 5 days in your refrigerator.

**Just before serving:**

Toss beans gently and serve with chips.

| | |
|---|---|
| 1 bag | **baked tortilla chips** (*Tostitos®*) |

---

**EXCHANGE VALUES**

| 3 Starch | — Meat | — Veg. | — Fruit | — Milk | — Fat |
|---|---|---|---|---|---|

Nutrition information for — approximately 1/2 cup of dip with 10 baked corn chips

Preparation Time — 12 min.

| | | | |
|---|---|---|---|
| Calories .................................. 215 | Fat ............................................... 3 g | Fiber ............................................... 7 g | Sodium ............................. 665 mg | Total Carbohydrate ............. 42 g |
| Calories from Fat ............... 13% | Saturated Fat ...................... < 1 g | Cholesterol ....................... < 1 mg | Protein ....................................... 7 g | Sugars ........................................ 5 g |

## Party Survival Tip #3:
## Bring a low-fat dish

In addition to picking a recipe from this chapter, a vegetable tray or a platter of sliced fruit are also great ideas. My favorite quick fruit dip is lemon yogurt. You can mix it up yourself, using $1/2$ tsp lemon extract and $1^1/_2$ T sugar per 8 ozs plain non-fat yogurt. For a vegetable dip, I simply use bottled low-fat or fat-free Ranch dressing.

# Herbed Salmon Spread

This makes an excellent party appetizer. Serve inside a hollowed out loaf of round pumpernickle bread and eat with the bread cubes. This is also wonderful served with bagel or pita chips, or crackers. Try it as a lunchtime sandwich spread!

| 2 cups | plain non-fat yogurt |
|---|---|

**16 hours before serving:**

Line a strainer with a paper coffee filter or cheesecloth. Place over a bowl. Spoon yogurt onto coffee filter, cover and refrigerate for 10 to 14 hours.

Yogurt will now be thick. Discard the collected liquid beneath or use it in soups or breads. Remove yogurt from the filter and place in a small bowl.

| 1 can | (15 oz) red *or* pink salmon packed in water, drained |
|---|---|
| 1 T | *Miracle Whip®* Light |
| 1 T | fresh parsley, chopped |
| 1 T | green onion, tops and bottoms, chopped |
| ¹/₄ tsp | dill |
| ¹/₄ tsp | thyme |

**2 to 4 hours before serving:**

Gently mix into yogurt. Serve now or refrigerate 2 or more hours before serving.

Serve with *Bagel Chips* (page 29).

Note: If "water puddles" appear after the dip has sat awhile, simply stir.

---

**EXCHANGE VALUES**

| 1 Starch | 1 Meat | — Veg. | — Fruit | — Milk | — Fat |
|---|---|---|---|---|---|

**Nutrition information for — approximately 4 T spread on 4 *Bagel Chips***

Preparation Time — 12 min.

| Calories ..................... 140 | Fat ........................... 4 g | Fiber ..................................... .5 g | Sodium ........................... 260 mg | Total Carbohydrate ............. 16 g |
|---|---|---|---|---|
| Calories from Fat ............... 23% | Saturated Fat ................... < 1 g | Cholesterol ...................... 24 mg | Protein ..................................... 12 g | Sugars ..................................... 2 g |

## Tip

## Party Survival Tip #4: Use a plate

One thing that puts on weight, is eating more than you're aware of. Anytime you nibble on things directly from the bowl, you can end up eating more than if you put all the food on a plate. Therefore, **make a rule for yourself: everything goes on a plate.** Make it a small plate for even better results!

# Holiday Crab Dip

So simple and delicious yet very low in fat and calories.
Serve with homemade bagel chips or whole-wheat crackers.

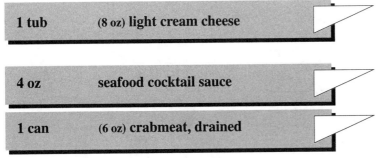

| **1 tub** | (8 oz) **light cream cheese** |
| --- | --- |

Allow to soften, then mash and spread across the bottom of a decorative serving platter.

| **4 oz** | **seafood cocktail sauce** |
| --- | --- |

Spread over the cream cheese.

| **1 can** | (6 oz) **crabmeat, drained** |
| --- | --- |

Sprinkle chunks over the sauce.

Circle the platter with whole-wheat crackers or *Bagel Chips* (page 29).

---

**EXCHANGE VALUES**

| 1.5 Starch | 1 Meat | — Veg. | — Fruit | — Milk | — Fat |
| --- | --- | --- | --- | --- | --- |

**Nutrition information for — approximately 4 T of dip and 4 *Bagel Chips***      **Preparation Time — 5 min.**

| Calories ...................................... 195 | Fat ...................................... 5.5 g | Fiber ...................................... 1 g | Sodium ............................. 590 mg | Total Carbohydrate ............. 24 g |
| --- | --- | --- | --- | --- |
| Calories from Fat ............... 26% | Saturated Fat ...................... 3 g | Cholesterol ...................... 35 mg | Protein ................................... 10 g | Sugars ...................................... 4 g |

## Party Survival Tip #5: Put foods to the "pinch, slip, and shine" test

**Tip**

One way to scout out fat is to look and do the pinch test for its "slip and shine." The following are appetizers that will undoubtedly give you a positive reading on that very test, therefore alerting you to avoid them:

- Egg rolls
- Buttery crackers
- Potato chips
- Pigs-in-a-blanket
- Chicken wings
- Meatballs
- Anything wrapped in bacon

These bagel chips pass the test with no sign of "slip and shine." On the contrary, a bag of commercial bagel chips has enough "slip" to shine several pairs of shoes!

# Bagel Chips

Looking for a snack that's a hit? These are absolutely terrific served with any dip, but especially, *Herbed Salmon Spread, Holiday Crab Dip* or *Benito Bean Dip.* Also makes a delicious "road trip" munchie all by itself.

**Preheat oven to 350°.**

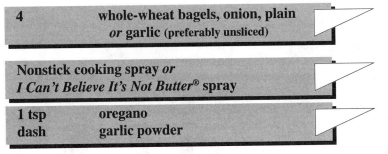

| 4 | whole-wheat bagels, onion, plain *or* garlic (preferably unsliced) |
|---|---|

Using a sharp serrated knife, slice bagel vertically (from top to bottom) into very thin slices. Arrange in single layer on baking sheet.

**Nonstick cooking spray** *or*
***I Can't Believe It's Not Butter*®** **spray**

Lightly spray bagel slices.

| 1 tsp | oregano |
|---|---|
| dash | garlic powder |

Sprinkle on bagel slices.

Bake for 12 minutes.

Let cool and enjoy! Store in an airtight container for up to 1 week.

---

**EXCHANGE VALUES**

1 Starch — Meat — Veg. — Fruit — Milk — Fat

| Nutrition information for — approximately 4 *Bagel Chips* | | | | Preparation Time — 20 min. | Oven Time — 12 min. |
|---|---|---|---|---|---|
| Calories ............................. 95 | Fat ............................. .5 g | Fiber ............................. 1 g | Sodium ............................. 190 mg | Total Carbohydrate ............. 19 g | |
| Calories from Fat ................ 5% | Saturated Fat ................ 0 g | Cholesterol ................ 0 mg | Protein ................................ 4 g | Sugars .................................... 0 g | |

## Party Survival Tip #6:
## Avoid drinking all your calories

"But I hardly ate a thing all holiday season!
How did I gain weight?"

**Think before you drink:**

Egg Nog (4 oz.) 355 calories

Wine (3 oz.) 85 calories

Beer, regular (12 oz.) 150 calories

Beer, light (12 oz.) 100 calories

Cider (12 oz.) 180 calories

Fruit punch (12 oz.) 180 calories

Piña colada (6 oz.) 325 calories

Opt for: club soda or sparkling water to
dilute punch or fruit juice, mineral water,
low-calorie soda or diet tonic water.

*Lickety-Split Meals*

# Spinach Dip in Pumpernickel

Here's a delicious dip that is always a hit at parties, minus the hit on your hips! Don't tell anyone it's lowfat; they'll never guess on their own.

Also good with rye bread.

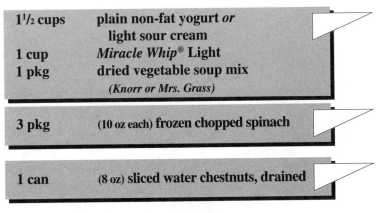

| | |
|---|---|
| 1½ cups | plain non-fat yogurt *or* light sour cream |
| 1 cup | *Miracle Whip®* **Light** |
| 1 pkg | dried vegetable soup mix *(Knorr or Mrs. Grass)* |
| 3 pkg | (10 oz each) **frozen chopped spinach** |
| 1 can | (8 oz) **sliced water chestnuts, drained** |
| 1 large | **round loaf of pumpernickel bread*** |

## 3 hours before serving:

Mix together so the dried soup can begin rehydrating.

Thaw the spinach in the microwave. Squeeze out all excess water. Stir into mixture.

Chop into small pieces. Stir into mixture. For best results, refrigerate 3 hours before filling the pumpernickel loaf and serving.

## Just before serving:

Using a knife, hollow out a large hole. Fill the hole with dip. Cube the bread you've removed to serve on the side for dipping. When the cubes are gone, invite guests to tear bread from the "bowl."

---

**EXCHANGE VALUES**

| 1 Starch | — Meat | 2 Veg. | — Fruit | — Milk | 1 Fat |
|---|---|---|---|---|---|

\* **If you can't find a large round unsliced loaf of pumpernickel bread, simply buy sliced pumpernickel, cube it and serve with the dip.**

**Nutrition information for — 4 T of dip on 6 cubes of bread (or 1 slice of bread)**      **Preparation Time — 30 min.**

| | | | | | |
|---|---|---|---|---|---|
| Calories ................. 160 | Fat ............................ 4 g | Fiber ...................... 4.6 g | Sodium ..................... 580 mg | Total Carbohydrate ............. 26 g |
| Calories from Fat ............... 23% | Saturated Fat ............... < 1 g | Cholesterol ................. < 1 mg | Protein ...................... 6 g | Sugars ...................... 4 g |

## Party Survival Tip #7:
## Mingle AWAY from the food

Standing beside a big bowl of cashews or Spanish peanuts can really throw a monkey wrench into your weight loss efforts. Think I'm kidding? Just try to stand or sit near an enticing bowl of nuts and NOT unconsciously eat a little handful here, another handful there. Although you swear it wasn't much, it was an unconscious downing of 10 grams of fat per handful!

**Suggestion:**

Take out 5 whole cashews (equivalent to 5 grams of fat) and line them up on your napkin or plate. Enjoy them one-by-one, with lots of time in between. Take a break and enjoy other foods like raw vegetables and fruit. Repeat with 5 more if you really want them. Decide that you're finished and move away from them!

# South of the Border Roll-ups

Thanks to my neighbor Suzy Crossley for the recipe to this popular appetizer.
It has been a hit at many neighborhood parties.

| | |
|---|---|
| 8 oz | light cream cheese |
| 8 oz | light sour cream |
| ½ packet | taco seasoning |
| 4-8 oz | hot salsa (to taste) |
| 1 can | (4 oz) chopped green chilies |

| | |
|---|---|
| 4 | green onions (tops & bottoms chopped) |
| 1 cup | reduced-fat shredded cheddar cheese |

| | |
|---|---|
| 10 | 8" flour tortillas |

**4 hours before serving:**

Mix together in a medium size bowl.

Gently stir in.

Lay out 5 tortillas at a time. Using ½ the cheese mixture, divide and spread evenly across the 5 tortillas. Roll up creating spirals inside. Repeat with remaining 5 tortillas.

Lightly dampen 10 sheets of paper towel. Wrap each roll in one. Refrigerate 3 to 4 hours.

**Just before serving:**

Unwrap each roll and slice 1" apart.

Arrange on decorative platter.

---

**EXCHANGE VALUES**

| 1 Starch | 1 Meat | — Veg. | — Fruit | — Milk | — Fat |
|---|---|---|---|---|---|

**Nutrition information for — 4 pinwheel bites**          Preparation Time — 30 min.

| | | | | | |
|---|---|---|---|---|---|
| Calories .................... 142 | Fat ......................... 6 g | Fiber ..................... 1.7 g | Sodium .................... 655 mg | Total Carbohydrate ........... 15 g | |
| Calories from Fat ........ 35% | Saturated Fat ........... 3 g | Cholesterol ............ 14 mg | Protein ........................ 8 g | Sugars ........................ 4 g | |

## Party Survival Tip #8:
## Keep your focus away from the food

While good food is certainly an important part of an enjoyable party, be sure you keep it in perspective. Appreciate the other great things: socializing, the beautiful decorations, music, games, and activities.

## Why tofu?

See page 50 to find out!

# Simple Tofu Bites

Serve these at your next party. When your guests ask what these delicious little cheese chunks are, watch their jaws drop when you tell them it's tofu!

*Use as meatslices for sandwiches or sprinkle the chunks on a tossed salad.*

| 16 oz | firm tofu |
|-------|-----------|

**3 or more hours before serving:**

Slice the tofu into small bite size chunks, or into $1/8$" "lunchmeat" slices for sandwiches.

| 2 T | soy sauce, reduced-sodium *or* Tamari sauce |
|-----|---------------------------------------------|
| $1/2$ tsp | low-sodium *Spike®* or *Mrs. Dash®* seasoning mix |

Mix the soy or Tamari sauce with the seasoning. Marinate the tofu chunks in the mixture for 2 or more hours.

**Preheat oven to 425°.**

**45 minutes before serving:**

When marinating time is almost up, heat oven to 425°. Spray a nonstick baking sheet with cooking spray. Place the tofu on the baking sheet. Bake 30 minutes. Tofu should become slightly browned.

Line platter with red tipped lettuce leaves and layer on the chunks. Stab chunks with toothpicks and serve hot or cold.

Note: This simple marinade works great with chicken too.

---

**EXCHANGE VALUES**

| — Starch | 1 Meat | — Veg. | — Fruit | — Milk | — Fat |
|----------|--------|--------|---------|--------|-------|

**Nutrition information for — approximately 8 chunks**　　　　　**Preparation Time — 5 min.**　　**Oven Time — 30 min.**

| Calories ..................... 75 | Fat .......................... 3 g | Fiber ..................... not available | Sodium ........................... 310 mg | Total Carbohydrate .............. 4 g |
| Calories from Fat ............... 37% | Saturated Fat ...................... 0 g | Cholesterol ........................ 0 mg | Protein ................................. 9 g | Sugars ..................................... 1 g |

## Party Survival Tip #9:  Stop Eating Early

Even if you stay late, decide in your mind *when* you will quit eating. This strategy can do wonders to prevent that continuous "just because it's there" munching, saving you hundreds of calories.

*Lickety-Split Meals*

# Tzatziki & Vegetables

My thanks to Carol Brickenden and Stacy Rafalko for this simple and delicious dip for vegetables. It is also the traditional Greek sauce used in pita sandwiches. Try using this instead of butter or mayonnaise in a sandwich.

| | |
|---|---|
| 2 cups | plain non-fat yogurt |

| | |
|---|---|
| ¹/₂ | cucumber, peeled, seeded & shredded |
| 2 large | cloves of garlic, minced |
| ¹/₂ tsp | dill* (dried) |
| ¹/₄ tsp | salt |
| 2 tsp | lemon juice |
| 1 tsp | olive oil |

**12 to 24 hours before serving:**

Line a strainer with a paper coffee filter or cheesecloth. Place over a bowl. Spoon yogurt onto coffee filter, cover and refrigerate for 12 to 24 hours.

Yogurt will now be thick. Discard the collected liquid beneath or use it in soups or breads. Remove yogurt from the filter and place in a small bowl.

**1 hour before serving:**

Mix into yogurt.

Serve with a variety of fresh vegetables like: fresh green beans (lightly steamed), green, red or yellow peppers, carrots, celery, zucchini, yellow squash, tomatoes, cucumbers, radishes, broccoli and cauliflower. Also delicious with pita triangles and *Bagel Chips* (page 29).

---

**EXCHANGE VALUES**

— Starch  — Meat  — Veg.  — Fruit  .5 Milk  — Fat

\* Can use 1 tsp fresh dill instead.

| Nutrition information for — approximately 4 T | | | Preparation Time — 8 min. | |
|---|---|---|---|---|
| Calories .................................... 40 | Fat ............................... < 1 | Fiber ........................................ < 1 | Sodium .............................. 115 mg | Total Carbohydrate ............... 5 g |
| Calories from Fat ............... 15% | Saturated Fat ...................... < 1 | Cholesterol .......................... 1 mg | Protein ...................................... 3 g | Sugars ..................................... 3 g |

## Party Survival Tip #10:
## No matter what, stay positive

Even if you did overdo it at the party, keep things in perspective. You do not need to be "perfect" all the time, and one event does not make you an overweight person, or give you high cholesterol. Say "It's no big deal," and start your next day back on your healthy fitness regime.

# Marinated Sesame Chicken Kabobs

**ALSO GREAT DINNER ENTREE!** | **SERVES**

Here's a great way to add a lean protein source to your finger-food party menu. Festive, delicious and easy to eat, your guests will love them!

12 FOR APPETIZERS (2 6-INCH SKEWERS PER PERSON)

6 FOR DINNER (2 12-INCH SKEWERS PER PERSON)

**Preheat BBQ grill or oven broiler.**
**Position oven rack 6 inches from broiler.**

| | |
|---|---|
| ¼ cup | **Tamari *or* soy sauce** (reduced-sodium) |
| 1 tsp | **sesame oil** |
| 1 T | **firmly packed brown sugar** |
| ½ tsp | **ginger** (fresh grated is best) |
| 8 grinds | **fresh ground pepper** |
| ¼ tsp | **minced garlic** |
| 2 T | **sesame seeds** |

| | |
|---|---|
| 6 | **skinless, boneless, chicken breast** (halves) |

**Optional additions**
**Whole mushrooms, green & red pepper chunks, onion wedges, cherry tomatoes, pineapple chunks**

Kids' Favorite

### 5 hours before serving or night before:

Mix together in a large bowl for marinating.

Slice the chicken into small 2" x ½" strips. Thoroughly coat with marinade, cover and refrigerate for 5 hours or overnight.

### 10 minutes before serving:

If using these, mix with the chicken and marinate a few minutes before assembling. (Over-exposure to the salty marinade causes vegetables to "wilt.")

Using 6" bamboo skewers for appetizers* and 12" for dinner entrées, begin assembling K-bobs. Pierce 1 end of the chicken strip, then hook it around and pierce the other end. Or pierce the whole strip lengthwise (use a weaving motion if desired). Alternate with the colorful vegetables if using. Broil or grill 6 to 8 minutes or until chicken is fully cooked.

Serve warm or cold on a lined tray of red tipped lettuce leaves.

\* **Simply cut 12" skewers in half.**

**EXCHANGE VALUES**

| — Starch | 2 Meat | — Veg. | — Fruit | — Milk | — Fat |
|---|---|---|---|---|---|

| Nutrition information for — (2) 6-inch skewers (without optionals) | | | | Preparation Time — 40 min. | |
|---|---|---|---|---|---|
| Calories ......................................... 85 | Fat ....................................... 2 g | Fiber ....................................... < 1 g | Sodium ............................. 217 mg | Total Carbohydrate ............... 2 g |
| Calories from Fat ................. 20% | Saturated Fat ..................... < 1 g | Cholesterol ........................ 33 mg | Protein ................................ 14 g | Sugars ..................................... 2 g |

# 1-Minute Mini-Meals

We've all been there. It's 6:50 p.m., and you're walking in the door. You have a 7:00 meeting to go to and it takes 5 minutes to get there. You have 5 minutes, so frantically you scrounge through the fridge and cupboards for anything to eat. The only thing you're thinking is "FOOD NOW!"

There's no time for cooking anything, you'll just have to "grab." Is there something you can throw together in 1 minute, that suffices as a meal and happens to be healthy *and* taste good? In the past, ¹/₂ a bag of *Doritos*® would have done the trick. But not anymore! Assuming you've shopped using the *Lickety-Split* grocery list, you're in business to make ANY of these tasty and "good for you" 1-Minute Mini-Meals!

# Tip

## True or False?

*"Popcorn should be reserved as a snack and a snack only. It would be unhealthy to serve popcorn as the grain in your meal."*

**Answer: FALSE!**

Popcorn is corn and corn is a healthy contribution to a meal, right? Corn is actually a grain (sorry, not a vegetable) and grain or starch should be a major part of every meal. Who says potatoes, rice, pasta and bread are the only grains allowed at meal time? As long as your popcorn is healthfully prepared (including the truly low-fat versions of microwave popcorn), it's fine to include popcorn in a meal. My personal favorite combinations are beans and popcorn, and soup and popcorn!

# Quick Nachos

Spread 20 *Baked Tostitos*® on a microwave safe plate.

Sprinkle with $1/4$ cup reduced fat shredded cheddar cheese.

 Microwave on high 45 to 60 seconds.

Eat with fat-free refried beans and salsa along with baby carrots and fruit juice.

SERVES 1

# Quick Quesadilla

Place a flour tortilla on a plate.

Sprinkle with 2 T reduced-fat shredded cheddar cheese.

 Microwave 20 seconds on high.

Meanwhile, chop a tomato for topping. (Salsa may also be used.)

 Roll and eat.

SERVES 1

# Cheese Pita Pizza

Spread 2 T spaghetti sauce on a pita.

Sprinkle with 2 T reduced-fat shredded mozzarella cheese and 2 tsp Parmesan cheese.

(Add any vegetables you have lying around, too!)

 Microwave until cheese is melted.

SERVES 1

# Zon's Stress Reliever: Beans and Popcorn

Place a bag of *Orville Redenbacher*® *Smart Pop* in the microwave on high.

Open a single serving can of *Eden*® flavored beans.

 Eat the beans while waiting for the popcorn.

 Chase beans with $1/2$ a bag of popcorn.

SERVES 1 TO 2

*Lovers' tip: Prepare separate sleeping quarters
     for evening to follow.*

# Beans & Crackers

Open a can of baked beans and eat with crackers.

 Any baked beans are OK, however *Eden*®*'s* baked beans can't be beat for being the most nutritionally smart. And their single serving size pop-top can is so convenient.

Chase with a handful of baby carrots.

SERVES 1 TO 2

# Fiesta Bean Burrito

Spread $1/2$ cup fat-free refried beans and 1 T salsa in a flour tortilla.

 Roll and eat.

SERVES 1

## Tip

**Great ideas from people like you!**

**How do you eat right when your job has you on the road ALL the time?**

"Restaurants used to be my downfall, but not anymore. My secret is I no longer look at the menu. That took care of the fried mozzarella sticks and chicken wings staring me in the face. Now, instead of ordering from the menu, I ask the server, 'Can you make me a broiled chicken breast, with lots of steamed vegetables, no butter, some marinara sauce and a baked potato? No more surprises and it's NEVER too much fat.'"

—SUE KLOC, 41,
Management Analyst
Celebrating the loss of 20 pounds and
normalization of her high blood pressure
without drugs.

See page 136 for the steps Sue took!

## Snappy Sandwich Roll

Spread mustard on 1 flour tortilla or Lavash flat bread.

Add 2 oz 97% fat-free lunch meat *or* low-fat cheese.

Place a couple carrots and celery sticks lined up end to end.

 Roll and eat.

SERVES 1

## Low-Fat Yogurt & Grapenuts

Pour ⅓ cup *Grapenuts*® into 8 ozs flavored yogurt.

 Stir and eat.

*Tip:* *If all you have is plain yogurt, simply stir in 1 to 2 T fruit jam or preserves.*

SERVES 1

## English Muffin Melt

Toast an English muffin.

Lay ½ a slice of low-fat cheese on each half.

 Microwave 15 seconds.

Add a tomato slice, if you like. Eat with an apple.

SERVES 1

## Cottage Cheese & Fruit

Open a can of pineapple, peaches or apricots.

Place fruit over a scoop of low-fat cottage cheese.

 Eat with wheat crackers.

SERVES 2

## Applesauce and Cottage Cheese

Place a plop of each side by side.

Sprinkle with cinnamon, if desired.

 Slightly mix together as you eat.

SERVES 1

## Easy Cheesy Tomatoes

Open a 14½ oz can of stewed tomatoes.

Pour into a bowl with 1 oz reduced-fat shredded mozzarella cheese, 1 tsp Parmesan cheese and a dash each of oregano and pepper.

 Microwave until cheese is melted.

 Eat with crackers.

SERVES 1 TO 2

## Super Soup in a Flash!

Looking for a delicious and nutritious canned soup, but don't know which brand to buy? Be sure to try one of my favorite brands: *Shari's™ Organic*. Top quality, NOT too high in sodium, loaded with fiber, and DELICIOUS! Just open a can, heat and eat!

# Pop Quiz!

*Your fruit bin and baskets are typically:*

A. Stocked with the season's best selection, replenished at least once if not twice each week.

B. Full after shopping, but empty for days between trips, since it's hard to get to the store.

C. Home to a few apples or oranges, or other fruits with a long shelf life.

D. What bin or basket?

**Correct Answer: A.**

With all the anti-aging compounds in fresh fruit, it's hard to name a habit more beneficial to your health than eating 3 to 4 pieces of fruit each day. And in order to eat fruit, you have to BUY fruit. Establish the habit of making a midweek stop at a produce market so you'll always have enough!

**P.S. Fruit is fast food!**

# Pepper Strips and Low-fat Cottage Cheese

Slice 1 red or green pepper.

Pour a puddle of light Thousand Island dressing.

Plop ½ cup cottage cheese on the side for 2-step dipping.

 Eat with a nectarine, pear or orange.

SERVES 1

# Pita Wedges and Veggies Dipped in Hummus

Rinse some fresh broccoli flowerets and baby carrots.
Slice a pita into 8 triangles.

 Dip pita triangles and veggies into hummus and eat.

*Note:* *You buy the ready-made hummus in a case near the deli section of your grocery store.*

AN 8 OZ TUB OF HUMMUS SERVES 2 TO 4

# Bagelwich

Slice a bagel and throw on 2 oz turkey with some mustard.

 Eat with a handful of baby carrots and radishes.

SERVES 1

# Sardines and Crackers

Pop open a 3¾ oz can of sardines in mustard sauce.

 Eat with reduced fat *Triscuits*® or *Wheat Thins*® and a handful of baby carrots.

SERVES 1

# Garden Lentil Salad and Crackers

Eat salad directly from container.

 Eat with 6 to 10 crackers.

*Note:* *You buy this delicious ready-made salad from the deli section of your grocery store. (I like the* Oasis Mediterranean Cuisine's *Garden Lentil Salad.)*

SERVES 1 TO 2

# Mediterranean Lavash Roll-up

Spread ¼ cup hummus and ½ cup tabouli on a Lavash flat bread (or flour tortilla).

 Roll and eat.

*Note:* *You buy the ready-made hummus and tabouli in a case near the deli section of your grocery store.*

SERVES 1

# Pop Quiz!

**Tip**

*Which best describes your vegetable consumption yesterday?*

A. Cup of vegetable soup, large stir-fry including peppers, broccoli, and carrots

B. Small iceberg salad with tomato fragment, $^1/_2$ cup overcooked green beans

C. Ketchup, pickles, and French fries

If you answered anything besides A, you're in big trouble! With all the cancer and heart disease fighting compounds in vegetables, your body needs the help of these protectors to stay disease free. Say yes to a double serving of vegetables at dinner, and munch on raw vegetables at lunch. Your body will thank you with a reduced risk of cataracts, clogged arteries, and cancer!

**P.S. Raw veggies are fast food!**

## Turkey Rolls with Potato Chips

Spread hot mustard on 2 slices of 97% fat-free turkey lunchmeat.

Place a couple carrots lined up end to end.

 Roll and eat.

Chase with 15 *Baked Lay's*® potato chips and a juice box.

Serves 1

## Quick Chicken Sandwich

Open a 10 oz can of cooked chicken.

Mix with 2 to 3 T *Miracle Whip*® Light and 1 T Dijon mustard.

 Spread ⅓ of chicken mixture on a slice of bread and eat with an apple, pear or nectarine.

Serves 3

## Baked Tostitos® and Spicy Pintos

Pop open a single serving can of *Eden*® *Spicy Pintos* and eat with *Baked Tostitos*®.

 Chase with 5 spoonfuls of applesauce.

Serves 1

## Simple Salad Supper

Pour pre-cleaned salad greens into a bowl.

Pop open a single-serving can of *Eden*® garbanzo beans.

 Drain and sprinkle on top of salad.

Add a plop of low-fat cottage cheese, a bunch of canned beets and other fresh veggies.

Top with light Thousand Island dressing and croutons.

Serves 1

## String-Cheese Standby

Eat 1 *or* 2 string-cheese pieces with crackers and an apple, orange or pear.

Serves 1

## Salmon Pita Sandwich

Open a 7 oz can of salmon and drain.

Mix with 2 T *Miracle Whip*® Light. (Smash bones with a fork.)

 Stuff into a pita.

Add lettuce and tomato, and eat.

Serves 2 to 3

## Pop Quiz!

**Tip**

*Which best describes the high calcium foods you consumed yesterday?*

A. Milk on cereal, 6 oz. yogurt and 1 oz. low-fat cheese on broccoli

B. Cheese on pizza, ice cream

C. No dairy; you avoid it because of allergy or intolerance.

**Correct Answer: A.**

Calcium is a VERY important anti-aging food. It helps prevent osteoporosis (weak and porous bones), a common disease of aging. If you answered A, great. If you answered B, the amount of calcium is not only insufficient, but your intake also contains excessive saturated fat and calories. C means you just plain need to start taking a calcium supplement. Don't delay. Start doing it now!

## Tuna Cracker Sandwiches

Pop open a single serving can of tuna and drain.

 Make cracker sandwiches and eat with a can of low-sodium *V-8*®.

Serves 1

## Left-Over Rice and Veggie Salad

Chop green or red pepper and carrots.

Add to bowl of left-over rice.

Toss with a salad dressing like *Henri's*® *Private Blend TAS-TEE*® **low-fat dressing.** (This is a coleslaw type, which works great.)

About 1¹/₂ cups serves 1

## Hard-Boiled Egg with Crackers

Crack and peel 1 *or* 2 of the eggs you've previously hard-boiled.

 Eat with 8 reduced-fat *Triscuits*® and an apple.

Serves 1

## Tuna in a Pita

Spread 1 T *Miracle Whip*® **Light inside a pita.**

Pop open a single serving can of tuna and drain. **Stuff into pita.**

 Add any vegetables that you have.

Serves 1

## Peanut Butter Rice Cake

Spread 1 T peanut butter thinly on a couple of rice cakes.

 Eat with a banana.

Serves 1

## Corny Chicken Salad

Rinse and drain a 10 oz can of cooked chicken and a 15 oz can of corn.

Flake chicken and toss together in a bowl with 3 T lite *or* fat-free Italian dressing.

 Eat with widely cut strips of red pepper.

Serves 2 to 3

## Dashboard Dining Tip

Keep a *Ziplock®* bag full of napkins, plastic forks, spoons, and one sharp knife in your car's glove box. You are now in a better position to grab and eat a healthy lunch from a grocery store. (Bye-bye fast food restaurants!) I recommend the following favorites:

- Low-fat deli salads
- Pre-packaged salads like lentil or garbanzo bean
- Bagel with sliced low-fat deli meat
- Yogurt
- Low-fat cottage cheese and low-fat crackers
- Fresh fruit
- Veggies off the salad bar

*Lickety-Split Meals*

## Quick 2-Bean Salad

**Rinse and drain a 15 oz can of kidney beans and a 14$^1/_2$ oz can of green beans.**

**Transfer to a bowl and toss with $^1/_4$ cup lite *or* fat-free Italian dressing.**

 Eat with crackers.

SERVES 2

## Quick Black Bean and Corn Salad

**Rinse and drain a 15 oz can each of black beans and corn.**

**Transfer to a bowl and toss with 2 cups of salsa.**

 Eat as a salad, rolled up in a tortilla, or as a dip with *Baked Tostitos*®.

SERVES 2 AS A MAIN MEAL SALAD, *OR*
SERVES 4 AS A TORTILLA ROLL-UP

# 5-Minute Meals

It just astounds me how many people go out to eat. "I don't have time to cook," they say. But eating out takes SO MUCH time! Even going through a drive-through takes time. My husband and I firmly believe that the fastest way to get a meal is to make it yourself. The secret is keeping the right ingredients on hand, and of course, use *this* book!

When we want a meal in 5 minutes, we mentally pick from these 3 things:

- **Roll-ups** (bean burrito or a lavash roll-up) or
- **Quick Pita Sandwich** or Pita Pizza (see Pizza chapter, page 102) or
- **Canned beans** (mix with canned corn or tuna)

Once you decide, you'll be eating 5 minutes later!

# Tip

## What is fiber and where do you find it?

Fiber is the portion of plant foods that you can not digest, also known as "roughage."

It is not found in any animal foods.

| Yes | No |
|-----|-----|
| **Plant foods** | **Animal foods** |
| Fruits | Chicken |
| Vegetables | Beef |
| Grains | Pork |
| Whole grain flours | Veal |
| Whole grain baked goods | Fish |
| Dried beans and peas | Milk |
| Nuts and seeds | Eggs |

# Benito Bean Burritos

**SERVES**

Burritos without the *refried* beans. Soon to be a household favorite!

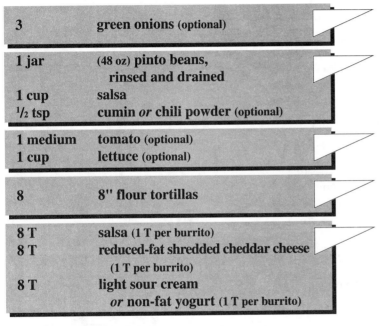

| | | |
|---|---|---|
| 3 | green onions (optional) | Chop in the food processor. |
| 1 jar | (48 oz) pinto beans, rinsed and drained | Add to processor and blend thoroughly.* |
| 1 cup | salsa | Heat the spread in the microwave for 2 or more minutes. |
| ½ tsp | cumin *or* chili powder (optional) | |
| 1 medium | tomato (optional) | Rinse and chop for extra toppings, if desired. |
| 1 cup | lettuce (optional) | |
| 8 | 8" flour tortillas | Microwave for about 5 seconds per tortilla. |
| 8 T | salsa (1 T per burrito) | Use as desired for topping your burrito. |
| 8 T | reduced-fat shredded cheddar cheese (1 T per burrito) | |
| 8 T | light sour cream *or* non-fat yogurt (1 T per burrito) | |

Chop in the food processor.

Add to processor and blend thoroughly.*
Heat the spread in the microwave for 2 or more minutes.

Rinse and chop for extra toppings, if desired.

Microwave for about 5 seconds per tortilla.

Use as desired for topping your burrito.

Assemble by spreading approximately ¼ cup Benito Spread on tortilla and layer on any additional ingredients you choose. Fold in the ends and roll up.

Slice 2 apples into wedges and place on table with baby carrots.

If you must eat on the run, just roll your burrito up in a paper towel, and take it with you. Don't forget your apples & carrots.

**EXCHANGE VALUES**

2 Starch — Meat 1 Veg. — Fruit — Milk — Fat

\* **This step can be replaced by simply opening a can of fat-free refried beans. My husband and I still prefer the flavor of this old fashioned method.**

**Nutrition information for — 1 burrito**

| | | | | |
|---|---|---|---|---|
| Calories ................. 255 | Fat ......................... 4 g | Fiber ......................... 14 g | Sodium ..................... 800 mg | Total Carbohydrate ............ 42 g |
| Calories from Fat ............... 14% | Saturated Fat ................. 1.6 g | Cholesterol ..................... 6 mg | Protein ......................... 15 g | Sugars ......................... 4 g |

# Why is fiber so important?

- Yields no calories! Helps control your weight by filling you up on fewer calories.

- Plays an important role in intestinal health. (Your intestinal tract is 24 feet long and needs to be kept clean!) Helps keep you "regular."

- Greatly reduces your risk of cancer, especially colon cancer.

- Helps lower blood cholesterol.

- Helps lower blood sugar levels for people with diabetes.

*Lickety-Split Meals*

# Great Northern Tuna Salad Stuffer

Quickly mix this up for a delicious pita pocket stuffer, flour tortilla roll-up, or on top of a tomato or bed of salad greens. Friends will rave!

Keeps in refrigerator for 4 days. Use for lunches all week.

| 1 large can | (12 oz) **water packed tuna, drained** |
| 1 jar | (24 oz) **Great Northern beans, rinsed & drained** |

Toss together in a medium-sized bowl.

| ½ tsp | **dill** |
| ¼ cup | **light Thousand Island dressing** |

Add and mix gently.

| **Optional:** | |
| 1 | **green onion, chopped** |
| ½ | **red pepper, chopped** |
| ¼ | **cup fresh parsley, chopped** |

Add if you have time.

Serve ¾ cup stuffed into 2 pita halves, rolled in a flour tortilla, placed on top of a tomato or salad greens, or simply eaten with crackers.

---

**EXCHANGE VALUES**

| 1 Starch | 2 Meat | 1 Veg. | — Fruit | — Milk | — Fat |

**Nutrition information for — 3/4 cup including the optional veggies**

| Calories ................................. 185 | Fat ................................. 2 g | Fiber ................................. 8 g | Sodium ............................ 535 mg | Total Carbohydrate ............. 21 g |
| Calories from Fat ............... 10% | Saturated Fat ...................... .2 g | Cholesterol ...................... 18 mg | Protein ............................. 21 g | Sugars ................................. 0 g |

# Tip

## How much fiber do you need?

The recommended intake is 20-30 (or more) grams per day.

On the average, people eat only 11 grams of fiber per day, with some people eating even less than that. (YIKES!)

# Almond Chicken Salad

This makes a very special luncheon dish served in 1/2 of a cantaloupe.
It's also great for sprucing up a brown bag lunch.

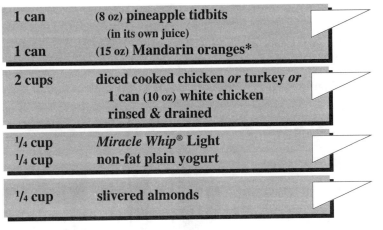

| | |
|---|---|
| 1 can | (8 oz) **pineapple tidbits** (in its own juice) |
| 1 can | (15 oz) **Mandarin oranges*** |

Open cans and drain. Reserve pineapple juice for another use.

| | |
|---|---|
| 2 cups | **diced cooked chicken** *or* **turkey** *or* **1 can** (10 oz) **white chicken rinsed & drained** |

Place in a medium bowl with the fruit.

| | |
|---|---|
| ¼ cup | *Miracle Whip*® **Light** |
| ¼ cup | **non-fat plain yogurt** |

Mix together in a 2 cup measuring cup. Fold into fruit and chicken.

| | |
|---|---|
| ¼ cup | **slivered almonds** |

Gently mix in.

Use to make a sandwich, stuff a pita, top lettuce greens, or fill half a cantaloupe.

---

**EXCHANGE VALUES**

| — Starch | 3 Meat | — Veg. | 1.5 Fruit | — Milk | — Fat |
|---|---|---|---|---|---|

**\* Try substituting 1 cup of grape halves for variety.**

**Nutrition information for — approximately 1 cup**

| Calories ..................... 315 | Fat ..................... 10 g | Fiber ..................... 1.4 g | Sodium ..................... 195 mg | Total Carbohydrate ..................... 25 g |
|---|---|---|---|---|
| Calories from Fat ............... 30% | Saturated Fat ..................... 1.3 g | Cholesterol ..................... 72 mg | Protein ..................... 30 g | Sugars ..................... 22 g |

# How can you get all 20-30 grams of fiber each day?

**Think "10 + 10 + 10"** ·············· **To achieve this each day, EAT:**

10 grams from fruit ··············· 3 or more pieces of fruit

10 grams from vegetables ··············· 3 or more ½ cup servings of vegetables

10 grams from whole grains ··············· 4 or more servings of whole grain bread, cereals, brown rice, oatmeal, etc.

**Also include beans on a weekly basis:**

Pinto, kidney, garbanzo, navy, lima beans, and lots of peas and corn.

This *Black Bean and Corn Salad* at 7 grams of fiber per serving helps get you to your daily goal of 20-30 grams in a hurry!

# Black Bean & Corn Salad

This is so simple, it's almost obscene! Thanks to Karen Pender for this incredibly simple and delicious dish! She brought it to a 4th of July potluck picnic where many of us fell in love with it.

| | | |
|---|---|---|
| **2 cups** | **frozen corn *or* 1 can (16 oz) corn** | Place in a strainer to drain. If using frozen corn, run warm water over it to thaw. Transfer to a medium bowl. |
| **1 can** | **(16 oz) black beans** | Rinse in a strainer, then add to bowl. |
| **1 cup** | **fresh tomato salsa\*** | Add to bowl and mix contents gently. |

Eat as a salad, or rolled up in a tortilla as a quick sandwich.

Also makes a wonderful accompaniment for outdoor-grilled chicken or fish.

**Optional additions**
| | |
|---|---|
| **¹/₂ tsp** | **cumin** |
| **¹/₂ tsp** | **chili powder** |
| **3 dashes** | **cayenne pepper** |

---

**EXCHANGE VALUES**

| 2 Starch | — Meat | 1 Veg. | — Fruit | — Milk | — Fat |
|---|---|---|---|---|---|

**\* If you only have canned salsa, try adding some chopped fresh tomatoes and minced parsley for fresh color and flavor.**

**Nutrition information for — approximately 1 cup**

| | | | |
|---|---|---|---|
| Calories ..................... 150 | Fat ......................... .5 g | Fiber ........................ 7 g | Sodium ........................... 516 mg | Total Carbohydrate ............. 35 g |
| Calories from Fat ............... 2% | Saturated Fat ............... < 1 g | Cholesterol ................... 0 mg | Protein ............................. 7 g | Sugars ...................................... 4 g |

## Tip

**Why buy Lavash?**

1. It's very nutritious since you can buy 100% whole-wheat Lavash bread that has no added fat.

2. It allows you to make a sandwich out of leftover stir-fry or just about anything!

3. It's a nice change from eating "sandwiches" all the time.

4. It easily allows you to include all kinds of vegetables.

5. It's perfect for eating on the run!

# Turkey & Hot Mustard Roll-ups

I don't know what we would do without these Lavash breads. Be sure to try this.
A great way to get a meal on the run!

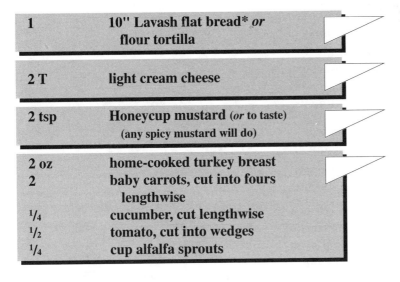

| 1 | 10" Lavash flat bread* *or* flour tortilla |
|---|---|
| 2 T | light cream cheese |
| 2 tsp | Honeycup mustard (*or* to taste) (any spicy mustard will do) |
| 2 oz | home-cooked turkey breast |
| 2 | baby carrots, cut into fours lengthwise |
| 1/4 | cucumber, cut lengthwise |
| 1/2 | tomato, cut into wedges |
| 1/4 | cup alfalfa sprouts |

Lay out on flat surface.

Spread across entire Lavash or tortilla.

Spread on top of the cream cheese.

Place each in a row side by side.

Get ready to roll! Starting from the edge of a long row, roll it up.
If eating later, wrap in plastic wrap.

To eat as a sandwich, peel back a few inches of plastic wrap, eat, peel some more, eat… you get the idea!

To eat as an appetizer, let them "set" in the refrigerator for 2 or 3 hours. Then remove the plastic wrap. Slice the rolls, 1 to 1 1/2" apart, using a sawing motion.

Serve on a platter garnished with red-tipped lettuce or purple kale.
P.S. Make more!

Note: If you use a processed turkey instead of home-made, the sodium for this sandwich soars to 1,225 mgs!

*Also an excellent party appetizer.*

\* **Find Lavash (sometimes spelled lawash) in the deli or bakery sections of your grocery store. It's a large flat bread like a tortilla.**

### EXCHANGE VALUES

| 4 Starch | 3 Meat | 1 Veg. | — Fruit | — Milk | — Fat |
|---|---|---|---|---|---|

**Nutrition information for — 1 entire roll-up**

| | | | |
|---|---|---|---|
| Calories ......................... 490 | Fat ............................. 9 g | Fiber ........................ 5 g | Sodium ........................ 760 mg | Total Carbohydrate ........... 73 g |
| Calories from Fat ........... 16% | Saturated Fat .......... 4 g | Cholesterol ............ 62 mg | Protein ........................ 31 g | Sugars ............................ 10 g |

**Go Mediterranean!**

The Mediterranean diet has become increasingly popular, spotlighting the health benefits of legumes, vegetables, olive oil, and garlic. Purchasing ready-made hummus and tabouli is a great way to conveniently reap these benefits.

**Hummus:** Ground chickpeas, sesame seed paste, lemon, and garlic. Excellent for dipping with pita bread triangles or crackers.

**Tabouli:** Bulgur (wheat kernels that have been steamed, dried, and crushed), parsley, lemon, olive oil, and garlic. Excellent as a side salad or stuffed into a pita or rolled in a lavash.

The combination of hummus and tabouli together in these sandwiches is awesome! You must try it!

# Mediterranean Roll-ups

You'll never be saying "Where's the meat?" in this delicious super-fast vegetarian sandwich. Just stop by the specialty section of your grocery store deli for prepared Tabouli and Hummus, and a package of Lavash.

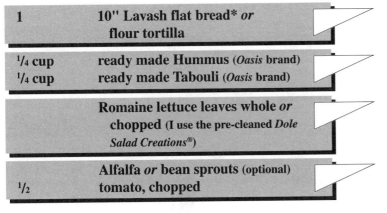

| 1 | 10" Lavash flat bread* *or* flour tortilla |
| --- | --- |
| ¼ cup ¼ cup | ready made Hummus (*Oasis* brand) ready made Tabouli (*Oasis* brand) |
| | Romaine lettuce leaves whole *or* chopped (I use the pre-cleaned *Dole Salad Creations®*) |
| ½ | Alfalfa *or* bean sprouts (optional) tomato, chopped |

Lay out on a flat surface.

Pile each in a long row, side by side.

Add generously.

Add as desired.

Get ready to roll! Starting from the edge of a long row, roll it up. If eating later, wrap in plastic wrap.

To eat as a sandwich, peel back a few inches of plastic wrap, eat, peel some more, eat… you get the idea!

To eat as an appetizer, let them "set" in the refrigerator for 2 or 3 hours. Then remove the plastic wrap. Slice the rolls, 1 to 1½" apart, using a sawing motion.

Serve on a platter garnished with red-tipped lettuce or purple kale. P.S. Make more!

*Also an excellent party appetizer.*

---

**EXCHANGE VALUES**

5 Starch   1 Meat   1 Veg.   — Fruit   — Milk   — Fat

\* **Find Lavash (sometimes spelled lawash) in the deli or bakery sections of your grocery store. It's a large flat bread like a tortilla.**

**Nutrition information for — 1 entire roll-up**

| | | | | |
| --- | --- | --- | --- | --- |
| Calories ............... 478 | Fat ........................... 8 g | Fiber ....................... 10 g | Sodium ........................... 800 mg | Total Carbohydrate ............. 91 g |
| Calories from Fat ........ 14% | Saturated Fat ............ < 1 g | Cholesterol ............................ 0 g | Protein ................................ 14 g | Sugars ...................................... 5 g |

# Test Your Weight Loss IQ:

*If you change from drinking 2 cups of 2% milk each day, to drinking 2 cups of 1/2% milk each day, you'll lose:*

A. 6 pounds in a year

B. 10 pounds in a year

C. 12.5 pounds in a year

**Answer:** C. 12.5 pounds in a year!

■ ■ ■ ■ ■ ■ ■ ■ ■ ■ ■ ■ ■ ■ ■ ■ ■ ■

# Vegetable & Spinach Dip Roll-ups

Have leftover spinach dip? Here's the perfect way to use it.

*Also excellent as a party appetizer.*

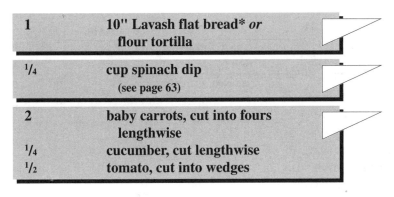

| 1 | 10" Lavash flat bread* *or* flour tortilla |
| --- | --- |

Lay out on a flat surface.

| ¹/₄ | cup spinach dip (see page 63) |
| --- | --- |

Spread across entire Lavash or tortilla.

| 2 | baby carrots, cut into fours lengthwise |
| --- | --- |
| ¹/₄ | cucumber, cut lengthwise |
| ¹/₂ | tomato, cut into wedges |

Line up the vegetables each in a row, side by side.

Get ready to roll! Starting from the edge of a long row, roll it up. If eating later, wrap in plastic wrap.

To eat as a sandwich, peel back a few inches of plastic wrap, eat, peel some more, eat… you get the idea!

To eat as an appetizer, let them "set" in the refrigerator for 2 or 3 hours. Then remove the plastic wrap. Slice the rolls, 1 to 1¹/₂" apart, using a sawing motion.

Serve on a platter garnished with red-tipped lettuce or purple kale. P.S. Make more!

---

**EXCHANGE VALUES**

| 4 Starch | — Meat | 2 Veg. | — Fruit | — Milk | — Fat |
| --- | --- | --- | --- | --- | --- |

\* **Find Lavash (sometimes spelled lawash) in the deli or bakery sections of your grocery store. It's a large flat bread like a tortilla.**

**Nutrition information for — 1 entire roll-up**

| Calories ................................. 410 | Fat ......................................... 6 g | Fiber .................................... 7 g | Sodium ............................. 800 mg | Total Carbohydrate ............. 80 g |
| --- | --- | --- | --- | --- |
| Calories from Fat ............... 12% | Saturated Fat ................... < 1 g | Cholesterol ...................... < 1 mg | Protein .................................. 13 g | Sugars ................................... 12 g |

# What IS tofu?

### Tip

Tofu is made from soymilk by adding a coagulant and pressing the curds into blocks like cheese. It's high in protein and happens to be the staple meat alternative in Asian countries.

**Why should we eat tofu?**

Soybeans contain a powerhouse of antioxidants and other disease-fighting agents. Thirty-four studies have shown that soy protein lowers cholesterol by 15% or more. In study after study, consumption of soy foods is associated with lower risk of heart disease, breast and prostate cancers, and osteoporosis.

*Eating soy is like taking a sip from the fountain of youth!*

**More ways to incorporate beneficial soy:**

**Soy milk** on your cereal (I personally like the *EdenSoy® Extra*, both vanilla and original). Try cooking your oatmeal in it. Makes pudding too!

**Black soy beans** (you can buy these canned and ready to eat from *Eden®* — see the coupons in the back). Rinse and drain, and add to chili or any dish that would use beans. They are very much like black beans, but black soy beans are incredibly high in the healthful soy compounds.

**Tofu** (see the recipes listed in the index on page 193).

**Commercial soy burgers** (a majority of these products have had most of the beneficial soy compounds removed, however, they are still healthier than eating meat).

# Eggless Salad Sandwiches

You can make this great summertime salad with chicken and tofu, or only tofu. Never tried tofu? Combined with the chicken, it's a tasty way to become a tofu believer!

| 12 oz | firm tofu |
| | *or* |
| 6 oz | firm tofu |
| | *and* |
| 1 can | (10 oz) **chicken breast meat, rinsed & drained** |

Drain water from tofu. Crumble the tofu with a fork in a medium bowl. If using chicken, add it to the bowl and flake it apart.

| 2 stalks | celery |
| ¹/₂ | onion |
| ¹/₂ | red pepper |

Chop vegetables. Add them to the bowl and mix.

| 2 T | Dijon mustard |
| ¹/₄ cup | *Miracle Whip*® Light |

Add to the bowl and mix well.

Serve in a pita pocket or on whole-wheat bread with lettuce and tomatoes. This is also delicious as a dip for crackers or celery sticks.

---

**EXCHANGE VALUES**

— Starch    1 Meat    1 Veg.    — Fruit    — Milk    — Fat

**Nutrition information for — approximately 1/2 cup of salad (without bread)**

| | | | | | |
|---|---|---|---|---|---|
| Calories ................................. 110 | Fat .......................................... 4 g | Fiber ........................................ 1 g | Sodium ............................ 250 mg | Total Carbohydrate .............. 5 g |
| Calories from Fat ............... 35% | Saturated Fat .................... < 1 g | Cholesterol ......................... 21 mg | Protein ................................. 12 g | Sugars ..................................... 2 g |

# 15-Minute Meals

It's a quarter to 6 and the family is starved. You were planning on having chicken, but you forgot to thaw it out. Is it still humanly possible to get a hot and satisfying chicken dinner on the table in 15 minutes?

Welcome to 15-Minute Meals! You'll discover how to turn frozen chicken breasts into *Crispy Chicken Dijon* or *Creamy Chicken Dijon over Noodles* all within 15 minutes! Or how about

stuffed baked potatoes, sloppy joes, or nachos? They're all here, and you'll know how to get the complete meal on the table in 15 minutes or less. Guaranteed!

Remember: If it takes a bit longer than 15 minutes, refer back to the introduction about how to "speedisize" your kitchen. To really achieve this kind of efficiency, it's imperative to have every drawer, cupboard and utensil in full cooperation.

# Tip

## Why make the effort to eat less fat?

1. To lower your risk of heart disease
2. To lower your risk of cancer
3. To control your weight
4. To have MORE energy!

# Veggie & Cheese Stuffed Baked Potatoes

Here's what we serve most often in our house. It's a real "no-brainer."

**SERVES**

1

**MENU**

STUFFED BAKED POTATOES

LIGHT CANNED PEACHES

| | |
|---|---|
| **1 large** | **potato** |

Scrub thoroughly and pierce 3 or 4 times with a fork. Place in microwave on high for 4 to 5 minutes. Make sure it's done by piercing with a fork. Cook more if necessary. Set aside.

| | |
|---|---|
| **1 cup** | **frozen California blend broccoli, cauliflower & carrots** |

Place vegetables in a microwave safe dish. Cover and cook for 6 to 8 minutes on high.

Split potato open and top with vegetables (overflowing the spud!)

| | |
|---|---|
| **¼ cup** | **reduced-fat shredded cheddar cheese** |

Sprinkle on top and microwave the entire potato for 1 more minute until melted.

Top potato with pepper if desired and serve with a side of cottage cheese, a dollup of plain yogurt or light sour cream, and light canned peaches.

---

**EXCHANGE VALUES**

| 2 Starch | 1 Meat | 2 Veg. | — Fruit | — Milk | — Fat |
|---|---|---|---|---|---|

**Nutrition information for — potato with vegetables and cheese, no toppings**

| | | | | |
|---|---|---|---|---|
| Calories ................................. 235 | Fat ............................. 3 g | Fiber ................................. 5 g | Sodium ............................ 280 mg | Total Carbohydrate ............. 37 g |
| Calories from Fat ............... 13% | Saturated Fat ...................... 2 g | Cholesterol ...................... 9 mg | Protein ............................... 14 g | Sugars ..................................... 1 g |

# Tip

## How many fat grams can I have each day?

It is recommended to consume between 30 and 60 grams of fat per day depending on your health needs*.

If you are less active and/or want to lose weight, choose closer to 30 grams.

If you are more active and/or want to maintain weight, choose closer to 60 grams.

* Studies by Dean Ornish, MD, author of *Reversing Heart Disease Without Drugs or Surgery*, suggest that a vegetarian diet as low as 15 grams of fat in combination with exercise and meditation, can reverse heart disease in diseased patients.

### Did you Know?

Every 5 grams of fat on a label you see = 1 teaspoon of lard or shortening!?!

Some Americans eat over 100 grams of fat per day!

That's almost a 1/2 cup of lard or shortening EACH DAY!

# Chicken Dijon Stuffed Baked Potatoes

Here's another great way to make a quick meal out of a baked potato. The sour cream replaces the mayonnaise for a perfect complement atop a potato.

| | |
|---|---|
| **3 large** | **baking potatoes** |

Scrub thoroughly and pierce each potato 3 or 4 times with a fork. Microwave on high for 8 minutes. Cook more if necessary.

Place a steamer with water on high heat.

| | |
|---|---|
| **1 bunch** | **asparagus** (about 18 spears) |
| | *or* **broccoli** |
| **1** | **red pepper** |

Rinse vegetables. Cut off asparagus ends. Slice pepper into long strips. Place all in the steamer, which should be boiling by now. Steam 8 to 10 minutes.

| | |
|---|---|
| **1 can** | **(10 oz) white chicken meat, drained** |

Drain and place in a medium-size microwave safe bowl. Flake meat with a fork.

| | |
|---|---|
| **¼ cup** | **light sour cream** *or* **non-fat plain yogurt** |
| **1 T** | **Dijon mustard** |
| **1** | **green onion, chopped** *or* **1 tsp dried onion flakes** |

Add to chicken along with sour cream and mustard. Mix well.

When potatoes are done, microwave the chicken mixture for 1½ to 2 minutes on high.

To serve, cut potatoes in ½, spoon the chicken salad into the middle of the potatoes and top with the steamed vegetables.

Serve with applesauce.

---

**EXCHANGE VALUES**

2 Starch    3 Meat    2 Veg.    — Fruit    — Milk    — Fat

**Nutrition information for — 1 stuffed baked potato**

| | | | | |
|---|---|---|---|---|
| Calories ............................. 300 | Fat ............................. 4.5 g | Fiber ............................. 4 g | Sodium ............................. 300 mg | Total Carbohydrate ............ 40 g |
| Calories from Fat ............... 8% | Saturated Fat ..................... 2 g | Cholesterol ..................... 48 mg | Protein ............................. 27 g | Sugars ............................. 3 g |

# Tip

## True or False?

*Nachos are a fattening appetizer, and could never pass as a "healthy dinner."*

TRUE for most restaurant nachos, FALSE for your own homemade!

Sitting down to a mounding plate of nachos covered with beans, cheese, and sour cream sounds like a major binge, right? Not at all, thanks to all the new low-fat foods available. Baked tortilla chips (like *Tostitos*®) can count as a healthful

serving of grain. Add vegetables, beans, salsa, and non-fat sour cream or yogurt, and you have a *most* delicious, satisfying, and completely guilt-free meal!

Compare this to a *restaurant* serving of *Nachos Supreme*, at 800 calories and 55 grams of fat!

Note: To achieve the recommended vegetable quota at dinner, munch on raw vegetables while you're making this up.

# Guiltless Nachos Supreme

Here's my favorite Friday night "veg-out" dinner. My husband and I munch on raw carrots, broccoli and cauliflower as we're making this up.

| SERVES | MENU |
|---|---|
| 2 | NACHOS |
| DOUBLES & | RAW VEGGIES |
| TRIPLES EASILY | GRAPES |

**Turn broiler on and keep oven door ajar.**

| | |
|---|---|
| 1 T | water |
| ¼ cup | onion *or* 2 green onions, chopped |
| ½ cup | green pepper, chopped |
| 1 cup | pinto *or* black beans (drained, rinsed) |
| 1 tsp | chili powder |

Chop vegetables, then heat all ingredients in a nonstick pan for about 3 minutes, stirring frequently.

Also a great party appetizer!

| | |
|---|---|
| 30 | (3 oz) baked tortilla chips *(Tostitos®)* |

Spread out onto a baking sheet.

Layer sauté over chips.

| | |
|---|---|
| ½ cup | reduced-fat shredded cheddar cheese |

Sprinkle on top of nachos.

Broil 6" from heating element for 4 to 6 minutes, or until cheese melts and browns slightly.

Play "Macho, Macho Man" by the Village People, dance around and sing, "Nacho, Nacho Man." Throw in a few jumping jacks and sit-ups while you're at it.

| | |
|---|---|
| ¼ cup | salsa |
| ¼ cup | light sour cream *or* non-fat plain yogurt |

Serve on the side for dipping. Fresh grapes make the ideal dessert.

**Sodium alert!** While 1,145 mg of sodium can work into a day's guideline of 3,000 mg, it is a bit much for other people needing to stay under 2,000. Therefore, to reduce sodium, use *Eden®* brand canned beans (which are low in sodium). Other sodium saving options are fresh (low sodium) salsa and unsalted baked corn tortillas.

## EXCHANGE VALUES

| 4 Starch | 2 Meat | 2 Veg. | — Fruit | — Milk | — Fat |
|---|---|---|---|---|---|

**Nutrition information for — ½ the recipe, 15 chips with salsa and light sour cream**

| | | | | |
|---|---|---|---|---|
| Calories .................................. 430 | Fat ............................................. 8 g | Fiber ....................................... 15 g | Sodium ........................ 1,145 mg | Total Carbohydrate ............. 70 g |
| Calories from Fat ............... 16% | Saturated Fat ...................... 4 g | Cholesterol ........................ 20 mg | Protein ................................. 22 g | Sugars ..................................... 5 g |

## "The Clean-Plate" Syndrome

# Tip

Try to refrain from asking your children to clean their plates. Insisting they finish their food when their stomachs are full, is teaching them to ignore their innate "obesity fighting" signal. Instead, say to them, "When your stomach tells you you've had enough, you can be excused." Then cover unused portions and refrigerate for the next meal or snack time.

# Turkey Joes

These Joes are fast and healthy. You can make your own Sloppy Joe sauce to save on the sodium, but when you need it fast, the can will do.

**SERVES** 6

**MENU**

Turkey Joes

Sunshine Carrot-Raisin Salad

Applesauce

| 1 lb. | extra-lean ground turkey breast |
| 1 | onion, chopped |

Brown in a nonstick skillet.

| 1 can | (16 oz) Sloppy Joe sauce (*Manwich®*) |

Add to the skillet. Cover and cook over medium high heat and simmer for 3 more minutes.

| 6 | whole-wheat hamburger buns |

Ladle ⅙ of the batch on top of each hamburger bun.

Serve with *Sunshine Carrot-Raisin Salad* (page 140) and applesauce on the side.

---

**EXCHANGE VALUES**

2.5 Starch    2 Meat    1 Veg.    — Fruit    — Milk    — Fat

**Nutrition information for — 1 Turkey Joe with bun**

| | | | | | |
|---|---|---|---|---|---|
| Calories .................................. 275 | Fat ................................. 2.5 g | Fiber ..................................... 4.5 g | Sodium ............................ 795 mg | Total Carbohydrate ............. 40 g |
| Calories from Fat ................. 8% | Saturated Fat .................... < 1 g | Cholesterol ........................ 36 mg | Protein ................................. 25 g | Sugars ..................................... 4 g |

# Tip

## Buying chicken: Save yourself time, money and headaches

I've found buying bags of *individually frozen*, skinless, boneless chicken breasts saves a lot of time, money, and effort. This product is so convenient because you can reach into the *Ziploc®* bag and grab however many you need. The chicken breasts are a uniform size and thickness. No need to plan ahead; they thaw in minutes on your cutting board. For even quicker results, add to the pan while still frozen. (They will thaw *and* cook in no time.) How terrific!

Look for this type of chicken in the freezer section of your grocery store.

### Sodium Alert

Check the label and avoid brands containing over 200 mg of sodium per serving. (Sometimes they go overboard injecting with a salt-water solution to promote juiciness.)

*Lickety-Split Meals*

# Crispy Chicken Dijon

Add this to your "must try" list. It's absolutely terrific!

| | | |
|---|---|---|
| **2 medium** | **sweet potatoes** (*or* **4 regular potatoes**) | Scrub and place in microwave for 12 minutes on high. |
| **1 box** | **(10 oz) frozen green beans, broccoli,** *or* **pea pods** | Place steamer basket in a pan and add 1" of water. Place over medium-high heat. Add vegetables and cover. When you notice it's boiling, set timer for 8 minutes. |
| **1 box** | **(10 oz) frozen sliced carrots** | |
| **¹/₂ cup** | **dry bread crumbs, unseasoned** | Take out 2 cereal bowls and place the bread crumbs in one, the mustard in the other. |
| **¹/₄ cup** | **Dijon mustard** | |
| **1 T** | **olive oil** | Heat over medium heat in a non-stick skillet. |
| **4** | **(4 oz each) boneless skinless chicken breast (halves)** | Dip chicken in mustard, then roll in the crumbs. Brown each side in the skillet 4 to 5 minutes. |

If vegetable timer goes off before you're ready, remove from heat and partially remove lid (to allow steam to escape but to keep the vegetables warm.)

Check to see if the chicken is done.

Serve with vegetables and a potato.

---

**EXCHANGE VALUES**

2 Starch    4 Meat    2 Veg.    — Fruit    — Milk    — Fat

**Nutrition information for — 1 chicken breast half, 1/2 sweet potato, 1 cup vegetables**

| | | | | |
|---|---|---|---|---|
| Calories ........ 380 | Fat ........ 8.5 g | Fiber ........ 6 g | Sodium ........ 360 mg | Total Carbohydrate ........ 42 g |
| Calories from Fat ........ 20% | Saturated Fat ........ 1.7 g | Cholesterol ........ 73 mg | Protein ........ 32 g | Sugars ........ 13 g |

# Simple Cutting Tip

Cutting chicken into strips is easy when the chicken is still mostly frozen. Set individually frozen chicken breasts on your cutting board to thaw for about 5 minutes. Then cut quickly and easily with a chef's knife (the kind with a big wide blade). Be careful, they can be a little slippery!

# Creamy Chicken Dijon over Noodles

Unexpected guests? Proudly serve this delicious 15 minute "company food" meal.
Guests will rave and family will feel like guests!

MENU

CREAMY CHICKEN DIJON

EGG NOODLES

ASPARAGUS

SLICED TOMATOES & CUCUMBERS

FRESH FRUIT CUP

**Place a large kettle full of water on to boil.**

| For 4 | For 6 | |
|---|---|---|
| 1 T | 1½ T | olive oil |
| 1 tsp | 1½ tsp | minced garlic (2 cloves) |
| 1 lb | 1½ lb | skinless, boneless, chicken breast strips |

Sauté 7 or 8 minutes until chicken is no longer pink.

*Delegate Someone to: Prep asparagus, tomatoes, cucumbers and fruit.*

| For 4 | For 6 | |
|---|---|---|
| 8 oz | 12 oz | dry egg noodles |

Meanwhile… add to boiling water.
Set timer for 6 minutes.

| For 4 | For 6 | |
|---|---|---|
| 1 small | 1 large | bunch fresh asparagus |

Meanwhile… wash asparagus. Trim off ends, cut diagonally into 1½" slices, and set aside.

| For 4 | For 6 | |
|---|---|---|
| 1 can | 2 cans | (7 oz each) mushrooms, drained |

Add to chicken and cook 1 minute.

| For 4 | For 6 | |
|---|---|---|
| ¼ cup | ⅓ cup | *Dijon* mustard |
| ½ cup | ¾ cup | light sour cream *or* non-fat yogurt |

Meanwhile… mix together using a 2 cup measuring cup. Add to bubbling chicken and mushrooms.

When timer goes off, toss asparagus in with the bubbling noodles. Set timer 2 minutes. At the sound of the timer, quickly drain.

Serve the Creamy Chicken Dijon over the noodles with asparagus, and place sliced tomatoes, cucumbers and a fresh fruit cup on the side.

**EXCHANGE VALUES**

| 2 Starch | 4 Meat | 2 Veg. | — Fruit | — Milk | — Fat |
|---|---|---|---|---|---|

**Nutrition information for — 1 chicken breast half, 1-1/2 cups noodles & asparagus, 1/4 cup sauce**

| | | | | | | |
|---|---|---|---|---|---|---|
| Calories .................................... 460 | Fat ........................................ 11 g | Fiber ........................................ 4 g | Sodium ............................ 440 mg | Total Carbohydrate ............. 48 g |
| Calories from Fat ............... 22% | Saturated Fat ..................... 3.5 g | Cholesterol ..................... 130 mg | Protein ................................ 40 g | Sugars ...................................... 6 g |

## Pop Quiz!

**Which of the following best describes your consumption of cooked dried beans?**

A.  Each week: A cup of bean soup, garbanzo beans on a salad, a bean burrito, and a serving of mixed vegetables (including lima beans).

B.  2 bean entrées per week including another serving from the left-overs for lunch on the following day (4 servings per week).

C.  Refried beans in Mexican food, once a week.

D.  Chili twice a year, baked beans twice a year.

E.  Beans? Are you crazy? I tasted them when I was 7 years old and hated them!

**Correct answer: A and B**

Dried beans are among the best foods on the planet! They are jam-packed with disease fighting phyto-chemicals, vitamins, minerals, and cholesterol-lowering fiber. They are rich in protein and are, therefore, a wonderful meat alternative. When beans *replace* meat at a meal, the benefit is magnified even more.

**Do yourself a favor: Think beans, 4 times a week!**

# White Beans with Tomato, Basil & Parmesan

| SERVES | MENU |
|---|---|
| 4 AS A MAIN COURSE | WHITE BEANS WITH TOMATO, BASIL & PARMESAN |
| 8 AS A SIDE DISH | CORNBREAD OR 9-GRAIN BREAD |
| | RAW VEGETABLES & DIP |
| | LEMON SORBET |

Serve this hot or cold, as a main or side dish.
Great with cornbread or whole-grain bread and raw veggies.

**Note: If you're planning to have *Cornbread*, mix that up first.
Start this recipe once you have the cornbread in the oven.**

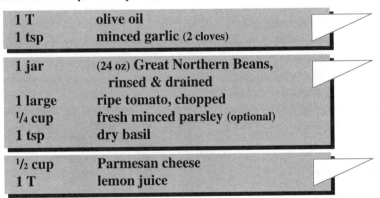

| | |
|---|---|
| 1 T | olive oil |
| 1 tsp | minced garlic (2 cloves) |

In a 12" nonstick skillet, sauté over medium heat for 3 minutes.

| | |
|---|---|
| 1 jar | (24 oz) **Great Northern Beans,** rinsed & drained |
| 1 large | ripe tomato, chopped |
| ¼ cup | fresh minced parsley (optional) |
| 1 tsp | dry basil |

Stir in and cook about 7 minutes longer.

Meanwhile… slice bread and prep raw veggies.

| | |
|---|---|
| ½ cup | Parmesan cheese |
| 1 T | lemon juice |

Mix in just before serving.

Serve with *Cornbread* (page 151) or 9-grain bread, raw vegetables and dip. Try lemon sorbet for dessert.

---

**EXCHANGE VALUES**

| 2 Starch | 1 Meat | — Veg. | — Fruit | — Milk | — Fat |
|---|---|---|---|---|---|

**Nutrition information for — maincourse serving, 1 cup**

| | | | | |
|---|---|---|---|---|
| Calories .................... 240 | Fat ........................ 6.5 g | Fiber ...................... 13 g | Sodium .................... 550 mg | Total Carbohydrate ......... 32 g |
| Calories from Fat ......... 24% | Saturated Fat ......... 2.5 g | Cholesterol .............. 8 mg | Protein ...................... 14 g | Sugars ........................ 1 g |

# Tip

| "The Big Eater" |

*Do you remember being praised for eating more food than anyone else?*

When your child does eat a big meal, avoid the temptation to say, "good boy" or "good girl." Instead, keep your comments low-key and focused on their "gut" feelings, like, "Wow, you were hungry tonight, weren't you?" Responses like these go a long way in preventing the overeating habit.

# Cheesy Potato Skillet with Mixed Vegetables

Talk about a "no-brainer," this is fast and satisfying after a super hectic day.

**MENU**

CHEESY POTATO SKILLET WITH MIXED VEGETABLES

WHOLE-WHEAT GARLIC CHEESE TOAST (OPTIONAL)

SLICED APPLES, ORANGES OR KIWIS

| | |
|---|---|
| **1 T** | **oil** (olive *or* canola) |
| **16 oz** | **frozen mixed vegetables** (peas, corn, carrots) |

Place in a non-stick skillet over medium-high heat for 4 minutes. Stir frequently.

(During this time, consider making the *Whole-Wheat Garlic Cheese Toast,* page 150.)

| | |
|---|---|
| **16 oz** | **frozen *Ore Ida*® O'Brien Potatoes** (hash browns with onions and peppers) |

Add and cook 6 minutes longer, stirring frequently.

(Look for fruit to serve like oranges, apples and kiwi.)

| | |
|---|---|
| **¹/₂ cup** | **reduced-fat shredded mozzarella cheese** |
| **10 grinds** | **fresh ground pepper** |
| **2T** | **Parmesan cheese** |

Sprinkle over vegetables, turn off heat, cover, and let stand 1 minute.

Serve with orange sections, apple wedges, or kiwi slices and *with Whole-Wheat Garlic Cheese Toast.*

---

**EXCHANGE VALUES**

| 3 Starch | 1 Meat | 2 Veg. | — Fruit | — Milk | — Fat |
|---|---|---|---|---|---|

Nutrition information for — one generous serving (1/2 the recipe) NOTE: If serving with *Whole-Wheat Garlic Cheese Toast,* serve less.

| | | | | |
|---|---|---|---|---|
| Calories ......................................... 436 | Fat ......................................... 11 g | Fiber ......................................... 15 g | Sodium ............................. 450 mg | Total Carbohydrate ............. 70 g |
| Calories from Fat ............... 21% | Saturated Fat ..................... 3.5 g | Cholesterol ........................ 14 mg | Protein ......................................... 20 g | Sugars ......................................... 11 g |

# Tip

## Beans, Beans the Magical Fruit...

I suppose it's time to talk about ... GAS. If you find yourself avoiding beans because of this problem, try these tips:

1. Many people's digestive tracts gradually adjust in their ability to produce the necessary enzymes to digest beans. **Therefore, add beans to your diet in *small* servings several times per week.** Not eating beans on a consistent basis and then digging into a big batch of chili and beans is what shocks your system, causing excessive gas.

2. Start with easier-to-digest beans like lentils and split peas.

3. **Consider a supplement like "Beano."** It provides the enzyme that your body is not sufficiently producing. Available at your pharmacy.

4. If all else fails, take frequent walks. Whatever it takes, get your body used to eating a small portion of beans, FOUR times per week!

# Gingered Black Beans with Squash

I'm always on the lookout for recipes using the nutrition dynamo Winter squash.
This recipe comes from *Easy Eden®* by Lorna Sass and is delightful served over rice.

| SERVES | MENU |
| --- | --- |
| 6 | GINGERED BLACK BEANS WITH SQUASH OVER RICE |
| | APPLE WEDGES |

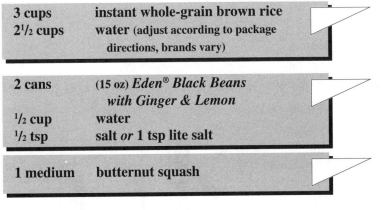

| | |
| --- | --- |
| 3 cups | instant whole-grain brown rice |
| 2½ cups | water (adjust according to package directions, brands vary) |

Place rice and water in a 2 quart microwave-safe dish. Cover and cook for 12 minutes on high.

| | |
| --- | --- |
| 2 cans | (15 oz) *Eden® Black Beans with Ginger & Lemon* |
| ½ cup | water |
| ½ tsp | salt *or* 1 tsp lite salt |

In a large saucepan, place over medium-high heat.

| | |
| --- | --- |
| 1 medium | butternut squash |

Peel, seed, and cut into chunks. Place in a food processor and pulse a few times to create pieces slightly larger than the beans.

Add squash to the beans and simmer 5 minutes or until squash is done.

| | |
| --- | --- |
| 3 T | white wine |
| ½ cup | sliced green onions (tops & bottoms) |

Stir in and serve over rice.

Serve with apple wedges.

## EXCHANGE VALUES
4 Starch    1 Meat    1 Veg.    — Fruit    — Milk    — Fat

**Nutrition information for — ⅙ of the recipe**

| | | | | |
| --- | --- | --- | --- | --- |
| Calories ............ 338 | Fat ............ 1 g | Fiber ............ 5.5 g | Sodium ............ 440 mg | Total Carbohydrate ............ 68 g |
| Calories from Fat ............ 3% | Saturated Fat ............ 0 g | Cholesterol ............ 0 mg | Protein ............ 13 g | Sugars ............ 5 g |

Gingered Black Beans with Squash                    *Lickety-Split Meals*

# Tip

## What does tofu taste like?

No one can say tofu tastes bad. It simply has no taste at all! The good news is, tofu takes on the flavors of whatever spices or flavorings you use with it. In fact, a good rule of thumb is to increase spices and seasonings by one-half whenever using tofu.

See page 50 for information about what tofu is and its benefits.

---

**\*Super Time Saving Tip**

Skip microwaving the potatoes and chopping the pepper and onion by using 2 cups of *Ore Ida® Potatoes O'Brien* (a frozen hash brown product, called for in previous recipe). It has no fat, just chopped potatoes, onions, and peppers, and saves you loads of time!

*Lickety-Split Meals*

# Cheesy Scrambled Tofu

This is the very first recipe I learned to make (and like!) using tofu. Makes a great dinner or breakfast. You can save a lot of fat grams by using your favorite fat-free cheese.

| | |
|---|---|
| 2 | potatoes* |

Scrub potatoes clean. Poke each twice with a fork. Wrap them in damp paper towels. Microwave on high 6 to 8 minutes.

| | |
|---|---|
| ½ | green pepper* |
| ½ | onion* |

Meanwhile… chop vegetables and begin to sauté in a nonstick pan using nonstick spray.

**Optional extras**

| | |
|---|---|
| 1 cup | frozen corn |
| 1 | chopped tomato |
| 1 cup | sliced mushrooms |
| 1 cup | fresh *or* frozen snow peas |

Add any optional extras.

| | |
|---|---|
| 4 slices | whole-wheat bread, *or* |
| | 4 English muffins |

Make toast.

| | |
|---|---|
| 12 oz | firm tofu |
| 1 tsp | cumin, dill *or* oregano |
| | (pick your favorite) |

Crumble tofu and add it to the sauté. Add tofu and your choice of spice to the pan. It is important for the tofu to absorb the flavors from the vegetables and spice. When potatoes are done, chop them and add to sauté 5 minutes.

| | |
|---|---|
| ¼ cup | reduced-fat shredded cheddar cheese |
| ¼ cup | reduced-fat shredded mozzarella cheese |

Sprinkle both kinds of cheese on top. Cover and cook 2 minutes more.

Meanwhile… set the table, set out fresh fruit, toast and jam.

---

**EXCHANGE VALUES**

| 2 Starch | 2 Meat | — Veg. | — Fruit | — Milk | — Fat |
|---|---|---|---|---|---|

\* See my Super Time Saving Tip above.

**Nutrition information for — 1 serving, including optional extras and 1 slice of bread**

| | | | | | | | | |
|---|---|---|---|---|---|---|---|---|
| Calories | 265 | Fat | 5.5 g | Fiber | 6 g | Sodium | 385 | Total Carbohydrate | 40 g |
| Calories from Fat | 17% | Saturated Fat | 1.2 g | Cholesterol | 5 mg | Protein | 17 g | Sugars | 5 g |

# 30-Minute Meals

While researching the needs of families, I heard several shared wishes:

- "Easy meals for more quality dinner time at home"
- "To eliminate unnecessary steps"
- "To create less mess"
- "To put the entire meal on the table in 30 minutes"

Are you also in need of the Wizard? Welcome to the Land of Oz, where there's no place like home. It's back to the family, gathered around the table for a home cooked meal. All in only 30 minutes!

## Money Saving Tip for Brown Rice

**Tip**

While instant whole-grain brown rice combines nutrition with convenience, it can also be a bit pricey. Try this tip: On any day that you are going to be around the house for an hour, cook 3 cups of brown rice in 6 cups of water for 45 minutes to 1 hour. The rice will then keep in the refrigerator for 4 days, or in the freezer for up to 3 months. Either way, reheating the rice in the microwave is as fast as using instant rice, without the cost!

# Curried Chickpeas & Gingered Black Beans

SERVES 4

Ready for a nice twist for the old taste-buds? You know, I never thought I liked curry and avoided every recipe with it. What a mistake! The ginger and curry are awesome together and the presentation is beautiful. Try it!

**MENU**

CURRIED CHICKPEAS W/RICE
BROCCOLI & CARROTS
LEMON SORBET

| | |
|---|---|
| 2 cups | **instant whole-grain brown rice** |
| 1³/₄ cup | **water** (adjust according to package directions, brands vary) |

Place in microwave-safe dish.

| | |
|---|---|
| 1 head | **broccoli** (cleaned & cut into flowerettes) |
| 12 | **baby carrots** |

Add to rice. Cover and place in microwave.
Cook on high for 10 minutes.

| | |
|---|---|
| 1 small | **onion** |
| 1 T | **olive oil** |
| 2 tsp | **ginger** (fresh grated is best) |
| 2 tsp | **curry** |

Cut onion into small wedges. Heat oil on medium-high in a nonstick skillet. Add onion and spices. Cook 2 minutes. Meanwhile… open cans. Drain and rinse beans for next step.

| | |
|---|---|
| 1 can | **(14.5 oz) stewed tomatoes** |
| 1 can | **(15 oz) chickpeas, rinsed and drained** |
| 1 can | **(15 oz) blackbeans, rinsed and drained** |
| ¹/₃ cup | **chopped fresh parsley** (optional) |

Add to skillet and simmer 5 minutes.

| | |
|---|---|
| 1 T | **lemon juice** (optional) |

Stir in just before serving.

Serve beans over the rice and vegetables, with lemon sorbet for dessert.

## EXCHANGE VALUES

5 Starch   1 Meat   2 Veg.   — Fruit   — Milk   — Fat

**Nutrition information for — approximately 1 cup over 1 cup rice with 1 cup vegetables**

| | | | | | |
|---|---|---|---|---|---|
| Calories .................... 440 | Fat .......................... 6 g | Fiber ............................ 15.5 g | Sodium .......................... 766 mg | Total Carbohydrate ............ 87 g |
| Calories from Fat .............. 11% | Saturated Fat ................ < 1 g | Cholesterol ...................... 0 mg | Protein ............................ 17 g | Sugars .............................. 10 g |

# Tip

## Married with children?

Finding it hard to get a sitter for that once-a-week date your marriage desperately deserves? Follow the advice of my friends, Jay and Art Johnson. Pick 1 night a week for date night. Make the kids their favorite dinner while the two of you munch on raw veggies and dip. Get the kids to bed promptly at 8:00. Light candles. Make a simple, yet light and elegant dinner. Rent a movie. Presto! You have date night, without hiring a sitter!

Romantic dinner for two suggestions:

*Skillet Chicken and Vegetables in Wine* (this page!)

*Crispy Chicken Dijon* (page 56)

*Chicken Marsala with Brown Rice and Peas* (page 65)

*White Beans with Tomato, Basil & Parmesan* (page 58)

Our favorite, *Guiltless Nachos Supreme* (page 54)

# Skillet Chicken & Vegetables in Wine

Serve this scrumptious meal with a tossed salad and whole grain bread.

**SERVES**

4

**MENU**

SKILLET CHICKEN IN WINE
BAKED POTATOES
TOSSED SALAD
WHOLE-GRAIN BREAD
FROZEN YOGURT

| | |
|---|---|
| 4 | potatoes, sweet *or* regular |

Scrub thoroughly and pierce each potato 3 or 4 times with a fork. Microwave on high for 10 minutes. Cook more if necessary.

| | |
|---|---|
| 1 T | olive oil (garlic flavored if you have it) |
| 4 | skinless, boneless, chicken breasts |
| | (halves) |

Heat oil in nonstick pan on medium high. Add chicken to pan and cook until browned. Turn and brown other side.

| | |
|---|---|
| 1 | onion |
| 1 | red *or* yellow pepper |
| 1½ | cups frozen peas |

Meanwhile... cut peppers into strips and onion into wedges. Add to chicken, and sauté for 2 minutes.

| | |
|---|---|
| ¼ cup | white wine |
| ¼ tsp | thyme |
| ¼ tsp | rosemary |
| ¼ tsp | poultry seasoning |
| 5 grinds | fresh ground pepper |
| ½ tsp | salt |

Add to pan and cover. The wine should entirely evaporate in only a few minutes. When "brown bits" begin collecting in the pan, the dish is done.

Serve with potatoes, salad, and whole grain bread.

If you still have room for dessert, treat yourself to a small scoop of vanilla frozen yogurt with chocolate syrup on top.

## EXCHANGE VALUES

2 Starch    4 Meat    1 Veg.    — Fruit    — Milk    — Fat

**Nutrition information for — 1 chicken breast half, 1 potato, 3/4 cup vegetables**

| | | | | | |
|---|---|---|---|---|---|
| Calories .................... 340 | Fat .......................... 5 g | Fiber .......................... 7 g | Sodium .......................... 430 mg | Total Carbohydrate ............ 36 g |
| Calories from Fat ............... 14% | Saturated Fat ..................... 1 g | Cholesterol ...................... 68 mg | Protein .................................. 34 g | Sugars ..................................... 5 g |

# Tip

## Germ-Free Cooking

The Center for Science in the Public Interest recommends that we assume *all* raw meat, poultry, and fish are contaminated with bacteria, and therefore to be handled properly. To prevent even a mild case of food poisoning "flu" in your home, do not allow any uncooked meat to come in contact with cutting boards, plates or utensils that will touch foods that will be eaten uncooked.

Follow these important safe-handling tips:

- Own 2 cutting boards. Reserve one for meats, the other for vegetables. This helps reduce the chances of cross contamination.

- Thoroughly wash your cutting boards and knives immediately after prepping your meat. (Delaying this chore is an invitation for cross contamination to occur.)

- Use a CLEAN plate for serving meat off the grill (not the plate you used to bring the meat *to* the grill). Use a clean utensil as well.

- Discard meat marinade after its use. (However, if you boil it, you can serve it as a dipping sauce.)

# Chicken Marsala

This is worth the extra effort to buy Marsala cooking wine. You'll think you're eating restaurant food! And you'll be glad to know this really only takes 20 minutes.

**MENU**

CHICKEN MARSALA
BROWN RICE
PEAS
WHERE'S THE LETTUCE? SALAD
SLICED PEARS & KIWI

| | |
|---|---|
| 2 cups | instant, whole-grain brown rice |
| 1¾ cup | water (adjust according to package directions, brands vary) |
| 2 cups | frozen peas |

Combine in a microwave-safe dish. Cover and cook on high 9 to 10 minutes.

| | |
|---|---|
| 1 | onion, cut into wedges |
| 1 T | olive oil |
| 1 tsp | minced garlic (2 cloves) |
| 1 can | (7 oz) mushrooms, drained |

Meanwhile… prep the onion. Then heat oil in a nonstick skillet. Add all to the skillet and begin sautéing.

| | |
|---|---|
| 4 | skinless, boneless, chicken breast (halves) |

Add to the skillet. Brown on each side 5 minutes.

| | |
|---|---|
| ⅓ cup | Marsala wine |

Add to skillet. It will begin evaporating quickly.

| | |
|---|---|
| ⅔ cup | chicken broth, ⅓ less sodium |
| ¼ tsp | salt (optional) |
| 4 tsp | cornstarch |
| 4 grinds | fresh ground pepper |

Mix together in a measuring cup. Add to skillet. Reduce heat to low. Simmer 5 minutes until chicken is done.

Serve the chicken and sauce over the rice and peas with *Where's the Lettuce? Salad* (page 138) and sliced fruit for dessert.

---

**EXCHANGE VALUES**

| 3 Starch | 4 Meat | 1 Veg. | — Fruit | — Milk | — Fat |
|---|---|---|---|---|---|

**Nutrition information for — 1 chicken breast half, 1 cup rice and 1/2 cup peas with sauce**

| | | | | | |
|---|---|---|---|---|---|
| Calories ............... 430 mg | Fat ............... 6 g | Fiber ............... 8 g | Sodium ............... 725 mg | Total Carbohydrate ............... 53 g |
| Calories from Fat ............... 13% | Saturated Fat ............... 1 g | Cholesterol ............... 68 mg | Protein ............... 37 g | Sugars ............... 7 g |

# Tip

## How to combat the afterwork snack attacks

A good way to prevent coming home ravenous and out of control is to take a banana (or similar snack) to work with you. Save it to eat later in the afternoon or on your drive home. Eating a snack at this time allows the nourishment to "hit your stomach," so you will feel energized, instead of famished, upon arriving home. Chasing it with a bottle of water is also very filling and supplies needed hydration, which many people are lacking at this time of day.

# Hungarian Chicken Paprikash

This is a nutri-sized version of Katherine Buss' original Hungarian recipe, and you won't believe how delicious it is. Katherine's granddaughter, Stacy Rafalko and I were able to cut 15 grams of fat per serving off the original recipe. Grandma, can you tell?

| | |
|---|---|
| **3 medium** | **onions, chopped** |
| **1½ T** | **olive _or_ canola oil** |

Sauté in oil over medium-high heat for 8 to 10 minutes.

**Meanwhile… place a large kettle of water on to boil.**

| | |
|---|---|
| **6** | **skinless, boneless, chicken breast** (halves) |
| **3 T** | **paprika** (Yes, that's T's, not tsp's) |
| **10 grinds** | **fresh ground pepper** |
| **2 T** | **low-sodium chicken bouillon** |
| **1½ tsp** | **salt** |
| **¾ cup** | **water** |

Add to onions and mix to coat chicken.
Cover and cook 15 minutes, turning chicken occasionally.

| | |
|---|---|
| **12 oz** | **egg noodles** |

Meanwhile… add to boiling water. Set timer for 10 minutes.

| | |
|---|---|
| **2 boxes** | (9 oz each) **frozen whole green beans** |

Place in a microwave-safe dish, cover, and microwave on high for 8 minutes. Use this time to prepare a tossed salad and set the table.

| | |
|---|---|
| **1½ cups** | **light sour cream** |

Remove chicken from heat and stir in sour cream.

Drain noodles. Pour chicken mixture over noodles and toss.

Serve with the green beans and salad.

Don't forget ginger snaps and grapes for dessert!

---

**EXCHANGE VALUES**

3 Starch    4 Meat    1 Veg.    — Fruit    — Milk    — Fat

---

**Nutrition information for — 1 chicken breast half with 1-1/2 cups of noodles and 1/2 cup of green beans**

| | | | |
|---|---|---|---|
| Calories ............... 500 | Fat ............... 12 g | Fiber ............... 4.3 g | Sodium ............... 721 mg | Total Carbohydrate ............. 53 g |
| Calories from Fat ............... 23% | Saturated Fat ............... 5 g | Cholesterol ............... 142 mg | Protein ............... 40 g | Sugars ............... 9 g |

# Tip

## Attention Macaroni and Cheese Fans!

Rescue a high-fat, high-calorie, low-fiber meal with the following 3 simple changes:

1. Use skim milk.

2. Reduce the margarine to 1 T (eventually none!) and make up the reduced liquid in extra milk. (Numerous clients agree that even finicky children do not notice this change.)

3. Reduce the portion of macaroni and cheese and serve ample vegetables and sliced fruit with the meal. (This helps increase the fiber while reducing your sodium intake.) You may choose to add vegetables right to the macaroni and cheese to get twice the benefit from the cheesy sauce.

# Easy Succotash Dinner

| | SERVES | MENU |
|---|---|---|
| You may think I'm crazy to call this dish a meal, but think about it! It's protein, grain, and vegetables all in one dish. It's as fast as macaroni and cheese, and much more delicious and nutritious. | 4 | SUCCOTASH<br>SALAD OR CARROTS STICKS<br>FROZEN YOGURT<br>AND GINGERSNAPS |

| | |
|---|---|
| 1 cup | water |
| 1 bag | (16 oz) **frozen corn** |
| 1 bag | (16 oz) **frozen lima beans** |

Place all together in a medium-sized pan. Bring to a boil on medium-high heat. Cover and simmer for 13 minutes. Be sure to set your timer, this is the exact time before all the water boils away.

Search your refrigerator for some lettuce, vegetables, or fruit to make a salad. Raw carrots will do if that's all you can find.

| | |
|---|---|
| 1 cup | **reduced-fat shredded cheddar cheese** |
| 10 grinds | **fresh ground pepper** |

At the sound of the timer, remove from heat and stir in. The cheese will melt in seconds.

Serve with salad or carrot sticks, frozen yogurt, and gingersnaps.

---

**EXCHANGE VALUES**

| 3 Starch | 2 Meat | — Veg. | — Fruit | — Milk | — Fat |
|---|---|---|---|---|---|

**Nutrition information for — 1-1/4 cup serving**

| | | | | |
|---|---|---|---|---|
| Calories ....................... 270 | Fat ......................... 4 g | Fiber ......................... 9 g | Sodium .......................... 310 mg | Total Carbohydrate ............ 44 g |
| Calories from Fat ............... 13% | Saturated Fat ................... 2 g | Cholesterol ..................... 9 mg | Protein ................................ 18 g | Sugars ....................................... 5 g |

## Can you think of any foods that may have contributed to your youthfulness?

*"For 30 years, we raised sweet potatoes, and boy did we eat a lot of them. I've always cooked up a pot of beans weekly (yes, with a ham bone)! But probably the biggest thing, has been my years of home-cooked meals, not processed restaurant foods."*

—My grandmother
MINNIE BURGESS, 90,
still climbing the stairs
of her home effortlessly,
countless times a day

*Lickety-Split Meals*

# Broiled Orange Roughy

| SERVES | MENU |
|---|---|
| 4 | BROILED ORANGE ROUGHY |
|   | VEGETABLE MEDLEY |
|   | BAKED POTATOES |
|   | 5 GINGERSNAPS |

Let's face it, who wants to cook on Friday night? (And it's time you had a break from pizza!) This meal comes together so fast—you won't even know you cooked!

**Turn broiler on. Don't forget to leave oven door ajar.**

| 4 | sweet potatoes *or* regular potatoes |
|---|---|

Scrub thoroughly and pierce each potato 3 or 4 times with a fork. Microwave on high for 8 minutes. Cook more if necessary.

| ¹/₂ head | cauliflower |
|---|---|
| ¹/₂ head | broccoli |
| 8 | baby carrots |

Clean and cut into pieces or save time and use frozen. Place in a steamer on top of the stove to cook for 8 to 10 minutes.

| 4 | (4 oz each) **frozen fish fillets** |
|---|---|
|   | (thin fillets of orange roughy) |
| 1 | lemon, quartered |

Place frozen fillets on broiling pan. Squeeze ¹/₄ of the lemon over each fillet.

| dash | paprika |
|---|---|
| dash | dill *or* oregano |

Sprinkle as much as you wish onto each fillet.

Broil 6" from heating element for 7 to 10 minutes.

Place potatoes and vegetables on the table and serve fish.

Don't forget the gingersnaps!

Note: Fish will not need to be turned to cook all the way through if fillets are thin. Fish is done when it flakes easily with a fork.

---

**EXCHANGE VALUES**

| 3 Starch | 3 Meat | 3 Veg. | — Fruit | — Milk | — Fat |
|---|---|---|---|---|---|

**Nutrition information for — 1 fish fillet, 1 potato, 1 cup vegetables**

| Calories ................................... 325 | Fat ............................. 1.5 g | Fiber ................................. 10 g | Sodium .......................... 137 mg | Total Carbohydrate ............ 57 g |
|---|---|---|---|---|
| Calories from Fat ................. 4% | Saturated Fat ...................... 0 g | Cholesterol ...................... 23 mg | Protein ............................ 23 g | Sugars .................................. 27 g |

Broiled Orange Roughy

*Lickety-Split Meals*

## Fish Facts

# Tip

It all started with studies showing that fish-loving Eskimos hardly ever get heart disease. Now we know the oil in fish reduces heart attack risk by warding off blood clots, lowering blood pressure and bringing down high triglycerides (blood fats). Other associations are being made about fish oil being helpful to arthritics.

A smart move: Replace prime rib with salmon to boost your health. Also, for convenience at home, consider cracking open a can of salmon, just as you would tuna, for salmon salad sandwiches.

Aim to eat fish 2-3 times per week!

# Salmon Burgers

These are delicious! A simple and tasty way to eat salmon, which is so good for you! Serve as burgers on hamburger buns with lettuce and tomato, or serve with a baked potato and green vegetables for a salmon patty dinner.

**SERVES** 4

**MENU**

SALMON BURGERS WITH WHOLE-GRAIN BUN

STEAMED ASPARAGUS OR GREEN BEANS

BAKED TORTILLA CHIPS

FUDGESICLE

| | |
|---|---|
| 1 can | (15 oz) **red** *or* **pink salmon, packed in water, drained** (*or* 2 cups flaked) |

In a medium-sized bowl, remove skin from fish and flake with a fork, mashing bones (great calcium).

| | |
|---|---|
| 8 | **crackers** (whole-wheat saltines) |
| ¼ cup | **diced red pepper** |
| 3 T | *Miracle Whip*® **Light** |
| 1 tsp | **lemon juice** (bottled *or* fresh squeezed) |
| 4 drops | **Tabasco sauce** |

Crush the crackers and add to the bowl.
Add remaining ingredients. Mix well. Set aside.

| | |
|---|---|
| 1 bunch | **Fresh asparagus** *or* **green beans** |

Clean and place in a microwave-safe dish.
Cover and microwave on high for 7 minutes.

Return to the salmon mix. Shape into 4 patties. Spray a nonstick skillet with cooking spray and place over medium heat. Cook salmon cakes, turning once, until lightly browned on each side.

| | |
|---|---|
| 4 | **hamburger buns** (preferably whole-wheat) |
| 4 | **lettuce leaves** |
| 1 | **tomato, sliced** |

Assemble into burgers.

| | |
|---|---|
| 40 | *Baked Tostitos*® |

Serve with asparagus and 10 chips on the side.
Don't forget the fudgesicle for dessert!

---

**EXCHANGE VALUES**

| 3 Starch | 3 Meat | 1 Veg. | — Fruit | — Milk | — Fat |
|---|---|---|---|---|---|

---

**Nutrition information for — 1 Salmon Burger with whole-grain bun, 6 asparagus spears and 10 baked corn chips**

| | | | | |
|---|---|---|---|---|
| Calories .................................. 415 | Fat ........................................ 13.5 g | Fiber ........................................ 6 g | Sodium ............................. 795 mg | Total Carbohydrate ............. 50 g |
| Calories from Fat ............... 27% | Saturated Fat ........................ 2 g | Cholesterol ......................... 76 mg | Protein ................................. 28 g | Sugars .................................... 4 g |

## Pepper power!

Among the vegetable superstars stands sweet peppers. Red, yellow, orange, and green, they pack a powerful punch of valuable nutrition. Even the natural "color" of the peppers is tremendously valuable to your body and its defenses against cancer and heart disease.

My advice to you: Buy, cook, and snack on them as often as possible!

### Super Time and Money Saving Tip:

When you find peppers on sale (particularly the red, yellow, and orange ones which can be quite pricey), buy as many as you can. Wash, seed, and chop them. Place them in zip-lock bags and freeze. (Add chopped onions if you'd like.) Every 20 minutes over the next hour, reach in and shake the bags. (This keeps them from freezing in one big chunk. Set the timer to remind you.)

You will now have fast and economical chopped peppers ready in your freezer for directly adding to any stir-fry or vegetable sauté. They keep up to 3 months. (However, use fresh peppers for raw dishes like salads.)

*Lickety-Split Meals*

# Unstuffed Peppers

Who has time for fancy stuffed peppers? This recipe skips that step, yet delivers the characteristic flavor in a fast and simple skillet dish.

SERVES

6

MENU

UNSTUFFED PEPPERS
TOSSED SALAD
MULTI-GRAIN BREAD
SLICED FRUIT

| | |
|---|---|
| 1 box | **(10 oz) frozen chopped spinach** |

Take spinach out of freezer and thaw most of the way in the microwave. Set aside.

| | |
|---|---|
| 1 | **onion** |
| 1 each | **green, red and yellow pepper** |
| 2 tsp | **minced garlic (4 cloves)** |
| 20 | **baby carrots** |

Cut all the vegetables into small wedges.

| | |
|---|---|
| 1 T | **olive oil (garlic *or* red pepper flavored is good)** |

Heat oil in a large nonstick kettle and sauté the vegetables and garlic.

| | |
|---|---|
| 1 lb | **extra-lean ground turkey breast** |

Crumble the turkey, break up the spinach, and add both to the sauté.

| | |
|---|---|
| 2 tsp | ***Mrs. Dash® or Spike®* seasoning** |
| 2 tsp | **oregano** |
| 1/4 tsp | **salt (optional)** |
| 2 cans | **(14.5 oz) stewed *or* crushed tomatoes** |
| 1 can | **(14.5 oz) chicken broth, 1/3 less sodium** |

While waiting for the meat to brown, add seasonings to sauté. Open the cans. Once the meat is completely brown, add broth and tomatoes.

| | |
|---|---|
| 2 cups | **instant whole-grain brown rice** |
| 1/2 cup | **Parmesan cheese** |

Once the mixture comes to a boil, add rice and cheese. Stir well. Cover and set timer for 5 minutes.

Meanwhile… search through the refrigerator for tossed salad "fixin's". Slice up bread. Slice apples, kiwi, oranges or any other fruit you have. When timer goes off, dinner is ready!

---

**EXCHANGE VALUES**

| 2 Starch | 3 Meat | 2 Veg. | — Fruit | — Milk | — Fat |
|---|---|---|---|---|---|

**Nutrition information for — 1-1/2 cup serving**

| | | | | | | | | | |
|---|---|---|---|---|---|---|---|---|---|
| Calories | 320 | Fat | 6 g | Fiber | 5.2 g | Sodium | 800 mg | Total Carbohydrate | 40 g |
| Calories from Fat | 17% | Saturated Fat | 2 g | Cholesterol | 40 mg | Protein | 28 g | Sugars | 9 g |

# Great ideas from people like you!

**Tip**

"Because cancer fighting compounds from my foods are of utmost importance to me, I focus on dried beans, whole grains, fruits, vegetables, and plenty of soy foods, including a pound of tofu every week. I assure this with my ritual morning shake, consisting of tofu, soy milk, carrots, fruit, fruit juice, wheat bran, wheat germ, and flax seeds. I developed this shake after my third cancer, as a way to get as many phytochemicals in my diet as possible."

—DIANA DYER, MS, RD, CNSD
Dietitian
Vibrant and healthy
3-time cancer survivor

P.S. To follow an example for creating your own cancer recovery and healing program, order Diana's book, *A Dietitian's Cancer Story: Information and Inspiration for Recovery and Healing from a 3-Time Cancer Survivor.* From diet to meditation, exercise, supplements, alternative and conventional cancer therapies, Diana shares it all in this wonderful and personal book. Order by sending a check for $6.50 made out to Diana Dyer at P.O. Box 130221, Ann Arbor, MI 48113. And tell her I said hello!

## Why tofu?

See page 50 to find out!

*Lickety-Split Meals*

# Tofu Fiesta

You can have this delicious, meatless/cheeseless meal on the table in no time at all!

| | |
|---|---|
| 2 | potatoes |

Scrub thoroughly and pierce each potato 3 or 4 times with a fork. Microwave on high for 7 minutes. Cook more if necessary.

| | |
|---|---|
| 1 | onion |
| 1/2 | green pepper |
| 1/2 | red pepper |
| 1 tsp | minced garlic (2 cloves) |
| 1 cup | frozen corn |
| 1/2 cup | chopped fresh parsley *or* cilantro (reserve 1/4 cup for garnish) |

Spray frying pan with nonstick cooking spray. Chop onion and peppers into wedges or strips. Sauté vegetables in pan over medium-high heat for 3 minutes.

| | |
|---|---|
| 12 oz | firm tofu |
| 2 cups | (canned) pinto beans, rinsed & drained |
| 1 1/2 tsp | chili powder |
| 1/2 tsp | cumin |

Add crumbled tofu and spices to the pan. Drain and rinse beans. Add to pan. Sauté 5 minutes more.

Meanwhile… retrieve cooked potatoes. Chop into small pieces and add to sauté.

| | |
|---|---|
| 2 cups | salsa (fresh salsa is best) |
| 1/4 cup | reserved chopped parsley *or* cilantro |

Add salsa. Cover and cook 3 minutes more. (Use this time to warm bread in the microwave.)

To serve the Tofu Fiesta, I sprinkle on any additional parsley or cilantro for garnish. Accompany with warm bread, a tossed salad, and a bowl of fruit for dessert.

**EXCHANGE VALUES**

| 2 Starch | 2 Meat | 2 Veg. | — Fruit | — Milk | — Fat |
|---|---|---|---|---|---|

**Nutrition information for — approximately 1 cup**

| | | | | |
|---|---|---|---|---|
| Calories ..................................... 310 | Fat ...................................... 3 g | Fiber ...................................... 14 g | Sodium ............................ 840 mg | Total Carbohydrate ............. 58 g |
| Calories from Fat ................. 8% | Saturated Fat ........................ 0 g | Cholesterol .......................... 0 mg | Protein ............................... 16 g | Sugars ...................................... 8 g |

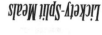

**Tip**

## What do you think is the secret to your youthfulness?

*"Since I feel my best on the days I get out and about, I sure think that's important. Each day I always eat 3-4 pieces of fruit and always have. I drink a lot of water, 2 glasses of 1/2% milk and hot water instead of coffee."*

—CHARLOTTE BROWNELL, 82
Still volunteering
at the thrift store
15 years and
counting

# Grilled Beef or Chicken Teriyaki

SERVES

4

When I was growing up, I remember mom let us pick what we wanted to have for our birthday dinner. I always chose "Beef Teriyaki." It's now my husband's favorite recipe for venison. This marinade is so versatile you can use it for any of your favorite meats or even for tofu!

**MENU**

GRILLED TERIYAKI

BROWN RICE

BROCCOLI & CARROTS

SLICED NECTARINES OR SIMPLE SUMMER FRESH FRUIT PIE

**Night before or in the early morning**

| | |
|---|---|
| ¼ cup | soy sauce, reduced-sodium |
| 1 T | firmly packed brown sugar |
| 2 T | water |
| 2 tsp | sesame oil |
| ½ tsp | ginger (fresh grated is best) |
| 5 grates | fresh black pepper |
| ¼ tsp | minced garlic (1 clove) |

Mix together in a bowl big enough to hold the meat you will be marinating.

| | |
|---|---|
| 1 lb | lean trimmed sirloin, flank steak, chicken breasts, venison, fish *or* 2 tubs (12 oz each) tofu cut into chunks *or* strips |

Add and toss to coat. Allow to marinate in the refrigerator 8 hours or overnight.

Consider making *Simple Summer Fresh Fruit Pie* (page 153).

**Preheat gas grill or broiler.**

**30 minutes before dinner**

| | |
|---|---|
| 2 cups | instant whole-grain brown rice |
| 1¾ cups | water (adjust according to package directions, brands vary) |

Place in microwave-safe dish.

| | |
|---|---|
| 1 head | broccoli (cleaned and cut into flowerets) |
| 12 | baby carrots |

Add to rice. Cover and place in microwave. Cook on high for 10 minutes.

Remove meat from marinade and grill or broil. Check meat frequently for doneness. Discard marinade.

Serve with rice, vegetables, and fruit or fruit pie for dessert.

**EXCHANGE VALUES**

| 2 Starch | 4 Meat | 2 Veg. | — Fruit | — Milk | — Fat |
|---|---|---|---|---|---|

**Nutrition information for — 4 oz. of beef, 1 cup rice, 1 cup vegetables**

| | | | | | |
|---|---|---|---|---|---|
| Calories .......... 475 | Fat .......... 16 g | Fiber .......... 4.5 g | Sodium .......... 390 mg | Total Carbohydrate .......... 44 g |
| Calories from Fat .......... 30% | Saturated Fat .......... 5.6 g | Cholesterol .......... 94 mg | Protein .......... 39 g | Sugars .......... 7 g |

# Oven · Exercise · Eat

## The road to dinner.

You've just gotten home with an hour to go before dinner. Your early morning meeting kept you from exercising this morning. How are you going to fit in your workout, before you're too pooped? Your personal experience tells you that inertia is five times stronger in the hours after dinner. If only you could fit exercise in BEFORE dinner.

Well, now you can, with Oven • Exercise • EAT! This is a collection of complete meal recipes that are quick to go in the oven, so you can exercise during the baking time and dinner is ready when you are done. Just flip through and see what looks good tonight. Note the length of prep-time and oven/exercise-time that works best for you. And assuming you've shopped using the *Lickety-Split* grocery list, you will have all the ingredients you need!

## Tip

### Keeping the Exercise in Oven/Exercise/Eat

If you're like most of us, you'll probably be tempted to use your bake time to do other seemingly important things, like laundry or housekeeping. But unless you've already exercised today, DON'T GIVE IN! A clean house has nothing over a clear mind and healthy body!

Have a great workout and enjoy a healthy and delicious meal, hot out of the oven when you're done!

# Oven-Baked Lentils & Rice

Yes, this recipe makes a huge batch. You're going to enjoy it so much that you'll be glad you made the extra for lunch "planned overs." It keeps in the refrigerator for 5 days and freezes well, too. Serve with steamed vegetables, salad, and whole grain bread.

**SERVES**

6

**MENU**

LENTILS & RICE
STEAMED VEGETABLES
SALAD
WHOLE-GRAIN BREAD

**Preheat oven to 350°.**

| | |
|---|---|
| 2 small | onions |
| 2 cans | (14.5 oz each) chicken broth, ⅓ less sodium |
| 1¾ cups | water |
| ½ cup | white wine |
| 1½ cups | lentils |
| 1 cup | brown rice (not quick-cooking) |
| 1 small jar | (2 oz) chopped pimentos |
| 1 tsp | dried basil |
| 1 tsp | dried oregano |
| ½ tsp | dried thyme |
| ¼ tsp | garlic powder |
| 15 grinds | fresh ground pepper |

Chop onions. Mix ingredients together in a large baking dish. Set timer for 90 minutes and bake uncovered.

*Meanwhile... how about 9 holes of golf? Remember, you don't need a cart!*

| | |
|---|---|
| 1½ cups | reduced-fat shredded mozzarella *or* Swiss cheese |

After 90 minutes of baking, sprinkle on and bake 15 minutes longer.

Use this time to steam vegetables, make a salad, slice some bread, and set the table.

---

**EXCHANGE VALUES**

2 Starch    1 Meat    — Veg.    — Fruit    — Milk    — Fat

**Nutrition information for — 1/6 of the recipe**

**Preparation Time — 10 min.**    **Oven / Exercise Time — 90 min.**

| | | | | | |
|---|---|---|---|---|---|
| Calories ............... 240 | Fat ............... 3.5 g | Fiber ............... 3 g | Sodium ............... 665 mg | Total Carbohydrate ............... 33 g |
| Calories from Fat ........... 13% | Saturated Fat ............... 1.7 g | Cholesterol ............... 10 mg | Protein ............... 15 g | Sugars ............... 2 g |

# Exercising Consistently: Here's How to Make Your Good Intentions Come True!

**Tip**

If you are just getting into an exercise routine, it's important to establish positive feelings of accomplishment, so you will want to continue and be consistent.

### WEEK #1

Try starting with only 5 minutes* of easy exercise, but **do it 5 times that week.** Perhaps marching in place in front of the TV, or spinning on your exercise bike. (Keep your intensity low.) You can always find 5 minutes! What's important is to do it **5 times per week. Do it at the same time each day, which will become your routine exercise time.**

### WEEK #2, 3, 4 and 5

*How does it feel to have exercised 5 times last week? Pretty good, huh?*

Now, over the next 4 weeks, **increase your exercise time.** Up to 7 minutes, then 10, 12, 15, 20, 25, 30. Keep your intensity fairly low. Be sure to keep up 5 times a week!

### WEEK #6

Now, don't you feel GREAT having exercised 5 times a week for 5 weeks? Congratulations!

Now you're ready to add intensity. Increase your walking speed or turn up the resistance on the stationary bike. Try to increase this by 10% each week.

* If you are particularly fit, you can start with 10 minutes, but not more. The point is NOT to do all you are physically capable of doing, but rather to establish the concrete habit for CONSISTENCY. Most people agree, *consistency* is the hardest part!

**Reminder:** ALWAYS CHECK WITH YOUR DOCTOR FIRST BEFORE STARTING ANY EXERCISE PROGRAM!

# Pizzucchini

Here's a delicious summer dish, that uses up your extra zucchini and tomatoes. *Pizzucchini* gets its name from smelling like pizza while baking. We serve this with corn on the cob and cantaloupe.

SERVES

6

MENU

PIZZUCCHINI WITH REDSKINS
CORN ON THE COB
CANTALOUPE

*Popular summer feast!*

**Preheat oven to 375°.**
**Spray a 9" x 13" baking pan with nonstick cooking spray.**

| | |
|---|---|
| 3 small | zucchini |
| 1 medium | onion |
| 4 medium | tomatoes |

Slice vegetables ¹/₈ inch thick.
Separate onion slices into rings.

| | |
|---|---|
| 6 T | Parmesan cheese |
| 1¹/₂ cups | reduced-fat shredded mozzarella cheese |
| 2 tsp | dried oregano |
| 1 tsp | garlic powder |

Mix together in a medium-size bowl.

Make 2 layers in the baking dish, using half the ingredients each time in the order listed: zucchini, onion, tomatoes, cheese mixture (repeat).

| | |
|---|---|
| 6 small | red-skin potatoes, cut in ¹/₂ |

Scrub potatoes and slip in around the edges of the casserole.

Cover and bake for 1 hour. (Remember to set timer.)

 *How about swimming?*

After 1 hour, remove cover and bake 15 minutes more. Use this time to cook some corn on the cob and slice some cantaloupe. Enjoy!

---

**EXCHANGE VALUES**

| 1 Starch | 1 Meat | 2 Veg. | — Fruit | — Milk | — Fat |
|---|---|---|---|---|---|

| Nutrition information for — 1/6 of the recipe | | Preparation Time — 20 min. | Oven / Exercise Time — 60 min. |
|---|---|---|---|

| | | | |
|---|---|---|---|
| Calories ......................... 200 | Fat ........................... 4.5 g | Fiber ........................... 4 g | Sodium ........................... 335 mg | Total Carbohydrate ............. 26 g |
| Calories from Fat .............. 20% | Saturated Fat .............. 2.5 g | Cholesterol .................. 14 g | Protein ........................ 14 g | Sugars ........................ 5 g |

# Tip

## Don't let the weather control your workout.

*Always* have a back-up plan for nasty weather. If the weather is nice, I walk, jog, rollerblade, or ride my bike. If not, I work out indoors doing aerobics, the *Health Rider®*, indoor bike, or *Nordic Track®*. Develop a plan that works best for you.

# Tuna Noodle Casserole

SERVES

4 OR 8

**MENU**

TUNA NOODLE CASSEROLE
TOSSED SALAD
WHOLE-WHEAT ROLLS
FUDGESICLE

Yes, it's your all-American favorite! This time it's made lower in fat and sodium, and without the time-wasting step of boiling the noodles first. Plan on a good workout tonight with 50 minutes of oven time!

**Preheat oven to 375°.**

| For 4 | For 8 | |
|-------|-------|---|
| 1 can | 2 cans | (10³/₄ oz each) **cream of mushroom soup** (*Campbell's® Healthy Request®*) |
| 1¹/₄ c | 2¹/₂ c | **skim milk** (fill the empty soup can) |
| 1 can | 2 cans | (6 oz each) **water packed tuna drained and flaked** |
| 1 tsp | 2 tsp | **dried onion flakes** |
| ¹/₂ tsp | 1 tsp | **dill** |
| ¹/₄ c | ¹/₂ c | **Parmesan cheese** |
| 1¹/₂ c | 3 c | **frozen peas** |
| 3 c | 6 c | **uncooked shells *or* noodles** |

Mix together in a casserole dish. Use a medium dish for serving 4 and a large dish for serving 8.

Add and mix.

Put in oven covered. Set timer for 50 minutes.

*How about heading outside for some "active" gardening or yard work?*

Check refrigerator for salad making possibilities, or try sliced cucumbers, tomatoes, and carrots.

Prepare salad or simply serve sliced cucumbers and tomatoes. Serve with whole-wheat rolls.

---

**EXCHANGE VALUES**

| 3 Starch | 2 Meat | — Veg. | — Fruit | — Milk | — Fat |

**Nutrition information for — 1/4 of the small batch, 1/8 of the large batch**

**Preparation Time — 10 min.**   **Oven / Exercise Time — 50 min.**

| Calories ............................... 315 | Fat ....................................... 4.6 g | Fiber ......................................... 4 g | Sodium .............................. 620 mg | Total Carbohydrate ............. 45 g |
| Calories from Fat ............... 13% | Saturated Fat ..................... 1.8 g | Cholesterol ........................ 18 mg | Protein ................................. 23 g | Sugars ....................................... 9 g |

**Tip**

## Want to create some fun and support between you and your spouse?

In a conspicuous place, hang 2 calendars side by side. Designate 1 for you and 1 for your spouse. Record your minutes of exercise each day. On Saturday or Sunday night, total up your minutes. The person with the least minutes gives a back-rub to the other. What competitive (and slightly romantic) fun!

# Tantalizing Turkey Loaf Dinner

This dinner is a far cry from the traditional artery-clogging classic. It's fast and tasty, too!
The applesauce replaces the moisture lost by using extra-lean ground turkey.

SERVES

4

**MENU**

TURKEY LOAF
BAKED POTATOES
BROCCOLI
FAT-FREE INSTANT PUDDING

**Preheat oven to 350°.**

| | |
|---|---|
| 4 | baking *or* sweet potatoes |

Scrub potatoes and place in oven.

| | |
|---|---|
| 1 small | onion |

Chop and place in a medium-sized bowl.

| | |
|---|---|
| 1 lb | extra-lean ground turkey breast |
| 2 | egg whites |
| ½ - 1 tsp | Italian seasoning (young children prefer less seasoning) |
| ¼ tsp | crushed red pepper (optional) |
| ½ cup | applesauce, unsweetened |
| ½ tsp | salt (omit if bread crumbs are seasoned) |
| ½ cup | dry unseasoned bread crumbs |
| 2 T grated | Parmesan cheese |

Add and mix together thoroughly, using your hands if necessary. *(Wash them first!)*

Spray an 8" x 8" baking dish with nonstick cooking spray.

Form meat into a loaf and place in the middle of the pan.

| | |
|---|---|
| 1 cup | spaghetti sauce *(Healthy Choice®)* |

Pour sauce over top. Place in oven and set timer for 75 minutes.

*Head out for 60 or more minutes of exhilarating exercise.*

| | |
|---|---|
| 4 cups | broccoli |

Upon returning from exercise, place into a microwavable dish, cover and cook on high for 5 minutes. *Stretch those muscles!* When the oven timer goes off, slice loaf into 8 equal parts. It's time to eat!

---

**EXCHANGE VALUES**

3 Starch    3 Meat    2 Veg.    — Fruit    — Milk    — Fat

| Nutrition information for — 2 slices turkey loaf, 1 small potato, 1 cup broccoli | | | Preparation Time — 20 min. | Oven / Exercise Time — 75 min. |
|---|---|---|---|---|
| Calories .......... 415 | Fat .......... 3 g | Fiber .......... 7 g | Sodium .......... 780 mg | Total Carbohydrate .......... 58 g |
| Calories from Fat .......... 7% | Saturated Fat .......... < 1 g | Cholesterol .......... 56 mg | Protein .......... 38 g | Sugars .......... 13 g |

# Tip

## Eat the skin on your potato because it's good for you... Or is it?

While nutritionists have advised to eat the potato skin because of its extra vitamins, minerals, and fiber, new findings are causing a second look at this advice. These days most commercial potatoes have been sprayed, to slow their sprouting and extend their shelf life. This spray has raised safety concerns. **Therefore, the advice to "eat the skin on your potato because it's good for you," holds true only for potatoes bought at your local farmers market or organically grown.**

What about all those extra vitamins, minerals, and fiber that you'll be throwing away? It's not enough to fret over; there is good nutrition throughout the potato.

# Oven Fries

SERVES | MENU

I can't begin to tell you how much my husband loves these! Easy to make, inexpensive and delicious low-fat versions of the high-fat American favorite. I'll leave it up to you to decide what to serve them with. Perhaps baked chicken legs and steamed vegetables?

4

BAKED CHICKEN LEGS
OVEN FRIES
STEAMED VEGETABLES

**Preheat oven to 375°.**

| 4 large | baking potatoes |
|---------|-----------------|
|         | **(try sweet potatoes, they're great!)** |

Thoroughly wash and scrub—peel if commercial potatoes. (See tip above.)
Cut lengthwise into wedges. Place in bowl.

*Husbands and kids love these!*

| 1 T | oil (canola *or* olive) |
|-----|-------------------------|

Drizzle over potatoes and toss.

Spray a cooking sheet with nonstick cooking spray.

Spread potato wedges on cooking sheet.

Set timer and bake for 50 minutes or until tender.

*Now head out the door
for a 20 minute brisk walk or jog!*

At the sound of the timer, transfer to a serving dish.

**Salt, pepper and ketchup**

Sprinkle salt and pepper on potatoes to taste. Serve with ketchup.

**Note: *Ore Ida®* now makes frozen Potato Wedges, which are almost exactly the same as these. Buying their product will save you from scrubbing and slicing potatoes (about 10 minutes), but are of course more costly than buying plain potatoes. The choice is up to you!**

## EXCHANGE VALUES

3 Starch — Meat — Veg. — Fruit — Milk — Fat

| Nutrition information for — 1/4 of the recipe, without ketchup, salt and pepper | | | Preparation Time — 10 min. | Oven / Exercise Time — 50 min. |
|---|---|---|---|---|
| Calories ................................. 250 | Fat ........................................ 3.5 g | Fiber ........................................ 5 g | Sodium ............................... 16 mg | Total Carbohydrate ............. 50 g |
| Calories from Fat ............... 13% | Saturated Fat ....................... .5 g | Cholesterol ......................... 0 mg | Protein ..................................... 5 g | Sugars ....................................... 3 g |

# Tip

## Why aren't you lifting weights?

**Don't have time?** This book takes care of that!

**Don't want clunky equipment cluttering up the living room?** All it takes is 2 pair of dumbbells and you can store them under the coach.

**Don't know how?** Buy a video! Find one in "The Complete Guide to Exercise Videos," a catalog put out by Collage Video (1-800-433-6769). I highly recommend the "8-Minute Arms" video as well as the other 8-Minute tapes they offer.

**Attention women. Afraid you'll get big muscles?** Don't worry! You'd have to lift heavy weights for 3 hours a day, every day for a year, before that could even possibly become a problem!

# LaZonya

My lasagna has lots of veggies, low-fat cheese, and unboiled noodles (to save time). Double the recipe and freeze one pan for another time (freeze <u>after</u> baking). The sauce is so tasty, I have you make extra. Freeze the extra sauce for a quick meal (topping a baked potato or pasta).

**SERVES**

12 PER PAN

**Preheat oven to 350°.**

| (1) 9 x 13 | (2) 9 x 13 | |
|---|---|---|
| ½ | 1 | **green and red pepper** |
| 2 | 4 | **carrots** |
| 2 | 4 | **small onions** |
| 1 c | 2 c | **fresh mushrooms** *or* **zucchini** (optional) |
| 1 tsp | 2 tsp | **minced garlic** (2 or 4 cloves) |
| 1 T | 2 T | **olive oil** |
| ¼ c | ½ c | **fresh chopped parsley** |
| 1 lb. | 2 lbs. | **extra-lean ground turkey breast** (optional) |
| 1 block | 2 blocks | (12 oz) **firm tofu crumbled** (optional) |
| 1 tsp | 2 tsp | **oregano** |
| ¼ tsp | ½ tsp | **red pepper flakes** |
| 2 jars | 4 jars | (26 oz each) **spaghetti sauce** (*Healthy Choice*®) |
| 1 box | 2 bxs | (10 oz) **frozen spinach** |
| 1 tub | 2 tubs | (15 oz) **light Ricotta cheese** (*or* **low-fat cottage cheese**) |
| ½ tsp | 1 tsp | **dried onion flakes** |
| 1 T | 2 T | **fresh parsley** (from earlier) |
| 1 T | 2 T | **Parmesan cheese** |

## THE SAUCE...

Clean. Chop peppers, chop or shred carrots, dice onions, and slice mushrooms/zucchini.

Heat oil on medium-high in your largest nonstick kettle and add garlic and vegetables.

Chop. Reserve 1 to 2 T for later in recipe. Add to kettle.

Add turkey and/or tofu by crumbling. (First time tofu users, try ½ tofu and ½ turkey. Your guests will never tell the difference.) Add spices. Cook, stirring frequently for 5 minutes or until turkey is done.

Add sauce and spinach. Simmer on medium while you prepare the cheese mixture. When ready, move sauce to assembly line and place a measuring cup near it for scooping.

## THE CHEESES...

Mix together in a medium bowl. Divide into 3 equal parts (1 for each layer) for use during the *LaZonya* assembly process. Place a teaspoon in the bowl for scooping.

Recipe continued on next page.

# Tip

## The benefits of lifting weights are endless!

1. Helps fight off osteoporosis.

2. Raises your metabolism (muscle burns more calories than fat does).

3. Helps you lose inches, look firmer, and feel great.

4. Helps reverse the aging process.

# LaZonya (Con't.)

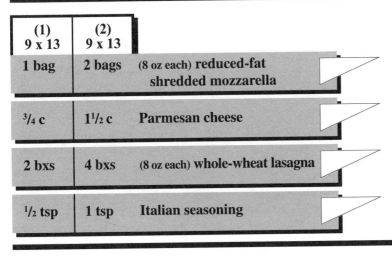

| (1)<br>9 x 13 | (2)<br>9 x 13 | | |
|---|---|---|---|
| 1 bag | 2 bags | (8 oz each) **reduced-fat shredded mozzarella** | Place opened bags in assembly line. |
| ³/₄ c | 1¹/₂ c | **Parmesan cheese** | Place in bowl. Place a tablespoon in bowl for use in assembly line. |
| 2 bxs | 4 bxs | (8 oz each) **whole-wheat lasagna** | Place opened boxes in assembly line. |
| ¹/₂ tsp | 1 tsp | **Italian seasoning** | Sprinkle on top layer when assembly is complete. |

## THE ASSEMBLY

**Preheat oven to 400°.**

1. Spray (1) or (2) 9" x 13" pans with nonstick cooking spray. Place 1³/₄ cups sauce in the bottom of each pan.

2. Layer: 3 hard noodles; 1³/₄ cups sauce, spread evenly; 12 rounded tsps Ricotta cheese; ¹/₂ cup mozzarella sprinkled evenly, and 3 T Parmesan cheese sprinkled. (Repeat layering 3 times.)

3. After the third Parmesan cheese sprinkle, complete the fourth and final layer with 3 hard noodles; 1¹/₂ cups sauce spread evenly; ¹/₂ cup mozzarella sprinkled evenly; 3 T Parmesan cheese; and ¹/₂ tsp Italian seasoning. **Remember, there should be leftover sauce for you to freeze for a quick meal later!**

4. Pour ¹/₄ cup of water (for each pan) all around the edges of the pan. This provides the needed steam to cook the noodles.

5. Cover with aluminum foil and bake 45 minutes.

*Capitalize on this time to get in a thorough resistance exercise workout.*

Uncover and bake 10 minutes longer. Meanwhile… prepare a salad and garlic toast.

Allow 10 minutes to set before serving.

*Use this time to stretch and set the table!*

---

**EXCHANGE VALUES**

| 2 Starch | 3 Meat | 2 Veg. | — Fruit | — Milk | — Fat |
|---|---|---|---|---|---|

---

| Nutrition information for — 1 square (1/12 of the pan) made with ground turkey and tofu | | | Preparation Time — 60 min. | Oven / Exercise Time — 50 min. |
|---|---|---|---|---|
| Calories .................................. 335 | Fat ......................................... 7.5 g | Fiber ........................................ 7.5 g | Sodium ............................. 713 mg | Total Carbohydrate ............. 43 g |
| Calories from Fat ............... 19% | Saturated Fat ..................... 3.5 g | Cholesterol ........................ 36 mg | Protein .................................. 29 g | Sugars .................................... 10 g |

# Tip

## Be sure to stretch! It only takes a minute!

**Benefits of stretching:**

1. Improves flexibility, mobility and range of motion.
2. Helps prevent injuries.
3. Promotes better circulation.
4. Reduces tension.
5. Helps prevent muscle stiffness and soreness after exercise.

**Rules for stretching:**

1. Gently hold a stretch for about 20 seconds.
2. Stretch only until you feel a comfortable stretch in the muscle.
3. Breathe normally. Do not hold your breath.
4. Never force a muscle to stretch too far when true pain is felt.
5. Never bounce while stretching! You want a constant, steady stretch.

# Mexican LaZonya

SERVES | MENU

(A.K.A. Bean and Vegetable Enchilada Bake) Teenagers will love how this dish resembles "Taco Bell" type food. If you have small children, you may want to reduce the cumin and chili powder by half.

**8**

MEXICAN LAZONYA

CINNAMON BUTTERNUT SQUASH

FROZEN YOGURT

**Preheat oven to 375°. Note: If serving *Cinnamon Butternut Squash* (page 149), get it started first.**

| 2 | onions, chopped |
|---|---|
| 2 | peppers (one green, one red), chopped |
| ½ head | cauliflower florets |
| 1 medium | zucchini *or* 3 carrots, chopped |

Prep the vegetables.

| 2 T | olive oil |
|---|---|
| 1 tsp | chopped garlic (2 cloves) |

Heat skillet and add oil. Add the garlic and the chopped vegetables (or frozen vegetables straight from the bag).

| 1 jar | (16 oz) salsa |
|---|---|
| 1 can | (16 oz) low-sodium tomato puree |

Add and set timer for 5 minutes.

| 1 T | ground cumin |
|---|---|
| 1 T | chili powder |
| 1 can | (15 oz) pinto, black *or* kidney beans, rinsed and drained |

Meanwhile… add to the simmering skillet.

When the timer goes off, it's time to assemble.

| 12 | corn tortillas |
|---|---|
| | (flour tortillas work fine too) |
| 1½ cups | reduced-fat shredded cheddar cheese |

### TO ASSEMBLE…

In a 9" x 13" baking dish, layer evenly: ⅓ of the sauce, 4 tortillas, and ½ cup cheese on top of tortillas (repeat 2 more times), **but wait to add last layer of cheese.** Cover with aluminum foil and place in oven. Set timer 25 minutes.

*How about jumping rope? Start with 5 minutes, working up to 20 when you can.*

Remove foil, add the remaining cheese, and bake 5 more minutes. *Stretch!*

Serve with Cinnamon Butternut Squash, tossed salad, or fresh vegetables with dip. Olé!

---

**EXCHANGE VALUES**

| 2 Starch | 1 Meat | 2 Veg. | — Fruit | — Milk | — Fat |
|---|---|---|---|---|---|

| Nutrition information for — 1 square (1/8 of the pan) | | | **Preparation Time — 40 min.** | **Oven / Exercise Time — 20 min.** |
|---|---|---|---|---|
| Calories .................................. 280 | Fat ............................................. 7 g | Fiber ..................................... 10.5 g | Sodium ............................. 675 mg | Total Carbohydrate ............. 41 g |
| Calories from Fat ................. 22% | Saturated Fat .......................... 2 g | Cholesterol .......................... 7 mg | Protein ..................................... 14 g | Sugars ........................................ 8 g |

# Tip

## Calories burned during exercise

Don't get depressed when you think...
I exercised for 20 minutes and all I burned
was 160 calories??? Just remember the
secret to consistency over time:

Twenty minutes of exercise 3 times a
week for a full year burns 24,960 calories,
which translates to **7 pounds of fat
burned in a year!**

Thirty minutes of exercise 5 times a week
for a year burns 62,400 calories, which
translates to **18 pounds of fat burned
in a year!**

Forty-five minutes of exercise 5 times a
week for a year burns 93,600 calories,
which translates to **27 pounds of fat
burned in a year!**

*As you can see, consistency pays!*

# Kickin' Chicken with Fries

| | SERVES | MENU |
|---|---|---|

Check this out! You get your workout in *and* your family fed all in less than 45 minutes! Your family will ask for this again and again!

SERVES: 4

MENU:
KICKIN' CHICKEN
OVEN FRIES
MIXED VEGETABLES
APPLESAUCE

**Preheat oven to 450°.**
**Arrange oven racks to accommodate both a cookie sheet and a 9" x 13" pan.**

Kids' Favorite

| 1 cup | salsa *or* Picante sauce |
| 1 T | firmly packed brown sugar |
| ½ T | Dijon mustard |

Mix together in a 2 cup measuring cup.

| 4 | skinless, boneless, chicken breast (halves) |

Place chicken in a 9" x 13" baking dish. Pour sauce over chicken. Put in oven.

| 1 bag | (24 oz) *Ore Ida*® potato wedges* |

Spread out on cookie sheet. Place in oven. Set timer for 25 minutes.

| 1 bag | (16 oz) mixed vegetables |
| 2 T | water |

Place in microwave safe dish, cover, and set to cook on high for 12 minutes. (You will be allowing the vegetables to sit in the oven 10 minutes longer.)

*Jump on your treadmill (or stationary bike) for a quick 22 minutes. (Take the first 2 minutes to warm up.)*

| 16 oz | applesauce, unsweetened |

At the sound of the timer, check chicken to see if it's done. Cook 5 more minutes if necessary. Open the applesauce and set the table.

It's Kickin' Chicken time!

\* If you prefer, make the home-made version of *Oven Fries* (page 78).

### EXCHANGE VALUES

| 4 Starch | 3 Meat | 2 Veg. | — Fruit | — Milk | — Fat |
|---|---|---|---|---|---|

| Nutrition information for — 1 chicken breast half, 1 cup fries, 1 cup mixed vegetables | | | Preparation Time — 15 min. | Oven / Exercise Time — 22 min. |
|---|---|---|---|---|
| Calories ................................. 490 | Fat ........................................ 7 g | Fiber ....................................... 10 g | Sodium ............................ 460 mg | Total Carbohydrate ............. 73 g |
| Calories from Fat ............... 12% | Saturated Fat ..................... 15 g | Cholesterol ........................ 68 mg | Protein ................................ 35 g | Sugars ................................... 24 g |

## How is it that people who can never find time to exercise can always find time to eat?

**The wonder of 336**

You may find it interesting to learn that there are 336 30-minute time segments in EVERY week. You need ONLY 3 to 5 of these 30-minute time segments each week for exercise.

This requires less than 5% of your time each week!

(While eating on the other hand, takes much more time, and we always find time for that!)

*Lickety-Split Meals*

# Delicate Baked Trout

The next time you walk by the fresh seafood counter, check out their fresh trout. My dear friend, Jay Johnson, taught me to add the milk in this recipe to keep the flavor delicate and mild. (Not at all fishy!)

SERVES 4

**MENU**

BAKED TROUT
OVEN FRIES
CALIFORNIA VEGETABLES
9-GRAIN ROLLS

**Preheat oven to 350°.**

Kids'
Favorite

| | | |
|---|---|---|
| 1 bag | (24 oz) *Ore Ida®* potato wedges* | Spread out on cookie sheet. Place in oven. |
| 1½ lbs | fresh trout fillet | Rinse clean and place in a 8" x 8" baking dish. |
| ½ | lemon, squeezed (*or* 1 T from a bottle) | Drizzle or pour over the fish in the order given. |
| 1 tsp | oil (canola *or* olive) | |
| 1 cup | skim milk | |
| ⅛ tsp | salt | Sprinkle as needed. |
| 6 grinds | fresh ground pepper | Place in oven. Set timer for 35 minutes. |
| 3 dashes | paprika | |
| 2 bags | (16 oz each) **frozen California blend vegetables** | Place in microwave-safe dish, cover, and let set in microwave. |
| 1 T | water | |

*Pop in an exercise video for 30 minutes of aerobic work. Remember to warm up.*

When the timer goes off, cook vegetables in microwave on high for 10 minutes. Allow fish to continue baking until microwave finishes.

*Step in place for 1 minute for a cool-down. Grab 2 soup cans and do bicept curls & overhead presses. Follow with some sit-ups and 2 minutes of stretching.*

Set table. When vegetables are done, it's time to eat!

\* If you prefer, make the home-made version of *Oven Fries* (page 78).

---

**EXCHANGE VALUES**

2 Starch    3 Meat    3 Veg.    — Fruit    — Milk    — Fat

---

| Nutrition information for — 4 oz. trout, 1 cup fries, 1-1/2 cups vegetables | | | Preparation Time — 10 min. | Oven / Exercise Time — 35 min. |
|---|---|---|---|---|
| Calories ................................. 420 | Fat .............................. 11 g | Fiber ................................. 10 g | Sodium ........................... 221 mg | Total Carbohydrate ............. 51 g |
| Calories from Fat ............... 24% | Saturated Fat .................... 2.6 g | Cholesterol ...................... 62 mg | Protein ................................. 28 g | Sugars ...................................... 8 g |

## Super Time Saving Tip

Skip prepping the potatoes and onion by using 4 cups of *Ore Ida® Potatoes O'Brien* (a frozen hash brown product that I call for frequently). It has no fat (just chopped potatoes, onions, and peppers), tastes great, and saves you loads of time!

# Nature's Popsicle: Frozen Grapes

If you haven't experienced frozen grapes yet, you don't know what you're missing!

Take seedless grapes off their vine. (Use red, green, or both.)

Serve frozen or partially thawed.

THOROUGHLY wash the grapes and pat dry on a towel.

Place in a airtight bowl or zip-lock bag and freeze.

Icy, sweet and delicious!

■ ■ ■ ■ ■ ■ ■ ■ ■ ■ ■ ■ ■ ■ ■ ■ ■

# Chicken and Vegetables in Foil

**SERVES**

**MENU:**

A super simple dinner that can be cooked indoors or on the outdoor grill.
Your choice, Italian style or barbecue. Best of all, there's no messy cleanup!

4

BBQ OR ITALIAN CHICKEN

POTATO

BRUSSELS SPROUTS AND
CARROTS

WHOLE-GRAIN BREAD

FROZEN GRAPES

**Preheat oven to 400°.**
**Tear off 2 large pieces of foil just larger**
**han the size of a cookie sheet.**

| | |
|---|---|
| **1 cup** | **bottled BBQ sauce** *or* <br> **³/₄ cup lite** *or* **fat-free Italian dressing** |

Spread ¹/₂ the sauce in the
center of one piece of the foil.

| | |
|---|---|
| **4** | **skinless, boneless, chicken** <br> **breast (halves)** |
| **4 medium** | **potatoes, scrubbed** *or* **peeled,** <br> **thinly sliced\*** |
| **1** | **onion, sliced into rings\*** |

Layer on the foil in order given. Spread on remaining sauce.

| | |
|---|---|
| **1 box** | **(10 oz) frozen Brussels sprouts** *or* <br> **cabbage wedges** *or* **broccoli/** <br> **cauliflower mix** |
| **1 box** | **(10 oz) frozen carrots** |

Place in a strainer and run hot tap water over them for 1 minute.

Drain and add to foil.

| | |
|---|---|
| **8 grinds** | **fresh ground pepper** |

Sprinkle with fresh ground pepper. Place the remaining piece of foil on
top. Seal with double folds. Place in oven and set timer for 75 minutes.

*How about a nice long bike ride outdoors? Reserve the last
15 minutes for push-ups and sit-ups. (How many of those are
you up to by now?) Stretch!*

Serve with rolls and frozen grapes (see above).

| EXCHANGE VALUES | | | | | |
|---|---|---|---|---|---|
| 3 Starch | 3 Meat | 3 Veg. | — Fruit | — Milk | — Fat |

**\* See my Super Time Saving Tip above.**

| Nutrition information for — 1/4 of the recipe | | | Preparation Time — 15 min. | Oven / Exercise Time — 75 min. |
|---|---|---|---|---|
| Calories .................................. 400 | Fat ............................................ 3 g | Fiber ...................................... 10 g | Sodium ............................. 660 mg | Total Carbohydrate ............. 58 g |
| Calories from Fat .................. 6% | Saturated Fat .................... < 1 g | Cholesterol ........................ 68 mg | Protein .................................. 35 g | Sugars ...................................... 16 g |

Chicken and Vegetables in Foil

**Oven • Exercise • Eat**
**84**

*Lickety-Split Meals*

# Tip

## Is your headache a sign of mild dehydration?

Do you ever arrive home with a headache? Did you know that this is often the first sign of dehydration? Hydrating your body may relieve your headache. You'll need to be adequately hydrated in order to feel good and perform well, especially during your workout. **The best habit is drinking fluids all day long.** If you haven't, play catch-up and down a glass of water when you get home.

**And be sure always to replace fluids after exercising!**

# Simple Baked Chicken and Rice

Got 10 minutes? That's all it takes to get this tasty favorite in the oven, leaving you with 1 whole hour of rejuvenating "all to yourself" exercise time.

**SERVES**

4

**Preheat oven to 375°.**

| | |
|---|---|
| 1 can | **(10.75 oz) cream of mushroom soup** *(Campbell's® Healthy Request®)* |
| 1 can | **(14.5 oz) reduced-sodium chicken broth** |
| 1/3 cup | **light sour cream** *(or plain yogurt)* |

Stir together in a 9" x 13" baking dish.

| | |
|---|---|
| 1 bag | **(16 oz) California blend frozen vegetables** |
| 1 can | **(10 oz) cooked white chicken, rinsed and drained** |
| 1 1/2 cups | **instant whole-grain brown rice** |
| 1 tsp | **dried onion flakes** |
| 10 grinds | **fresh ground pepper** |

Add and stir.

Cover and put in oven to bake. Set timer for 45 minutes.

*Tennis anyone? Remember to end with a thorough stretch session.*

At the sound of the timer, uncover and continue baking 10 minutes. Meanwhile… set table, slice bread and open the can of apricots. It's dinnertime!

---

**EXCHANGE VALUES**

| 2 Starch | 2 Meat | 3 Veg. | — Fruit | — Milk | — Fat |
|---|---|---|---|---|---|

**Nutrition information for — 1/4 of the recipe**

**Preparation Time — 10 min.**   **Oven / Exercise Time — 1 hour**

| | | | |
|---|---|---|---|
| Calories ........................... 340 | Fat ................................. 5.5 g | Fiber .......................... 7 g | Sodium ........................ 800 mg | Total Carbohydrate ........... 50 g |
| Calories from Fat ............ 15% | Saturated Fat ................. 2.5 g | Cholesterol ............... 38 mg | Protein ......................... 23 g | Sugars ............................... 9 g |

# Still wondering which exercise video to buy?

Call Collage Video at 1-800-433-6769
and ask for their free catalog entitled:
*The complete guide to exercise videos.*
This includes excellent descriptions of the
346 best videos on the planet. They even
boast that their telephone video consultants
have used the tapes themselves so they can
tell you the details. Now that's service!

# Chicken and Bean Enchiladas

| | SERVES | MENU |
|---|---|---|
| | 8 | BAKED ENCHILADAS |

My thanks to Stacy Rafalko for this neat recipe. Feel free to leave out the chicken or cheese if you prefer. These are easy and tasty!

**SERVES** 8

**MENU**

BAKED ENCHILADAS

CORN

SLICED CANTALOUPE, HONEYDEW OR WATERMELON

**Preheat oven to 350°.**

| | |
|---|---|
| 2 cups | ***Benito Bean Dip*** (page 57) *or* |
| 1 can | **(16 oz) fat-free refried beans** |
| 1 can | **(10 oz) chunk white chicken, rinsed & drained** |

Gently combine in a medium size bowl, enough to break chicken up.

| | |
|---|---|
| 8 | **8" flour tortillas** |

Place ⅓ cup of bean mixture in a long single row on a tortilla. Roll up. Place in a 9" x 13" baking dish. Repeat with remaining 7 tortillas.

*Kids' Favorite*

| | |
|---|---|
| 1 can | **(10 oz) enchilada sauce** *(Old El Paso®)* |

Pour over enchiladas.

| | |
|---|---|
| ½ cup | **reduced-fat shredded cheddar cheese** |

Sprinkle over all. Place in oven. Set timer for 30 minutes.

*Throw on your sweat pants and a T-shirt, and start your favorite exercise video.*

When the timer sounds, allow the enchiladas to cool a few minutes while you prepare corn and slice melons. Try to stretch while you work.

| | |
|---|---|
| ½ cup | **light sour cream** |
| | **minced fresh onion** (optional) |
| | **chopped green pepper** (optional) |

Serve enchiladas with 1 T of sour cream over each and optional onion and green pepper.

***Buen Appetito!***

---

**EXCHANGE VALUES**

| 2 Starch | 2 Meat | 1 Veg. | 1 Fruit | — Milk | — Fat |
|---|---|---|---|---|---|

---

**Nutrition information for — 1 enchilada with 1 T sour cream, 1/2 cup corn, 1 cup watermelon cubes**    **Preparation Time — 20 min.**    **Oven / Exercise Time — 30 min.**

| | | | |
|---|---|---|---|
| Calories .................................... 360 | Fat ....................................... 7 g | Fiber ......................................... 8 g | Sodium ............................ 600 mg | Total Carbohydrate ............. 58 g |
| Calories from Fat ............... 16% | Saturated Fat ................... 2.3 g | Cholesterol ........................ 23 mg | Protein ............................... 20 g | Sugars ................................... 18 g |

## Do houseguests cramp your exercise routine?

Why not invite them to join you? Make an early morning walk followed by a nutritious breakfast part of a perfect visit. It's amazing what a positive impact you can have on your family and friends!

Likewise, if *you* are the guest, look for opportunities to get your exercise in. Even if you go by yourself, it can provide a break for you *and* your host.

# Creamy Chicken Enchiladas

**SERVES** 6

Creamy, comforting, and "to die for" is the best way to describe this. My complete thanks to Diane Petersen for contributing this favorite recipe from her mom, Barb Filler.

**Preheat oven to 325°.**

| 6 | skinless, boneless, chicken breast (halves), **cut into strips** |
| 1 can | **(4 oz) chopped green chilies** |

Brown chicken in nonstick skillet with nonstick spray. Add green chilies during last 2 minutes.

| 1 cup | **light sour cream** |
| 1 can | **(10³/₄ oz) cream of chicken soup** *(Campbell's® Healthy Request®)* |

Meanwhile… in a medium sauce pan, mix together and heat over medium-low.

| 1 can | **(2.25 oz) sliced black olives** (optional) |
| 1 cup | **reduced-fat shredded cheddar cheese** |

Open olives and cheese and place in assembly line.

Spread ¹/₂ cup of soup mix on bottom of 9" x 13" pan.

| 10 | **8" flour tortillas** |

Lay out 5 tortillas on a clean countertop. Put 1 T sauce in a line down the center of each. Follow with: 2 T chicken, 1 T cheese, and 1 tsp olives. Roll up and place in 9" x 13" pan. Repeat with remaining 5 tortillas. Pour remaining sauce over the tortilla rolls. Sprinkle with remaining cheese. Place in oven and set timer for 20 minutes.

| 1 box | **(10 oz) cut green beans** |
| 1 box | **(10 oz) crinkle cut carrots** |

Place in microwave-safe bowl. Cover and let set in microwave.

*Is the weather nice? How about a nice nature walk? Otherwise, plug in an exercise video.*

When oven timer sounds, begin microwaving vegetables 10 minutes on high. (Allow enchiladas to continue baking.) *Do some sit-ups, push-ups, and stretches.* Slice apples and kiwi. When vegetables are done — it's dinner time!

## MENU

- CREAMY CHICKEN ENCHILADAS
- CUT GREEN BEANS
- CRINKLE CUT CARROTS
- APPLE WEDGES
- KIWI SLICES

*Kids' Favorite*

### EXCHANGE VALUES

| 2 Starch | 4 Meat | 2 Veg. | 1 Fruit | — Milk | — Fat |
|----------|--------|--------|---------|--------|-------|

Nutrition information for — 1-1/2 enchiladas, 1 cup vegetables, 1/2 an apple and kiwi

**Preparation Time — 30 min.**  **Oven / Exercise Time — 30 min.**

| Calories ............................ 480 | Fat ............................... 12 g | Fiber .......................................... 7 g | Sodium ............................ 800 mg | Total Carbohydrate ............. 55 g |
| Calories from Fat ............... 23% | Saturated Fat .................... 4.8 g | Cholesterol ......................... 80 mg | Protein .............................. 37 g | Sugars ............................... 17 g |

## Tip

### Arriving home starved: What to do

If you arrive home starved, you'll need something to hold you over until dinnertime. For a snack that's great exercise fuel, it's hard to beat a piece of fruit or glass of fruit juice. Or try a few crackers, ½ a bagel, or 2 rice cakes. Be sure to chase it with a glass of water. This will give you energy and valuable hydration until dinnertime, while holding off hunger throughout your workout.

### Encore! Left-over Spanish Rice Roll-up

Spoon leftover *Spanish Red Beans and Rice* (hot or cold) onto a lavash bread.

Add extra salsa, lettuce, tomatoes, and roll it up. Delicious!

# Spanish Red Beans & Rice

Every household needs a Spanish red beans and rice dish! Just like mom used to make. Feel free to make this with black beans if you prefer.

SERVES

4

**MENU**

SPANISH RED BEANS & RICE

TOSSED SALAD

PEARS

Kids' Favorite

**Preheat oven to 350°.**

| | |
|---|---|
| 1 can | (15 oz) **red, kidney *or* black beans, rinsed & drained** |
| 1 can | (14½ oz) **stewed tomatoes** |
| 1½ cups | **instant whole-grain brown rice** |
| ¾ cup | **salsa** |
| 1 cup | **water** |
| 4 - 5 drops | *Tabasco*® **sauce** |
| 1 tsp | **cumin** |
| ½ tsp | **oregano** |

Mix together in a large casserole dish.

Cover and put in oven to bake. Set timer for 55 minutes.

*I don't know about you, but the anticipation of this recipe puts me in the mood for rollerblading. What strikes you?*

| | |
|---|---|
| ½ cup | **reduced-fat shredded cheddar cheese** |

When the timer sounds, sprinkle cheese on the beans & rice and allow to melt while you set the table.

Serve with a tossed salad and fresh or canned pears.

---

**EXCHANGE VALUES**

3 Starch   1 Meat   — Veg.   — Fruit   — Milk   — Fat

| Nutrition information for — 1/4 of the recipe | | | Preparation Time — 10 min. | Oven / Exercise Time — 50 min. |
|---|---|---|---|---|
| Calories ........................ 280 | Fat ............................ 3 g | Fiber ........................... 8 g | Sodium .................... 900 mg | Total Carbohydrate ......... 50 g |
| Calories from Fat ......... 10% | Saturated Fat ............ 1.5 g | Cholesterol .............. 5 mg | Protein ......................... 15 g | Sugars ............................... 1 g |

# Tip

## Halloween Survival: "Boo"tiful Alternatives to Candy

- Stickers
- Hand stamps and removable tattoos
- Dimes or nickels (you can actually "save" money this way!)
- Shoelaces
- Barrettes
- Ponytail holders
- Pencils
- Erasers

- Crayons
- Plastic spiders and other bugs
- Sugar-free gum
- Peanuts (small individual packages)
- Cereal (small individual boxes)
- Raisins (small boxes)

# Ratatouille*

An especially excellent dish to make in the fall, or anytime eggplant and zucchini are readily available. This makes a large batch since the flavor improves each day with reheating.

**SERVES**

8

**MENU**

RATATOUILLE WITH POTATOES

WHOLE-GRAIN BREAD
AND/OR
PUMPKIN SURPRISE PIE
(MAKE AHEAD)

**Preheat oven to 350°.**

| | |
|---|---|
| 1 medium | eggplant unpeeled, cut into 1" cubes |
| 8 medium | potatoes, scrubbed clean, cut in ½ |
| 1 | red pepper, chopped |
| 1 | green pepper, chopped |
| 4 small | zucchini (2 can be yellow crooked neck squash), sliced in half lengthwise and then into 1" slices |
| 2 large | onions, sliced |

Prep vegetables and arrange in a large baking dish.

Crockpot option: Cook on high for 3 hours or low for 8 hours. You may need to halve the recipe to make it fit.

| | |
|---|---|
| 2 tsp | minced garlic (4 cloves) |
| ½ cup | fresh minced parsley |
| 1 tsp | dried basil, crushed |
| ¾ tsp | salt |
| 2 cans | (14.5 oz each) stewed tomatoes |
| 2 T | olive oil |

Mix together in a medium bowl — then pour over vegetables. Gently toss.

Cover and bake for 2 hours.

*This allows ample time for a long fall hike. Aren't the colors beautiful? After exercising, you'll still have time to whip up the* Pumpkin Surprise Pie *and get it into the oven for 1 hour.*

## *Option: Chicken Ratatouille

Place 8 skinless drumsticks, thighs, or breasts under the vegetables before baking.

When timer sounds, remove *Ratatouille* and allow to sit 30 minutes more, still covered. *Meanwhile… do push-ups, sit-ups and stretch.*

Serve with a sprinkle of Parmesan cheese, and whole-grain bread or *Pumpkin Surprise Pie* (page 164).

---

**EXCHANGE VALUES**

| 2 Starch | — Meat | 3 Veg. | — Fruit | — Milk | 1 Fat |
|---|---|---|---|---|---|

---

**Nutrition information for — 1/8 of the recipe (without chicken)**   **Preparation Time — 20 min.**   **Oven / Exercise Time — 2 hours**

| | | | | | |
|---|---|---|---|---|---|
| Calories .................................. 280 | Fat ........................................ 4 g | Fiber ........................................ 9 g | Sodium ............................ 450 mg | Total Carbohydrate ............. 58 g |
| Calories from Fat ............... 12% | Saturated Fat ....................... .5 g | Cholesterol .......................... 0 mg | Protein ................................ 7 g | Sugars ................................... 13 g |

# Halloween Survival Tips for KIDS

1. Try not to dole out candy piece by piece throughout the day. Repeated exposure to sugar is more likely to cause cavities. Rather, shoot for once a day and have them brush their teeth afterwards.

2. Don't let kids hide their candy underneath their beds. They'll be snacking all night without brushing their teeth.

3. Gently remind kids that candy is not a "grow food." This is why you are asking them to limit themselves to 2 or 3 pieces a day, in order to leave room for plenty of "grow" food.

4. Have them count out 30 (or so) pieces they want to keep and give the rest to families less fortunate.

# Jack in the Pumpkin

| | SERVES | MENU: |
|---|---|---|

This delicious and hearty Mexican style dish is baked in a hollowed-out pumpkin, providing for the ultimate autumn holiday dish! It's also fun to use small pumpkins for single serving bowls for each guest. This dish is equally delicious baked in a casserole dish.

**SERVES** 6

**MENU:**

JACK IN THE PUMPKIN

MARINATED VEGETABLE SALAD

CANNED PEACHES

Great Autumn dish! Kids' Favorite!

**Preheat oven to 375°.**

| 1 cup | wild/brown rice mixed ($^1/_4$ wild, $^3/_4$ brown) |
| 2 cups | water *and/or* broth |
| 1 | onion, chopped |

Cook for 45 minutes until done.

| 1 medium | pumpkin (pie pumpkin is best) |

Meanwhile… wash and carefully carve open a lid that provides a fairly wide opening. Be sure to carve with your knife at an angle, so that as it cooks, the lid does not slip through the opening. Scoop out all the seeds and pulp and discard. Set aside bowl and lid.

| 1 T | oil (olive *or* canola) |
| 1 tsp | minced garlic (4 cloves) |
| $^1/_2$ | red, green and yellow bell pepper, chopped |
| 2 | onions, chopped |

Combine in a large stir-fry pan and sauté.

Recipe continued on next page.

# Halloween Survival Tips for ADULTS

**Tip**

1. If you have the tendency to eat most of your Halloween candy before October 31, then refrain from buying until the day before.

2. Buy candy you don't like (if there is such a thing!)

3. Increase your exercise during this period.

4. Use positive self-talk. If you've nibbled a bit more than you wanted to, say "no big deal." Make a decision to end the "haunting" and give the candy away!

*Lickety-Split Meals*

| | |
|---|---|
| ³/₄ cup | medium *or* hot salsa (strain so salsa is thick) |
| 2 cups | frozen corn, thawed |
| 2 cans | (16 oz) black beans, drained |
| ¹/₄ cup | chopped fresh parsley |
| 2 tsp | cumin seed |
| 1 tsp | oregano |
| ¹/₈ tsp | cayenne pepper |
| ¹/₄ tsp | salt |

Add to sauté along with the cooked rice. Bring to a simmer for a few minutes. There should be minimal liquid.

Carefully spoon mixture into the pumpkin. Place the pumpkin on a cookie sheet, with the lid along side.

Bake for 1 hour and 15 minutes. Consider making a colorful *Marinated Vegetable Salad* (page 139).

*How about a long fall bike ride? Use the extra time for toning exercises like sit-ups, push-ups, leg lifts, and of course, stretching!*

Remove from oven. Place pumpkin lid on top of pumpkin, if desired, and serve proudly. Meat from inside the pumpkin will be tender and tasty to eat as well as its contents.

---

**EXCHANGE VALUES**

| 3 Starch | 1 Meat | 2 Veg. | — Fruit | — Milk | — Fat |
|---|---|---|---|---|---|

**Nutrition information for — approximately 1 cup, without pumpkin**     Preparation Time — 1 hour     Oven / Exercise Time — 75 min.

| | | | | |
|---|---|---|---|---|
| Calories ................................. 290 | Fat ........................................ 3.5 g | Fiber ........................................ 11 g | Sodium ............................. 650 mg | Total Carbohydrate ............. 60 g |
| Calories from Fat ................. 9% | Saturated Fat ................... < 1 g | Cholesterol ......................... 0 mg | Protein ................................ 11 g | Sugars ....................................... 6 g |

# Tip

## When is the best time of day to exercise you ask?

The BEST time to exercise is whenever you can and will do it CONSISTENTLY, whether that's morning, noon, or night. I recommend mornings, as your energy level is high. Once you are finished, your commitment to fitness has been fulfilled and your self-esteem soars. Take it from a converted "I hate mornings" person, it IS possible to change your habits!

Studies also suggest you will burn a few more calories all day due to an elevated metabolism. Furthermore, fewer interruptions increase the odds of your being consistent.

**P.S. So if you can swing it, exercise in the morning. If not, no PROBLEM. This *Oven/Exercise/Eat* chapter was written for you!**

# Chili Cornbread Pie

A simple one-dish meal that will make your kitchen smell awesome!
Serve with carrot sticks, celery, and peppers.

| SERVES | MENU |
|---|---|
| 6 | CHILI CORNBREAD PIE |
| | CARROT STICKS |
| | CHOCOLATE CHIP BAR COOKIE (MAKE AHEAD) |

**Preheat oven to 375°.**

| 2 cans | (15 oz each) **chili beans\*** *(Eden®)* |
| 1 can | (16 oz) **corn, drained** |
| ½ | **onion, chopped** (optional) |
| 1 tsp | **cumin** |

Combine in a 9" x 13" baking dish.

| 1 cup | **cornmeal** |
| 1 cup | **unbleached flour** |
| 1 T | **baking powder** |
| ¼ cup | **sugar** |

Combine in a medium bowl using a fork
to be sure baking powder is evenly distributed.

| 1 cup + 2 T | **skim milk** *or* **soy milk** |
| 1 T | **canola oil** |

Add to dry ingredients and stir just until blended.

Pour the batter over the bean mixture.

Place in oven to bake. Set timer for 30 minutes.

*Climb upon your stepper for 20 minutes.
When the timer goes off, you're done
and it's time to eat!*

**EXCHANGE VALUES**

| 5 Starch | 1 Meat | — Veg. | — Fruit | — Milk | — Fat |

**\* If you are a cilantro fan, add ¼ cup to the beans and corn.**

| Nutrition information for — 1/6 of the pie | | | | Preparation Time — 15 min. | Oven / Exercise Time — 30 min. |
|---|---|---|---|---|---|
| Calories .................................. 435 | Fat ................................ 4 g | Fiber ................................ 11.5 g | Sodium ............................ 675 mg | Total Carbohydrate ............. 80 g |
| Calories from Fat ................. 8% | Saturated Fat .................... < 1 g | Cholesterol ...................... < 1 mg | Protein ............................ 18.5 g | Sugars ................................ 14 g |

# Pasta

**P**erhaps known as the health food of the '90's, pasta has been touted *everywhere*. It's the "pre-game" meal of choice for athletes, a favorite among vegetarians, and a new low-fat "diet" food for the weight-conscious. And you thought starchy foods were fattening! What's the deal?

The nutritional plus comes from the fact that if you're eating a big plate of pasta, you're probably NOT eating a 12-ounce steak. This is good. If the pasta is tossed with a low-fat tomato sauce, instead of an artery-clogging Alfredo sauce, then this is really good! And if there are lots of vegetables tossed in the sauce, this is *really really* good!

The overall goal is to decrease the amount of animal sources in our diet, and increase the amount of vegetables and grains. Eating pasta (which is a grain), with a chunky tomato sauce with vegetables and a tossed salad on the side, is a great way to do exactly that.

Combining all of this with the fact that pasta meals are fast and a favorite to both children and adults, makes pasta a definite winner! Do you feel like spaghetti, corkscrews, penne or angel hair? Red or white sauce? How about *Southwest Chili* or *Oriental Noodles* for a change? You'll never get tired of having pasta once a week!

## Tip

### But isn't pasta fattening?

Following these 5 steps, pasta is NOT fattening.

1. Use a low-fat recipe for the sauce (like the ones in this chapter).

2. Include as many vegetables in the sauce as you can.

3. Choose whole-wheat pasta whenever possible (for added fiber, vitamins and minerals).

4. Eat a tossed salad before the pasta for appetite control.

5. Eat until your stomach says "satis-fied" instead of "full." Even pasta becomes fattening when you eat TOO MUCH!

# Veggie Sghetti

Occasionally we make this with turkey, but always with lots of vegetables. The vegetables replace the meat beautifully. Use any leftover sauce to top baked potatoes later in the week.

**SERVES**

6

**MENU**

VEGGIE SGHETTI

TOSSED SALAD

WHOLE-WHEAT GARLIC CHEESE TOAST

**Put a large pot of water on to boil.**

| 4 cups | any of the following: carrots, chopped green, red *or* yellow pepper, chopped zucchini, chopped mushrooms, chopped |
| 1 box | (10 oz) frozen chopped broccoli, cauliflower *or* spinach |

Clean and chop or use all chopped frozen, to save time and energy.

Delegate someone to: Make salad and garlic toast.

| 12 oz | spaghetti *or* any shape pasta — preferably whole-wheat |

As soon as water boils, stir in pasta and set timer for 10 minutes.

| 1 T | olive oil |
| 1 | onion, cut into wedges |
| 1 tsp | minced garlic (2 cloves) |
| 1 lb | extra lean ground turkey breast (optional) |

Heat oil in a large nonstick sauce pan. Add onion, garlic, and above vegetables. Add and brown turkey if using.

| 1 jar | (26 oz) spaghetti sauce (*Healthy Choice®*) |
| 2 tsp | oregano |
| 2 tsp | basil |
| dash | red pepper flakes (to taste) |

Add to vegetables. Bring to a simmer.

Meanwhile… make a tossed salad and *Whole-Wheat Garlic Cheese Toast* (page 150).

When timer sounds, drain pasta and serve with sauce.

***Bón Appetit!***

---

**EXCHANGE VALUES**

2.5 Starch — Meat 3 Veg. — Fruit — Milk — Fat

---

**Nutrition information for — about 1-1/2 cups of sauce & veggies over 1 cup pasta**

**Preparation Time — 30 min.**

| | | | |
|---|---|---|---|
| Calories .................................. 305 | Fat ........................................ 3.5 g | Fiber .................................. 11.5 g | Sodium ............................ 416 mg | Total Carbohydrate ............ 54 g |
| Calories from Fat ............... 10% | Saturated Fat .................... 1.3 g | Cholesterol .......................... 0 mg | Protein .................................. 14 g | Sugars .................................. 13 g |

# When is pasta NOT good for you?

The following are all examples of a "bypass special" wearing the pasta disguise…

1. Restaurant Lasagna, including Spinach Lasagna and Vegetarian Lasagna. (It's the truck load of cheese.)

2. Restaurant Fettuccine Alfredo (butter, oil, and cream — enough said.)

3. Most white sauces (unless it's a low-fat recipe like the one below!)

*Lickety-Split Meals*

# Pasta Primavera

You and your guests will never believe that this cream sauce is practically fat-free.
Do you want chicken, shrimp, or vegetables only? I use the shrimp or chicken options
when entertaining and vegetables only for every day.

| SERVES | MENU |
| --- | --- |
| 6 | PASTA PRIMAVERA |
| | CRANBERRY SALAD (MAKE AHEAD) |
| | FLAMING BANANAS FOSTER |

**Put a large pot of water on to boil.**

| 10 cups | vegetables — any combination of fresh *or* frozen |
| --- | --- |
| | broccoli |
| | carrots |
| | cauliflower |
| | green, red *or* yellow pepper |
| | zucchini |
| | yellow squash |
| | mushrooms |
| | pea pods |

Clean & chop the fresh vegetables you happen to have and fill in with frozen vegetables. To save time, use all frozen vegetables. Set aside.

| 8 oz | pasta (fettuccine *or* linguine) |
| --- | --- |

As soon as water boils, stir in pasta and set timer for 10 minutes. When timer sounds, drain and keep warm.

| 1 T | olive oil |
| --- | --- |
| 1 | onion, cut into wedges |
| 1 - 2 tsp | minced garlic (2 cloves) |

Heat oil in a large non-stick fry pan or wok. Add garlic and onion. Cook 1 minute.

Recipe continued on next page.

# When is pasta NOT good for you? (Continued)

4. When the pasta is tossed with lots of oil (restaurants commonly do this).

5. When the marinara sauce is made with too much oil to sauté the vegetables.

6. When the "sprinkled" Parmesan cheese exceeds a sprinkle.

7. When the recipe includes sausage and other artery clogging meats.

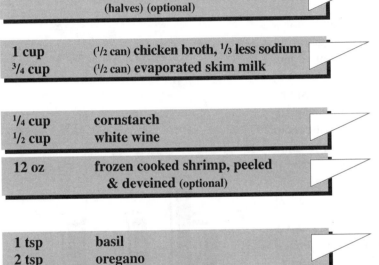

| | | |
|---|---|---|
| **4** | **skinless, boneless, chicken breast,** (halves) (optional) | Cube chicken and sauté 5 minutes (or skip this step). When chicken is almost finished cooking, add the vegetables and stir. |
| **1 cup** | (¹/₂ can) **chicken broth, ¹/₃ less sodium** | Meanwhile… in a small bowl, mix the ¹/₂ cans of chicken broth & evaporated skim milk. *(Combine the remaining broth and milk in an airtight container, label, and freeze for the next time you make this.)* |
| **³/₄ cup** | (¹/₂ can) **evaporated skim milk** | |
| **¹/₄ cup** | **cornstarch** | Add to broth mixture and stir well. |
| **¹/₂ cup** | **white wine** | |
| **12 oz** | **frozen cooked shrimp, peeled & deveined** (optional) | Remove tails if necessary. Add to the vegetables (or skip this step). Add the milk/broth mixture to the vegetables. Simmer until thick and bubbly. |
| **1 tsp** | **basil** | Add seasonings and cheese, followed by the cooked, drained pasta. Toss gently. |
| **2 tsp** | **oregano** | Serve with *Cranberry Salad* (page 144) and remember to save room for *Flaming Bananas Foster* (page 167). |
| **10 grinds** | **fresh ground pepper** | |
| **¹/₄ tsp** | **salt** | |
| **¹/₂ cup** | **Parmesan cheese** | |

---

**EXCHANGE VALUES**

2 Starch   2 Meat   3 Veg.  — Fruit  — Milk  — Fat

| Nutrition information for — about 1-1/2 cups sauce & shrimp (no chicken) over 1 cup pasta | | | Preparation Time — 45 min. | |
|---|---|---|---|---|
| Calories ..................... 370 | Fat ........................ 6 g | Fiber ...................... 6 g | Sodium ..................... 520 mg | Total Carbohydrate ............. 50 g |
| Calories from Fat ............. 15% | Saturated Fat .............. 2 g | Cholesterol .............. 117 mg | Protein ..................... 26 g | Sugars ....................... 8 g |

## True or False

# Tip

*"Eating 2 cups of regular pasta (not a whole-wheat variety) is like eating 4 slices of white bread."*

Depressing, but TRUE.

Most pasta is made from refined wheat. It does not contain the fibrous bran, or the nutrient-dense germ (and so is similar to the white flour used for white bread). While eating white bread is better than eating a big steak, we all know it's better to eat WHOLE-WHEAT products. And that includes pasta! (See page 185 for more information about the nutrition lost when whole grain is refined.)

Look for whole-wheat pasta products in your grocery store. They may be in the normal pasta section or in the "health food" section.

# Southwest Chili Pasta

A delicious and colorful "South of the border" pasta dish. And it is quick!

SERVES 4

**MENU**

SOUTHWEST CHILI PASTA
TOSSED SALAD
FUDGESICLE

**Put a large pot of water on to boil.**

| | |
|---|---|
| 1 | **green pepper** |

Chop pepper and set aside.

Open cans that are called for below.
Drain beans, reserving liquid.

*Delegate someone to: make tossed salad*

| | |
|---|---|
| 8 oz | **pasta** (preferably whole-wheat) **any size or shape** |

As soon as water boils, stir in pasta and set timer for 10 minutes.

| | |
|---|---|
| 1 T | **olive oil** |
| 2 tsp | **minced garlic** (4 cloves) |

Heat oil, then sauté garlic and chopped pepper for 1 minute.

| | |
|---|---|
| 1½ tsp | **whole cumin seeds** *or* **1 tsp ground cumin** |

Add and sauté 10 seconds longer.

| | |
|---|---|
| 1 can | (15 oz) **black beans, drained** |
| 1 can | (15 oz) **kidney beans, drained** |
| 1 can | (14.5 oz) **stewed tomatoes** |
| 2 - 3 tsp | **chili powder** |

Add to pot and simmer for 10 minutes. If chili becomes too thick, thin it slightly with the reserved bean liquid.

When the timer sounds, drain pasta and serve with the chili over top.

Serve with tossed salad.

---

**EXCHANGE VALUES**

4 Starch   1 Meat   1 Veg.   — Fruit   — Milk   — Fat

**Nutrition information for — about 1-1/4 cups of beans and sauce over 1 cup pasta**   **Preparation Time — 25 min.**

| | | | | |
|---|---|---|---|---|
| Calories .................... 425 | Fat ........................ 5.5 g | Fiber ........................ 18 g | Sodium ............................ 665 mg | Total Carbohydrate ............. 77 g |
| Calories from Fat ............... 11% | Saturated Fat ................... 2 g | Cholesterol .................... 0 mg | Protein ............................ 20 g | Sugars ...................................... 11 g |

## Tip

### Great ideas for first-time whole-wheat pasta users:

1.  Serve with lots of chunky tomato sauce.

2.  Toss the pasta and sauce in the kitchen so the children will not speculate why the pasta is brown.

3.  Try cooking half white and half whole-wheat until you are used to it.

4.  Try the 50-50 pastas available from *Eden Foods*®. (See the coupons in the back.) Eden offers a wonderful line of pasta that uses $^1/_2$ "sifted" flour with $^1/_2$ whole-wheat flour. These products are delicious, and you really can't tell they are made with whole-wheat! They, of course, offer fine 100% whole-wheat pasta as well. Look in your health food store or health food section of your grocery store. If it's not there, ask for it!

# Herbed Italian Sausage over Pasta

**SERVES** | **MENU**

Here's a tasty change from the traditional spaghetti dinner and yet another use for your *Homemade Turkey Sausage* (page 17).

4

**Put a large pot of water on to boil.**

| | |
|---|---|
| 1 | **onion** |
| 1 each | **green and yellow pepper** |
| 10 | **baby carrots, chopped** (optional) |
| 1 sm | **zucchini, cut in half and sliced** (optional) |

Slice onion into small wedges and vegetables into thin strips or however you'd like.

| | |
|---|---|
| 8 oz | **pasta** (preferably whole-wheat) **any size *or* shape** |

As soon as water boils, stir in pasta and set timer for 10 minutes.

| | |
|---|---|
| 1 T | **oil** (olive *or* canola) |
| 4 | ***Homemade Turkey Sausage*** **patties** (from freezer) |

Add oil to a hot nonstick skillet and sauté vegetables for 2 minutes. Add turkey sausage, breaking up into crumbles. Cook until done.

| | |
|---|---|
| 1 jar | (26 oz) **spaghetti sauce** (*Healthy Choice®*) |
| 1 tsp | **Italian seasoning** |

Add to skillet and bring to a simmer.

When timer sounds, drain pasta. Pour sauce over pasta to serve.

Don't forget the tossed salad and *Whole-Wheat Garlic Toast* (page 150).

While the others clear the table, there's plenty of time to mix up a batch of *Smoothies* (page 16).

---

**EXCHANGE VALUES**

| 3 Starch | 2 Meat | 2 Veg. | — Fruit | — Milk | — Fat |
|---|---|---|---|---|---|

\* See *Breakfast* section (page 50).

**Nutrition information for — about 1-1/4 cups sauce & veggies over 1 cup pasta**          **Preparation Time — 25 min.**

| | | | | |
|---|---|---|---|---|
| Calories ................. 370 | Fat ..................... 5 g | Fiber ................ 12 g | Sodium .............. 785 mg | Total Carbohydrate ...... 59 g |
| Calories from Fat ...... 13% | Saturated Fat ...... 1.5 g | Cholesterol ........ 16 mg | Protein ............... 21 g | Sugars ................. 17 g |

# Tip

## Selecting a spaghetti sauce

The goal is to find a sauce that is 5 grams or less of fat and 800 mg or less of sodium *per cup*. Including lots of chunky vegetables is definitely a plus, too. Contrary to what you may be thinking, 5 grams of fat is NOT TOO MUCH. In fact, studies have indicated that the lycopenes (cancer-fighting compounds in tomatoes) are more available to your body cells when the tomatoes ARE cooked with a small amount of oil, vs. no oil. Besides, pour it over 2 cups of pasta and you only have 10% of calories from fat.

I have recommended *Healthy Choice*® in my recipes simply because it meets these recommendations, has a little fat, and is readily available. However, I encourage you to shop around for the sauce you like best. Take a look at my selected sampling on page 178, to get an idea of what's out there.

# Parmesan Turkey Cutlets over Angel Hair

**SERVES** | **MENU**

When you're serving pasta once a week, it's nice to vary the presentation. My thanks to Connie and Rich Bloom for this neat find. If you don't have angel hair, any pasta will do.

6

PARMESAN TURKEY CUTLETS OVER ANGEL HAIR

WHOLE-WHEAT GARLIC CHEESE TOAST

WHERE'S THE LETTUCE? SALAD

**Put a large pot of water on to boil.**

| | |
|---|---|
| 1 jar | (26 oz) **spaghetti sauce** (*Healthy Choice®*) |

Place in a small saucepan and heat over medium-low.

| | |
|---|---|
| ¼ cup | **Parmesan cheese** |
| ¼ tsp | **Italian seasoning** |
| 5 grinds | **fresh ground pepper** |

Mix together in a bowl.

| | |
|---|---|
| 12 oz | **angel hair pasta** |

As soon as water boils, stir in angel hair and set timer for 7 minutes.

| | |
|---|---|
| 1 lb | **fresh turkey breast cutlets** |
| | (6 slices, ¼" thick each) |
| 1 T | **olive oil** |

Heat oil in skillet over medium heat. Coat each turkey cutlet with cheese mixture and place in skillet. Cook 2 minutes on each side.

When timer sounds, drain pasta.

To serve, place 1 cup pasta on each plate, top with 1 turkey breast slice and ½ to ¾ cup sauce over top.

Serve with *Whole Wheat Garlic Cheese Toast* (page 150) and *Where's the Lettuce? Salad* (page 138).

*Delegate Someone to: Make Garlic Toast and Where's the Lettuce Salad*

---

**EXCHANGE VALUES**

3 Starch    3 Meat    1 Veg.    — Fruit    — Milk    — Fat

| Nutrition information for — 1 small turkey cutlet, 1 cup pasta, 1/2 cup sauce | | | Preparation Time — 30 min. | |
|---|---|---|---|---|
| Calories .................................. 385 | Fat .............................. 5 g | Fiber ................................ 3.5 g | Sodium ............................ 525 mg | Total Carbohydrate ............. 54 g |
| Calories from Fat ................ 11% | Saturated Fat ...................... 1 g | Cholesterol ...................... 50 mg | Protein .................................. 30 g | Sugars ................................... 10 g |

# Tip

## Great ideas from people like you!

*"The most important aspect about exercise for me is that it builds a confidence level that carries me through all aspects of my life. I feel exercise is a celebration of life and a blessing on the whole day.*

—KAY V. E., 44
2nd grade teacher and
consistent exerciser for 15 years
Once 168 pounds, now 125

# White Beans & Penne Pasta

My thanks to neighbors Eric & Anne Tooley for sharing this family favorite. While the topping of oil with rosemary seems fattening, the numbers still come out healthy and the taste is exceptional.

6

WHITE BEANS
AND PENNE PASTA

TOSSED SALAD

WHOLE-WHEAT GARLIC
CHEESE TOAST

| | |
|---|---|
| 1 T | olive oil |
| 1 large | onion, cut into wedges |
| 1 tsp | minced garlic (2 cloves) |

Sauté 3 or 4 minutes in a large nonstick pan over medium-high heat.

Delegate someone to: Make the tossed salad.

| | |
|---|---|
| 2 cans | (14.5 oz) stewed tomatoes |

Add and simmer 10 minutes.
Use this time to put together a tossed salad.

| | |
|---|---|
| 2 cans | (14.5 oz each) chicken broth, ⅓ less sodium |
| 1 jar | (24 oz) Great Northern beans, rinsed and drained |

Stir in and bring to a boil.

| | |
|---|---|
| 6 oz | Penne pasta |

Stir in and set timer for 10 minutes.

Meanwhile… make *Whole-Wheat Garlic Cheese Toast* (page 150).

| | |
|---|---|
| 2 T | olive oil |
| 1 tsp | dry rosemary (*or* 1 T fresh) |

Mix together in small microwave-safe bowl. Warm in microwave for 30 seconds.

Prepare the servings of pasta and drizzle rosemary oil over each serving. Top with Parmesan cheese if desired. Don't forget the salad and garlic toast.

**EXCHANGE VALUES**

| 3 Starch | 1 Meat | 2 Veg. | — Fruit | — Milk | 1 Fat |
|---|---|---|---|---|---|

**SODIUM ALERT! See page 31.**

| Nutrition information for — about 1-1/2 cups | | | Preparation Time — 35 min. | | |
|---|---|---|---|---|---|
| Calories ................................. 330 | Fat ........................................ 7 g | Fiber ............................... 10 g | Sodium ............................ 900 mg | Total Carbohydrate ............. 53 g | |
| Calories from Fat ............... 19% | Saturated Fat .................... < 1 g | Cholesterol .......................... 0 mg | Protein ................................. 13 g | Sugars ....................................... 8 g | |

# Tip

## What is Tamari?

Tamari (sometimes called Shoyu) is very similar to reduced-sodium soy sauce, but is lighter in color and flavor. Both Tamari and Shoyu are popular in natural food recipes because they are made the more natural and traditional way with long fermentation. Soy sauce, on the other hand, is a general term for the dark-brown flavoring liquids with a soybean base. Soy sauce is prepared unfermented from hydrolyzed vegetable protein, corn syrup, caramel color, and salt.

I suggest looking for Tamari or Shoyu for both their "natural product" quality and delightful taste. If you cannot find them, use reduced-sodium soy sauce in their place.

# Oriental Noodle Toss with Black Beans

The sesame oil really makes this. Excellent as a main dish or as a side dish to grilled or broiled salmon steak. Serve warm or at room temperature.

**SERVES**

4

**MENU**

ORIENTAL NOODLE TOSS WITH BLACK BEANS

TOSSED SALAD WITH CRUNCHY VEGETABLES

RASPBERRY SORBET

**Put a large pot of water on to boil.**

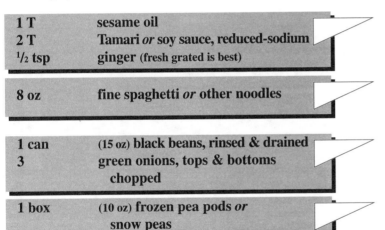

| 1 T | sesame oil |
| 2 T | Tamari *or* soy sauce, reduced-sodium |
| ½ tsp | ginger (fresh grated is best) |

Stir together in a medium-large serving bowl.

*Delegate someone to: Make tossed salad with crunchy vegetables.*

| 8 oz | fine spaghetti *or* other noodles |

As soon as water boils, stir in pasta and set timer for 6 minutes (9 minutes if not using a fine pasta.)

| 1 can | (15 oz) black beans, rinsed & drained |
| 3 | green onions, tops & bottoms chopped |

Add to bowl.

| 1 box | (10 oz) frozen pea pods *or* snow peas |

When timer sounds, add pea pods or snow peas to boiling noodles for 1 minute. Drain. Toss with the beans and sauce.

It's meal-time!

---

**EXCHANGE VALUES**

3 Starch  1 Meat  1 Veg.  — Fruit  — Milk  — Fat

| Nutrition information for — about 1-1/2 cups | | Preparation Time — 20 min. | |
|---|---|---|---|
| Calories ............... 345 | Fat ............... 5 g | Fiber ............... 9 g | Sodium ............... 530 mg | Total Carbohydrate ............. 64 g |
| Calories from Fat ............... 11% | Saturated Fat ............... < 1 g | Cholesterol ............... 0 mg | Protein ............... 15 g | Sugars ............... 3 g |

# Pizza

What's America's favorite food? Pizza! And what food often gets blamed for being fattening and artery-clogging? Pizza! But NOT anymore!

At first you would think pizza, made healthy and fast at home, would be a complete oxymoron. But thanks to the convenience of pita bread, (which make great individual pizza crusts) or ready-made crusts by *"Boboli®"* or *"Oliveri®"*, ready-made sauces and low-fat cheese, you can make your own healthy pizzas at home. And all in much less time than it takes to get pizza delivered!

The following recipes use ready-made sauces, lean meat (if any), low-fat cheese and ample vegetable toppings, which make the pizzas nutritionally smart. So stock up on your supplies. They're all on the *Lickety-Split* grocery list.

You will notice that some of the recipes instruct you to sauté the vegetable toppings first before placing on the pizza. Other recipes instruct you to place the toppings on raw (leaving them a little "more crunchy" when finished). It will not take long before you decide if more or less crunchy is your family's favorite. Simply add the sauté step if "more tender" is your preference.

I'm sure it's no surprise that the *Lickety-Split Weekly Menu Solution* lists Friday as your pizza night. The family's favorite by far! TGIF!

# Tip

## Pita: The perfect ready-made pizza crust

If you haven't used pita bread for pizzas yet, you haven't lived! Pitas allow every-one to make individual "custom" pizzas with the convenient ready-made "crusts." (Forget about the "pocket" and just lay them flat.) Be sure to look through all the recipes in this chapter, because you can adapt any of them to make a pita pizza in seconds.

Another fine benefit of pitas is that whole-wheat pitas are pretty easy to find (ask your grocer). This is a nutritional plus over the *Boboli®* or *Oliveri®* pizza crusts (which are unfortunately not available in whole-wheat).

**P.S.** Buy several packages of pitas for the freezer so you'll always have them on hand.

**P.S.S.** Be sure to involve the kids! They will love making their own pizzas!

# Pita Pizza

A quick and easy meal, that both kids and adults will love.
When you have more time, let the kids assemble their own pizzas.

**Turn oven on to broil. Leave the oven door ajar.**

| | | |
|---|---|---|
| 2 | whole-wheat pita breads | Lay out on a cookie sheet. |
| 6 T | spaghetti sauce *(Healthy Choice®)* | Spread $^1/_2$ of sauce onto each pita. |
| $^1/_4$ tsp | dried oregano | Sprinkle on top of each pita. |
| $^1/_4$ tsp | dried basil | |
| $1^1/_2$ cups | bite-size broccoli flowerets | Rinse, drain and place in a microwave-safe dish. Cover and cook $1^1/_2$ minutes on high. |
| $^1/_4$ | green pepper | Layer on the pita as desired. Add broccoli. |
| $^1/_4$ | onion | |
| 3 | mushrooms | |
| $^1/_2$ cup | reduced-fat shredded mozzarella cheese | Complete the pizzas by sprinkling each on top. Broil 6" from heating element for about 2 to 4 minutes, until cheese is melted and beginning to brown. |
| 2 T | Parmesan cheese | |
| dash | red pepper flakes (as desired) | Serve with tossed salad and fruit for dessert. |

### EXCHANGE VALUES

| 2 Starch | 1 Meat | 2 Veg. | — Fruit | — Milk | — Fat |
|---|---|---|---|---|---|

**Nutrition information for — 1 pita pizza**

**Preparation Time — 15 min.**

| | | | | |
|---|---|---|---|---|
| Calories .................................. 275 | Fat ........................................ 4 g | Fiber ...................................... 6.5 g | Sodium ............................ 600 mg | Total Carbohydrate ............ 43 g |
| Calories from Fat ............... 14% | Saturated Fat .................... 2.5 g | Cholesterol ......................... 14 mg | Protein .................................. 19 g | Sugars .................................... 6.5 g |

# Tip

## Pizza AND cookies?
## Are you sure this is a healthy cookbook?

The only thing better than pizza is pizza and cookies. Limit yourself to 2 slices of pizza, play some frisbee, and you can justify heading back to the kitchen for some dessert. *Chocolate No-Bakes* (page 160) are fast and 2 of them really hit the spot!

# Garden Vegetable Pizza

"Pre-steaming" the broccoli flowerets turns them bright green and keeps them from drying out. If you prefer your onion and peppers soft versus a little crunchy, microwave them along with the broccoli, adding 1 minute.

| SERVES | MENU |
|---|---|
| 4 | GARDEN VEGETABLE PIZZA |
| | WHERE'S THE LETTUCE SALAD |
| | CHOCOLATE NO-BAKE COOKIES |

**Preheat oven to 425°.**

| | | |
|---|---|---|
| 1 | ready-made pizza crust (*Boboli®*) | Spread sauce evenly onto crust. |
| 1 cup | (or more) spaghetti sauce (*Healthy Choice®*) | |

| | | |
|---|---|---|
| 1½ cups | fresh broccoli flowerets (cut into bite-size flowerets) | Rinse, drain and place in a microwave-safe dish. Cover and cook 1 minute on high. |

| | | |
|---|---|---|
| 1 small | onion, thinly sliced into rings | Prep vegetables and neatly arrange on pizza. |
| 5 | fresh mushrooms, sliced *or* 1 small can sliced mushrooms, drained | Top with broccoli flowerets. |
| ½ | red pepper, sliced into strips | |
| ½ | green pepper, sliced into strips | |
| 1 | fresh tomato, thinly sliced | |

| | | |
|---|---|---|
| 2 T | Parmesan cheese | Sprinkle evenly on pizza in order given. |
| 1 cup | reduced-fat shredded mozzarella cheese | Bake 10 to 12 minutes. |
| 4 dashes | (or more) hot pepper flakes | Meanwhile... make *Where's the Lettuce? Salad* (page 138). |
| 4 sprinkles | Italian seasoning | Cut into 8 slices and serve. |

**EXCHANGE VALUES**

| 3.5 Starch | 2 Meat | 2 Veg. | — Fruit | — Milk | — Fat |
|---|---|---|---|---|---|

**SODIUM ALERT! See page 31.**

**Nutrition information for — 2 slices**  **Preparation Time — 25 min.**

| | | | | |
|---|---|---|---|---|
| Calories ............................. 425 | Fat ......................................... 10 g | Fiber ......................................... 4.3 g | Sodium ......................... 1050 mg | Total Carbohydrate ............. 62 g |
| Calories from Fat ............... 19% | Saturated Fat ........................ 4 g | Cholesterol ......................... 16 mg | Protein ................................. 26 g | Sugars ....................................... 9 g |

# Solution to typical pizza problem #1:
# CHEESE and LOTS of it.

Making pizza at home means you can select part-skim mozzarella mixed 50-50 with the fat-free variety, for 3 grams of fat per ounce and use just 4 ounces (1 cup) of cheese for an entire pizza. This makes an incredibly low-fat pizza!

*Lickety-Split Meals*

# Hot & Spicy Pizza with Sausage

Here's another reason for making the "Homemade Turkey Sausage" from the Breakfast section. The sausage offers great flavor and convenience. Note vegetarians: Even without the sausage, this recipe is **very** delicious!

**SERVES**

4

**MENU**

HOT & SPICY PIZZA
WHERE'S THE LETTUCE SALAD
1 SCOOP FAT-FREE ICE CREAM

**Preheat oven to 425°.**
**Spray nonstick pan with nonstick spray.**

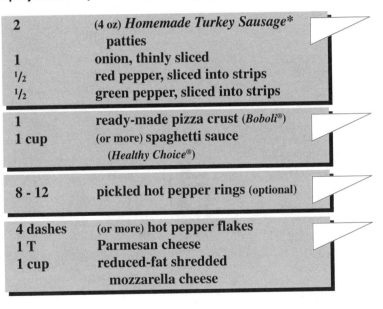

| | |
|---|---|
| 2 | (4 oz) *Homemade Turkey Sausage*\* patties |
| 1 | onion, thinly sliced |
| ½ | red pepper, sliced into strips |
| ½ | green pepper, sliced into strips |

Sauté until sausage is done, break up and crumble the patties.

| | |
|---|---|
| 1 | ready-made pizza crust (*Boboli*®) |
| 1 cup | (or more) spaghetti sauce (*Healthy Choice*®) |

Meanwhile… spread sauce evenly onto crust.
Spread sausage mixture over sauce.

| | |
|---|---|
| 8 - 12 | pickled hot pepper rings (optional) |

Evenly place onto pizza.

| | |
|---|---|
| 4 dashes | (or more) hot pepper flakes |
| 1 T | Parmesan cheese |
| 1 cup | reduced-fat shredded mozzarella cheese |

Add to pizza.

Bake 10 to 12 minutes.

Meanwhile… make *Where's the Lettuce? Salad* (page 138).

Cut into 8 slices and serve.

**SODIUM ALERT! See page 31.**

\* See *Breakfast* section (page 50)

---

**EXCHANGE VALUES**

3.5 Starch   3 Meat   2 Veg.   — Fruit   — Milk   — Fat

---

**Nutrition information for — 2 slices (without hot pepper rings)**

**Preparation Time — 30 min.**

| | | | |
|---|---|---|---|
| Calories ..................... 433 | Fat ......................... 9 g | Fiber ..................... 3.2 g | Sodium ..................... 1150 mg | Total Carbohydrate ............. 60 g |
| Calories from Fat .............. 18% | Saturated Fat ................. 3.8 g | Cholesterol ................. 25 g | Protein ..................... 30 g | Sugars ..................... 8 g |

**Tip**

**What is chutney?**

Chutney is the relish that traditionally accompanies Indian food, and is made of chopped fruits and spices like ginger, allspice, cinnamon, garlic, vinegar, and hot pepper. Look for it in the specialty section of your grocery store. Trust me: it's a delicious spicy-sweet dynamo.

# Chicken Chutney Pizza

My husband ordered this in a restaurant once.  I said, "What?  Are you crazy?"
And yes, crazy we both are now for Chutney Pizza! This stuff is *really* great!

**Preheat oven to 425°.**
**Spray nonstick pan with nonstick spray.**

| | |
|---|---|
| 1 | chicken breast halve, cut into small chunks (optional) |
| 1 small | onion, sliced into rings |
| ½ | red pepper, sliced into strips |
| ½ | green pepper, sliced into strips |

Sauté all together until chicken is no longer pink.

| | |
|---|---|
| 1 | ready-made pizza crust (*Boboli*®) |
| ⅓ cup | mango, pineapple *or* peach chutney |

Meanwhile… spread chutney sauce evenly onto crust.
When chicken is done, spread chicken mixture over sauce.

| | |
|---|---|
| 1 can | (8 oz) pineapple tidbits, in its own juice, drained |

Place on pizza.

| | |
|---|---|
| 1 cup | reduced-fat shredded mozzarella cheese |

Sprinkle on pizza.

Bake 10 to 12 minutes.

Meanwhile… make tossed salad.

Cut into 8 slices and serve.

---

**EXCHANGE VALUES**

4 Starch    3 Meat    — Veg.    1 Fruit    — Milk    — Fat

| Nutrition information for — 2 slices | | | | Preparation Time — 30 min. | |
|---|---|---|---|---|---|
| Calories ................... 530 | Fat ......................... 9 g | Fiber ........................................ 3 g | Sodium ........................... 850 mg | Total Carbohydrate ............. 78 g |
| Calories from Fat ............... 16% | Saturated Fat .................... 3.7 g | Cholesterol ...................... 48 mg | Protein .................................... 37 g | Sugars ....................................... 27 g |

## Solution to typical pizza problem #2: Fatty toppings

I probably don't have to tell you how bad pizza toppings like pepperoni (a.k.a. pig fat puddles) are for you. Saturated fat, sodium, preservatives....YUK!!! You'll also notice that I've included a meat topping that will surprise you: sautéed chicken breast strips. I have to admit, it sounded weird at first, but give it a try! In the meantime, for the true "hard-core pizza traditionalists," try this:

1. Opt for just 1 meat topping.

2. Choose leaner meat toppings like ham or Canadian bacon.

3. Select as many vegetable toppings as possible.

**Other pizza ordering tips.....**

4. Ask for the regular or thin crusts (more "dry") instead of deep dish which are often more greasy...notice the shine on your fingers?

5. Refrain from double cheese (you can do it!) and request "half the cheese you usually put on, please."

# Southwest Chicken Pizza

Since we like to have pizza once a week, this gives us some nice variety. Enjoy!

| SERVES | MENU |
| --- | --- |
| 4 | SOUTHWEST CHICKEN PIZZA<br>TOSSED SALAD<br>FRESH ORANGE SECTIONS |

**Preheat oven to 425°.**
**Spray a nonstick skillet with nonstick spray.**

| | |
| --- | --- |
| 2 | skinless, boneless, chicken breast (halves), **cut into strips** |
| 1 small | zucchini, sliced lengthwise, then crosswise ¼" thick |
| 1 small | onion, thinly sliced |
| 1 can | green chilies |
| 1 tsp | chili powder |
| 1 tsp | cumin |

Sauté all together until chicken is no longer pink.

| | |
| --- | --- |
| 1 | ready-made pizza crust (*Boboli®*) |
| 1 cup | thick salsa* |

Meanwhile… spread salsa evenly on crust.

Spread cooked chicken mixture on pizza.

| | |
| --- | --- |
| 1 cup | reduced-fat shredded cheddar cheese |
| 5 | black olives, sliced |

Add to pizza in order given.

Bake 8 to 10 minutes.

Meanwhile… prepare tossed salad and fresh orange sections.

Cut into 8 slices and serve.

**SODIUM ALERT! See page 31.**

\* If your salsa is thin, use a slotted spoon to lift out the thick parts.

**EXCHANGE VALUES**

| 3.5 Starch | 3 Meat | 2 Veg. | — Fruit | — Milk | — Fat |
| --- | --- | --- | --- | --- | --- |

**Nutrition information for — 2 slices**    **Preparation Time — 30 min.**

| | | | | | |
| --- | --- | --- | --- | --- | --- |
| Calories .......... 490 | Fat .......... 12 g | Fiber .......... 3 g | Sodium .......... 1350 mg | Total Carbohydrate .......... 59 g | |
| Calories from Fat .......... 22% | Saturated Fat .......... 4.3 g | Cholesterol .......... 47 mg | Protein .......... 36 g | Sugars .......... 5 g | |

*Lickety-Split Meals*

Southwest Chicken Pizza

# Tip

## Solution to typical pizza problem #3

**Pizza is usually the only food choice served at the meal.** I know what you're thinking. Pizza contains all of the necessary food groups right? But NOT in the right proportions to provide enough fiber and cancer-fighting nutrients to balance out all of the cheese fat. I remind you in each recipe that a serving of pizza is 2 slices (3 or 4 slices for *very* active people). In addition to this, you should serve it with salad or vegetables, and fruit. With this strategy, you can include pizza into a healthy diet every single week! TGIF!

# Polynesian Pizza

This pizza features the unexpected, BBQ sauce! Now
I know what you're thinking, but be brave. Try it!

**Preheat oven to 425°.**

| 1 | ready-made pizza crust (*Boboli®*) |
| ¹/₃ cup | BBQ sauce (*Open Pit®*) |

Spread sauce evenly onto crust.

| 1 | onion, thinly sliced into rings |
| ¹/₂ | red pepper, sliced into strips |
| ¹/₂ | green pepper, sliced into strips |
| 1 can | (8 oz) pineapple tidbits, in its own juice, well drained |

Layer on pizza. Reserve pineapple juice for another use.

| 1 cup | reduced-fat shredded mozzarella cheese |

Sprinkle evenly across pizza.

Bake 10 to 12 minutes.

Meanwhile… make *Crunchy Apple Salad* (page 141).

Cut into 8 slices and serve.

---

**EXCHANGE VALUES**

3 Starch    2 Meat    1 Veg.    1 Fruit    — Milk    — Fat

**SODIUM ALERT! Use pita bread instead of *Boboli®* crust and save about 250 mg of sodium.**

Nutrition information for — 2 slices

Preparation Time — 25 min.

| | | | | |
|---|---|---|---|---|
| Calories ............................... 425 | Fat ............................... 8.5 g | Fiber ............................... 2.5 g | Sodium ........................... 1130 mg | Total Carbohydrate ............. 66 g |
| Calories from Fat ............... 18% | Saturated Fat .................... 3.5 g | Cholesterol ....................... 14 mg | Protein ................................ 23 g | Sugars ............................... 13 g |

*Lickety-Split Meals*

**Polynesian Pizza**

# Is shrimp high in cholesterol or not?

Contrary to what you may have heard, shrimp, scallops, lobster, and crab (as long as they are not fried or sautéed in lots of fat) can definitely be part of a healthy diet. Here's what you need to know about seafood:

1. Seafood is naturally very low in total fat, including saturated fat.

2. Ounce for ounce, seafood has about the same amount of cholesterol as chicken.

3. Seafood contains the beneficial Omega III fatty acids (see page 69 for more information).

4. Stick with MODERATE portions (3 ounces or 7 medium shrimp) and avoid those "all you can eat" buffets.

5. Dip lobster in lemon not butter.

6. Avoid fried shrimp or broiled scampi or scallops that are swimming in butter!

7. Ask for "dry broiled" or steamed.

8. Of course, include lots of vegetables with your meal.

# Shrimp Pizza

Yet another delicious way to enjoy pizza at home.
The cocktail sauce provides a nice change.

**SERVES** | **MENU**

4 | SHRIMP PIZZA
SUNSHINE CARROT-RAISIN SALAD

*Appeteaser idea: Use mini pitas (like 2" round) to build tasty single serving appetizers, with one shrimp on each.*

**Preheat oven to 425°.**

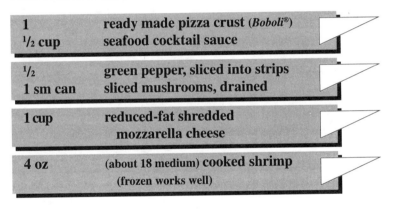

| | |
|---|---|
| 1 | ready made pizza crust (*Boboli®*) |
| ½ cup | seafood cocktail sauce |

Spread sauce evenly onto crust.

| | |
|---|---|
| ½ | green pepper, sliced into strips |
| 1 sm can | sliced mushrooms, drained |

Arrange evenly across sauce.

| | |
|---|---|
| 1 cup | reduced-fat shredded mozzarella cheese |

Sprinkle evenly across vegetables.

| | |
|---|---|
| 4 oz | (about 18 medium) **cooked shrimp** (frozen works well) |

Arrange shrimp over cheese. (If using frozen, cooked shrimp, run warm water over them to quick-thaw, then drain. Remove tails, if necessary.)

Bake 8 to 10 minutes.

Meanwhile… make *Sunshine Carrot-Raisin Salad* (page 140).

Cut into 8 slices and serve.

---

**EXCHANGE VALUES**

| 4 Starch | 2 Meat | — Veg. | — Fruit | — Milk | — Fat |
|---|---|---|---|---|---|

**SODIUM ALERT!** Use pita bread instead of *Boboli®* crust and save about 250 mg of sodium.

**Nutrition information for — 2 slices**

**Preparation Time — 25 min.**

| | | | |
|---|---|---|---|
| Calories ..... 420 | Fat ..... 9 g | Fiber ..... 2 g | Sodium ..... 1200 mg | Total Carbohydrate ..... 59 g |
| Calories from Fat ..... 18% | Saturated Fat ..... 3.6 g | Cholesterol ..... 70 mg | Protein ..... 29 g | Sugars ..... 7.5 g |

*Lickety-Split Meals*

Shrimp Pizza

## Stir-Fry

## "I highly recommend woking once a week. Not to be confused with walking of course, which should be done much more often!"

There are 3 complaints I hear quite often from clients:

- "4 ounces of meat looks SO tiny on my plate!"
- "Vegetables are boring without butter and salt."
- "If you want me to eat rice, I want a nice sauce to go over it."

Well, there's an easy way to end all 3 complaints in a hurry, and that's with a stir-fry!

But doesn't that sound like a lot of work? Don't you need special equipment? How do you make a nice flavorful sauce? Aren't commercially prepared sauces high in sodium? Can't you walk to China in the time it takes to chop all those vegetables?

As you're about to find out, stir-frying is a fast and simple way to get a delicious, vegetable packed meal on the table. You'll love how just a small amount of beef, chicken or pork (or no meat at all!) can flavor the entire dish. (Even meat lovers are fooled by the small meat portions!)

You can use your largest nonstick frying pan, or pick up a nonstick wok. (Whether it's electric or stove-top, I suggest a nonstick coating.) You can vary the vegetables you use according to what's in season and what your family likes. You can use frozen vegetables to eliminate time consuming chopping. And *yes*, you can shop for commercially-made sauces that don't break the sodium rules. (See page 186.)

Perhaps the best part is, you can select a different type of stir-fry each week, so "Saturday night stir-fry nights" are never boring. Happy woking!

Being overweight is like having a big weed in your yard. Going on a diet is like taking your weed wacker and nipping away at it. And sticking to the diet long enough, you can nip that weed right down to the ground.

But what happens after that? The weed grows back. Why? Because all weeds have roots.

The secret to permanent weight loss means succeeding within four critical habits. Not just "diet and exercise" mind you, but four! You can visualize the importance of these four areas similarly to the four wheels on a car. Without all four, it's impossible to drive anywhere and likewise impossible to navigate yourself to permanent weight loss.

### Secret #1 — The habit of eating healthy

The goal here is to achieve a healthful eating style that's natural to you, or second nature, which means you habitually gravitate to foods low in fat and high in fiber, at least 80% of the time. Whether you are eating out, at a party, buying groceries or just snacking, it's a natural habit for you to choose plenty of fruits, vegetables, and low-fat, high fiber foods. (Note: Acquire this habit slowly over time and keep in mind that 2 out of 10 meals or snacks do not have to be perfect!)

### Secret #2 — A consistent and dedicated exercise routine

It is imperative to have a regular exercise routine that you enjoy. The time you spend exercising should be a time of "peace" in your life with high priority. This is generally 30-60 minutes, 3-6 times per week. (The higher numbers yield the most weight loss, of course.) Incorporating resistance muscle training (for a further enhanced metabolism) and stretching (for needed flexibility and injury prevention) is ideal.

### Secret #3 — Emotional well-being

Learn to identify habits like stress eating, boredom eating, or emotional eating, and replace them with a more healthful coping response. Learn to listen and respond correctly to your internal appestat which tells you when you are hungry and when you are satisfied (versus just eating things because they are "there"). Plan menus which are completely satisfying to you.

### Secret #4 — A support system

You must create a support system that will help you hang on to and continue to establish healthy habits. This can be sharing weekly fitness goals with a spouse, friend, counselor, personal trainer, or coach. Being accountable to someone pays off with big rewards. It's also excellent to have an exercise buddy. Even simple encouragers like people at work who cover for you while you walk are important contributors to your support wheel. Any way you look at it, the support system is as important as any other!

*Lickety-Split Meals*

# The Easiest Stir-Fry Ever!

Looking for a "Stir-Fry for Dummies"? Here you go! Absolutely **no** chopping and **no** sauce making. Make it with chicken or without.

| | |
|---|---|
| 2 cups<br>1¾ cup | **instant whole-grain brown rice**<br>**water** (adjust according to package directions, brands vary) |

Place rice and water on stove. Cover, bring to a boil and reduce heat to medium low. Set timer for 5 minutes. When timer sounds, remove from heat and allow to sit, covered.

| | |
|---|---|
| 1 small<br>3 | **onion**<br>**skinless, boneless, chicken breast** (halves) (optional)* |

Meanwhile… cut onion into wedges and chicken into strips.

| | |
|---|---|
| 1 T | **oil** (canola or sesame) |

Heat in a nonstick wok. Add onion and chicken. Cook until chicken is browned.

| | |
|---|---|
| 2 bags | **(16 oz each) frozen mixed stir-fry vegetables** (*Freshlike Oriental Blend, Sugar-Snap Stir-Fry, Pepper Stir-Fry*) |

Add to wok. No need to thaw. Cook 11 to 13 minutes to desired tenderness. (It's ready when the water from the vegetables evaporates.)

| | |
|---|---|
| 1 jar<br>½ cup | **(10 oz)** *La Choy® Sweet & Sour Sauce*<br>**slivered almonds** *or* **chopped walnuts** *or* **cashews** |

Stir in. Let cook for 2 more minutes, then serve over the brown rice.

Save room for dessert.

---

**EXCHANGE VALUES**

| 3 Starch | 1 Meat | 2 Veg. | — Fruit | — Milk | — Fat |
|---|---|---|---|---|---|

\* As another option, a cube (12 oz.) of firm tofu cut into strips works great instead of chicken.

**Nutrition information for — 1/6 of the recipe over rice**

**Preparation Time — 20 min.**

| | | | | |
|---|---|---|---|---|
| Calories ................................ 390 | Fat ............................... 10 g | Fiber ......................................... 7 g | Sodium ............................ 220 mg | Total Carbohydrate ............. 54 g |
| Calories from Fat ............... 22% | Saturated Fat ....................... 1 g | Cholesterol ........................ 34 mg | Protein ......................................... 2 g | Sugars ....................................... 24 g |

# Isn't 800 mg of sodium too much???

For a cup of soup, or a $^1/_2$ cup of *Rice-a-Roni*®, yes.

For a complete entrée, no. Keep in mind these sodium facts:

- 2,000 to 3,000 mg are allowed each day.
- While 800 mg sounds like a lot, as an entire *entrée*, it fits into your day quite easily.
- Even 2 slices of bread contain 400 mg of sodium!

# Sweet & Sour Stir-Fry

Chicken, pork tenderloin, or tofu—it's up to you! The pineapple and nuts really make this dish.

| | |
|---|---|
| 2 cups | instant whole-grain brown rice |
| 1¾ cup | water (adjust according to package directions, brands vary) |

Combine in a microwave-safe dish. Cover and cook on high 7 minutes.

| | |
|---|---|
| 8 oz | pork tenderloin *or* 2 skinless boneless chicken breasts (halves) *or* 12 oz tofu (*or* try ½ meat, ½ tofu) |

Meanwhile… trim meat.
Slice into strips or cube tofu. Set aside.

| | |
|---|---|
| 1 | onion |
| 1 bunch | broccoli |

On a clean cutting board, cut vegetables into small pieces, keeping piles separate.

| | |
|---|---|
| 2 cans | (8 oz each) pineapple tidbits, in its own juice, drained |

Drain the juice into a 2 cup measuring cup.
Add orange juice or water to equal ¾ cup of liquid.

| | |
|---|---|
| 1 T | corn starch |
| 2 T | soy sauce, reduced-sodium |

Stir into the pineapple juice. Set mix aside.

| | |
|---|---|
| 1 T | oil (canola *or* sesame) |
| 1 tsp | minced garlic (2 cloves) |
| 1 tsp | ginger (grated tastes best) |

Heat a large skillet or wok. Add oil and spices. Then add meat and onions. Stir-fry 4 minutes, or until meat is cooked.

Stir pineapple juice mix and add to wok.

| | |
|---|---|
| 3 T | slivered almonds *or* chopped almonds *or* cashews |

Add the pineapple, broccoli, and almond slivers.

Cover and let simmer on medium-low heat for 3 to 4 minutes.

Serve immediately over rice, while broccoli is still bright green.

---

**EXCHANGE VALUES**

| 2 Starch | 2 Meat | 2 Veg. | 1 Fruit | — Milk | — Fat |
|---|---|---|---|---|---|

**Nutrition information for — 1/4 of the recipe using pork over rice**

**Preparation Time — 40 min.**

| | | | | |
|---|---|---|---|---|
| Calories .................................. 420 | Fat ............................... 11 g | Fiber ..................................... 6.3 g | Sodium ............................ 335 mg | Total Carbohydrate ............. 60 g |
| Calories from Fat ............... 22% | Saturated Fat ................... 1.5 g | Cholesterol ...................... 45 mg | Protein ................................ 25 g | Sugars ................................... 19 g |

## Great ideas from people like you!

# Tip

**As a 23 year veteran of the Michigan State Police, who passes the annual physical fitness test always at the highest (gold) level, how do you do it?**

*"I receive added motivation from reading books like* Personal Best *by George Sheehan. He refers to the Latin term `Arete, which is 'functioning as one should.' His analogy of being fit is 'being a good animal.' My training run is an exercise for my body, but even more an exercise for my mind. I find it an unequalled haven for concentration, creativity, and problem solving.'"*

—My brother,
CLIFF EDWARDS, 42
23 year veteran of the
Michigan State Police,
Never lost a race
that really counts
(chasing criminals)

*Lickety-Split Meals*

# Easy Pepper Steak Stir-Fry

A great way to pacify hard-core meat eaters with a small 3 oz. serving of steak.

| | |
|---|---|
| 2 cups | instant whole-grain brown rice |
| 1³/₄ cups | water (adjust according to package directions, brands vary) |
| 1 | zucchini, sliced into ¹/₂" rounds |
| 1 | yellow crooked neck squash, sliced into ¹/₂" rounds |

Combine in a microwave-safe dish. Cover and cook on high 9-10 minutes. (Steam the squash separately if you prefer.)

| | |
|---|---|
| 1 lb | top sirloin steak, well trimmed |

Slice "across the grain" into very thin strips. Set aside.

| | |
|---|---|
| 1 can | (14¹/₂ oz) beef broth |
| 3 T | cornstarch |
| 1 T | soy sauce, reduced-sodium |

Mix together in medium-size bowl. Stir and set aside.

| | |
|---|---|
| 1 T | oil (sesame) |
| 1 tsp | minced garlic (2 cloves) |
| 1 | onion, cut into wedges |
| 1 | red pepper, cut into strips |
| 1 | green pepper, cut into strips |
| 1 | yellow pepper, cut into strips |

After slicing onion and peppers, heat the oil in a large non-stick frying pan or wok. Add vegetables and stir-fry 2 minutes. Add beef and cook 2 minutes or until done.

Re-stir the broth and add to wok. Stir until thick and bubbly.

Serve over rice. Clean your palate with a scoop of rasberry sorbet.

---

**EXCHANGE VALUES**

| 2 Starch | 4 Meat | 3 Veg. | — Fruit | — Milk | — Fat |
|---|---|---|---|---|---|

**Nutrition information for — 1/4 of the recipe over rice**

**Preparation Time — 35 min.**

| | | | | |
|---|---|---|---|---|
| Calories ............... 455 | Fat ............... 11.5 g | Fiber ............... 5.3 g | Sodium ............... 570 mg | Total Carbohydrate ............ 48 g |
| Calories from Fat ......... 22% | Saturated Fat ......... 3 g | Cholesterol ......... 83 mg | Protein ............... 42 g | Sugars ............... 6 g |

# Tip

## Dining out tips for a Chinese restaurant

1. Order the plain steamed rice vs. the fried rice and you will save about 13 grams of fat!

2. For a 15 gram fat savings, skip the egg roll. Ask for double the rice instead.

3. Eat just half the order, save the rest for tomorrow. (The extra rice allows you to do this easily.)

4. Say: "Steam the chicken and vegetables, please, and add no sesame oil at the end."

5. Be brave and try a tofu dish. The Chinese know how to do tofu!

6. Ask that your meal be made without MSG.

# Saucy Almond Chicken Stir-Fry

You'll love all the extra sauce which thoroughly smothers the rice. The crunch of the almonds and water chestnuts makes for a delightful contrast.

SERVES | MENU

6

SAUCY ALMOND CHICKEN OVER BROWN RICE

SLICED APPLES, KIWI, AND ORANGES

| | |
|---|---|
| 3 cups | instant whole-grain brown rice |
| 2²/₃ cups | water (adjust according to package directions, brands vary) |

Combine in a microwave-safe dish. Cover and cook on high 9 to 10 minutes.

| | |
|---|---|
| 1 can | (14¹/₂ oz) chicken broth, ¹/₃ less sodium |
| 1 T | sugar |
| 2 T | vinegar (cider) |
| ¹/₄ cup | cornstarch |
| ¹/₄ cup | soy sauce, reduced-sodium |

Stir together in a medium-size bowl. Set aside.

| | |
|---|---|
| 1 T | sesame oil |
| 1 tsp | minced garlic (2 cloves) |
| ¹/₂ cup | slivered almonds |
| 4 | skinless, boneless, chicken breast (halves), cut into ¹/₂" pieces |

Heat oil and garlic in a large nonstick skillet or wok over medium-high heat. Add chicken and almonds. Cook 5 minutes or until chicken is done and almonds are golden brown.

| | |
|---|---|
| 1 | red pepper, cut into ³/₄" pieces |
| 2 | boxes (10 oz each) frozen pea pods *or* whole green beans |
| 1 can | (8 oz) sliced water chestnuts, drained |

Meanwhile… chop pepper and open containers. Add to stir-fry when chicken is done. Cook 3 to 4 minutes.

Re-stir the broth cornstarch mixture and pour in. Cook and stir until thick and bubbly.

Serve over rice with fruit on the side.

*Delegate Someone to: Chop red pepper and slice fruit.*

---

**EXCHANGE VALUES**

3 Starch    3 Meat    2 Veg.    — Fruit    — Milk    — Fat

**Nutrition information for — 1/6 of the recipe over rice**

**Preparation Time — 35 min.**

| | | | | | |
|---|---|---|---|---|---|
| Calories .................. 430 | Fat ............................ 10 g | Fiber ........................ 8 g | Sodium ...................... 620 mg | Total Carbohydrate ............ 58 g |
| Calories from Fat ........ 20% | Saturated Fat ............ 1 g | Cholesterol .............. 46 mg | Protein ........................ 30 g | Sugars ........................ 7 g |

## Electric Rice

You may want to consider buying an electric rice cooker. You'll no longer need to buy instant rice, and with very little effort you will have perfectly cooked rice that's held warm and ready for whenever you arrive home. Leftover rice can be stored in the refrigerator and used all week. (Be sure you have the storage space since it's a fairly large contraption.)

# "Unfried" Rice Dinner

Although initially you may want to serve this as a side dish, you will soon discover that this is a satisfying one dish meal. Perfect for a light supper.

**Note:** If you don't have leftover cooked rice on hand, put 2 cups of instant whole-grain brown rice in a microwave-safe dish with 1³/₄ cups of water. Cover and microwave 7 minutes on high while you prep vegetables.

| | SERVES | MENU |
|---|---|---|
| | 4 | "UNFRIED" RICE<br>ORANGE & KIWI SLICES<br>APPLESAUCE DUMPLINGS |

Great use for left-over cooked rice.

| | |
|---|---|
| 1 cup | shredded *or* finely chopped carrots<br>(about 15 baby carrots) |
| 3 | green onions, tops and bottoms, chopped |
| ¹/₂ | green pepper, chopped |
| 1 can | (7 oz) sliced mushrooms, drained |

Prep vegetables. For speed, use the food processor to coarsely shred or finely chop the carrots.

| | |
|---|---|
| 2 tsp | sesame oil |
| ¹/₂ tsp | ginger (grated tastes best) |
| ¹/₂ tsp | minced garlic (1 clove) |

Heat in a nonstick skillet over medium-high.
Add above vegetables, and stir-fry 1 to 2 minutes.

| | |
|---|---|
| 3 cups | cooked whole-grain brown rice |
| 1 cup | frozen peas |
| 3 T | soy sauce, reduced-sodium |

Stir in and cook 5 minutes.

| | |
|---|---|
| 2 | eggs, beaten |
| 5 grinds | fresh ground pepper |

In a small cup, beat eggs with a fork. Push rice mixture to side of skillet, add eggs and pepper to the open side. Allow eggs to set thoroughly. Cut the cooked eggs into rectangular bites.

Gently combine eggs with rice and serve with orange and kiwi slices. Consider *Applesauce Dumplings* (page 169) for dessert.

---

**EXCHANGE VALUES**

| 3 Starch | 1 Meat | 1 Veg. | — Fruit | — Milk | — Fat |
|---|---|---|---|---|---|

---

**Nutrition information for —**  **Preparation Time — 30 min.**

| | | | | |
|---|---|---|---|---|
| Calories .................................. 280 | Fat ................................. 6 g | Fiber .................................... 6.5 g | Sodium ............................ 675 mg | Total Carbohydrate ............. 47 g |
| Calories from Fat ............... 19% | Saturated Fat ...................... 1 g | Cholesterol ...................... 106 mg | Protein .................................. 12 g | Sugars ...................................... 8 g |

# Soups

No doubt about it, winter or summer, rain or shine, soup satisfies. The 30 or so minutes required to make a steamy pot of soup can yield high rewards. Just take a look at all the benefits of making soup at home:

- A tasty way to eat lots of healthy vegetables and beans.
- *You* control the sodium and fat content.
- Weight loss aide (soup before dinner can suppress your appetite).
- A pot can be stored in the refrigerator and single servings reheated all week.
- Individual servings can be frozen for another day.

So just when you thought you didn't have time to make soup from scratch, take a peek through this chapter. The time spent on a Saturday or Sunday afternoon will be well worth it!

## Weight loss tip: Eat negative calorie foods

Think "cooked and raw vegetables" every day. There's no science to this recommendation, it's just a reminder to eat 2 healthy doses of vegetables every day. When it comes to losing weight, you will want to have lots of these "negative calorie foods" (foods that require more calories to digest than they yield) at each meal. Each serving of *Miracle Soup* will take care of the "cooked" vegetable goal. Remember, almost all vegetables are negative calorie foods, so enjoy, enjoy, enjoy!

# Miracle Soup

SERVES | MENU

Ever heard of a negative calorie food? That's a food that burns more calories to digest than it yields. Hence, the name "Miracle," because this soup is great for weight loss. Enjoy a bowl with lunch *and* dinner! A pot lasts several days.

**16** | MIRACLE SOUP
LOW-FAT WHOLE-WHEAT CRACKERS OR A SANDWICH
SLICED FRUIT

| | |
|---|---|
| 6 cups | water |
| 1 quart | low-sodium vegetable juice |

Place in a large soup pot over medium-high heat.

| | |
|---|---|
| 3 large | onions |
| 1 | green pepper |
| 6 | celery stalks |
| 10 | carrots |
| 2 cans | (14.5 oz each) stewed tomatoes |
| 4 cups | shredded cabbage* |
| 1/2 cup | salsa |
| 1/4 tsp | garlic powder |
| 1/4 tsp | pepper |
| 1/2 tsp | red pepper flakes (optional) |
| 1 tsp | basil |
| 2 tsp | oregano |
| 1 envelope | dry onion *or* vegetable soup mix *or* 2 tsp low-sodium chicken bouillon |

Meanwhile… chop vegetables into bite-sized pieces. Toss vegetables and other ingredients into pot. Boil for 20 minutes, or until the vegetables are as done as you like.

Serve hot off the stove with low-fat whole-wheat crackers or a sandwich and fruit.

*Miracle Soup* keeps in the refrigerator for up to 5 days and also freezes well.

**EXCHANGE VALUES**

— Starch   — Meat   4 Veg.   — Fruit   — Milk   — Fat

\* Use your food processor or buy pre-shredded.

**Nutrition information for — about 1-1/2 cups**

**Preparation Time — 35 min.**

| | | | | |
|---|---|---|---|---|
| Calories .................. 85 | Fat .......................... 0 g | Fiber ....................... 4.5 g | Sodium ........................... 425 mg | Total Carbohydrate ............ 19 g |
| Calories from Fat ......... 0 % | Saturated Fat ............... 0 g | Cholesterol ............... 0 mg | Protein .............................. 3 g | Sugars ..................................... 11 g |

## Have a cold?

# Tip

I keep the following items in my medicine cabinet, in case a cold strikes…

1. Studies have shown that **zinc gluconate lozenges** (containing 13.3 mg of zinc) taken every 2 hours at the onset of a cold help decrease the duration from 7 days down to 4. The brand which the studies used was "Cold-Ease." (Since zinc can interfere with copper absorption, do not exceed 6 days of use.)

2. **Herbal remedy, ECHINACEA,** has also been determined to help boost immune functioning which in turn reduces the severity of a cold. (Do not take Echinacea routinely as it loses its effectiveness.) Medical experts recommend buying the extract for purity.

3. Taking **vitamin C** during a cold may also help alleviate the severity and symptoms. I keep 500 mg tablets on hand and take 1 or 2 twice a day, until the cold is gone.

*"The main objective of natural remedies is to stimulate a person's inherent ability to heal themselves."*

—My homeopath,

CAROLINE SMOYER, DHom
Salt Lake City, Utah

# Lentil Spinach Soup

If lentils aren't a favorite of yours yet, just give them time, they will be!
I love this refreshing, easy-to-make soup any time of the year, including
summer. It keeps in the refrigerator for up to 5 days and also freezes well.

**SERVES**

6

**MENU**

LENTIL SPINACH SOUP

CORNBREAD, CRACKERS
OR POPCORN

APPLESAUCE

| | |
|---|---|
| 2 | onions |
| 2 | carrots |

Chop into bite-size pieces.

| | |
|---|---|
| 1 T | olive oil |
| ½ tsp | minced garlic (1 clove) |

Sauté with vegetables in a medium soup pot for 2 minutes.

| | |
|---|---|
| 4 cups | water |
| 1¼ cups | dried lentils (½ pound) |
| 1 can | (14½ oz) stewed tomatoes |

Add water and lentils to pot. Cover and bring to a boil, then simmer
for 45 minutes. (Feel free to make some *Cornbread* [page 151] and
a salad now!)

| | |
|---|---|
| 1 pkg | (10 oz) frozen spinach |

Take out of freezer to thaw. Add to the soup after the 45 minute simmer.

| | |
|---|---|
| 1 T | lemon juice |
| 1 tsp | grated lemon peel *or* 2 tsp of red wine vinegar (optional) |

Add to soup and simmer 5 minutes longer.

Serve with cornbread, crackers or popcorn.

---

**EXCHANGE VALUES**

2 Starch     1 Meat     1 Veg.     — Fruit     — Milk     — Fat

| Nutrition information for — about 1-1/2 cups | | | Preparation Time — 1 hour | |
|---|---|---|---|---|
| Calories .................................. 215 | Fat .......................................... 3 g | Fiber ........................................ 8 g | Sodium ............................ 200 mg | Total Carbohydrate ............. 35 g |
| Calories from Fat ............... 11% | Saturated Fat .................... < 1 g | Cholesterol ......................... 0 mg | Protein ................................. 12 g | Sugars ...................................... 7 g |

# Secrets from a long-term weight maintainer ...

*"Every morning I weigh myself. I have a 4 pound window in which I vary. The day I go one pound over that window, a switch goes on in my brain that says 'cut back on what you're eating, and put in a longer run.'"*

— My mom,
GRACE EDWARDS, 60,
maintaining 123 lbs.
for 32 years

# Creamy Cauliflower Soup

A great way to enjoy cancer-fighting cauliflower, this creamy low-fat soup is delicious.
(Please note that the marjoram and savory make this soup, so substitutions are not recommended.)

**SERVES** 6

**MENU**

CREAMY CAULIFLOWER SOUP
SALTINES OR FRENCH BREAD
TOSSED SALAD

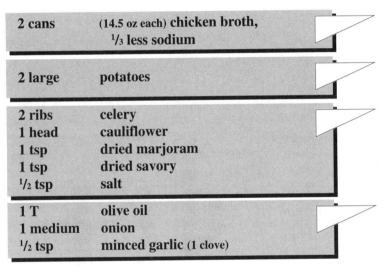

| 2 cans | (14.5 oz each) chicken broth, $^1/_3$ less sodium |
|---|---|

Bring to a boil.

| 2 large | potatoes |
|---|---|

Peel and cut into chunks. Add and simmer for 20 minutes.

| 2 ribs | celery |
|---|---|
| 1 head | cauliflower |
| 1 tsp | dried marjoram |
| 1 tsp | dried savory |
| $^1/_2$ tsp | salt |

After 20 minutes, slice and add to soup. Simmer 30 more minutes.

| 1 T | olive oil |
|---|---|
| 1 medium | onion |
| $^1/_2$ tsp | minced garlic (1 clove) |

Chop onion. Sauté all for 2 minutes, then add to simmering soup.

Purée soup in a food processor or blender (in small batches if required).

Serve with whole-wheat saltines or French bread and tossed salad.

---

**EXCHANGE VALUES**

1 Starch — Meat 1 Veg. — Fruit — Milk — Fat

| Nutrition information for — about 1-1/2 cups | | | Preparation Time — 1 hour | |
|---|---|---|---|---|
| Calories .................................. 125 | Fat ........................................ 3 g | Fiber ........................................ 5 g | Sodium ............................ 430 mg | Total Carbohydrate ............. 21 g |
| Calories from Fat ................ 17% | Saturated Fat .................... < 1 g | Cholesterol .......................... 0 mg | Protein .................................... 6 g | Sugars ........................................ 4 g |

# True or False?

*"As long as you don't add butter to popcorn, it's generally low-fat."*

**Answer:** FALSE!

Truck-loads of fat are often used to pop the popcorn, as is the case with:

- Movie popcorn

- Microwave popcorn (the regular varieties as well as some of the "lite" ones!)

- Home-made, where you use ¼ cup or more of oil in the pan or popper

Even without adding butter, the fat's already at near MAXIMUM CAPACITY!

# 3-Bean Turkey or Vegetarian Chili

This very fresh and light chili is a wonderful change from the heavy flavor of traditional chili loaded with fat.

SERVES

10

**MENU**

3-BEAN CHILI

WHOLE-WHEAT CRACKERS OR CORNBREAD

RAW VEGETABLES

Grat for football parties!

| | |
|---|---|
| 2 | onions |
| 1 | red pepper |
| 1 | green pepper |
| 4 | whole carrots *or* 1 cup shredded carrots |

Chop vegetables into small wedges.

| | |
|---|---|
| 1 T | olive oil |
| 1 tsp | minced garlic (2 cloves) |
| 1 lb | extra-lean ground turkey breast (optional) |

Heat oil in your largest kettle. Add garlic, chopped vegetables, and turkey. Sauté 5 minutes.

| | |
|---|---|
| 1 can | (15 oz) kidney beans |
| 1 can | (15 oz) garbanzo *or* pinto beans |
| 2 cans | (15 oz each) black beans |

While the vegetables are sautéing, open all the beans. Toss them in a colander, rinse, drain, and add to sauté.

| | |
|---|---|
| 2 T | cumin seed *or* 1 T ground cumin |
| 1 T | chili powder |
| 1 tsp | oregano |
| 1/4 tsp | red pepper flakes (optional) |
| 3 shakes | cayenne pepper (optional) |
| 1/4 cup | hot pepper rings from a jar (optional) |

Add all spices to sauté.

| | |
|---|---|
| 2 jars | (32 oz each) low-sodium *V-8*® juice |
| 1 can | (14.5 oz) stewed tomatoes |

Add to the pot and bring to a simmer for 10 to 20 minutes.

Serve with whole-wheat crackers or cornbread and raw vegetables.

---

**EXCHANGE VALUES**

| 2 Starch | 2 Meat | 1 Veg. | — Fruit | — Milk | — Fat |
|---|---|---|---|---|---|

**Nutrition information for — about 1-1/2 cups including ground turkey**

**Preparation Time — 35 min.**

| | | | | | |
|---|---|---|---|---|---|
| Calories .................................. 250 | Fat .................................... 3 g | Fiber ...................................... 9.5 g | Sodium .......................... 575 mg | Total Carbohydrate ............. 36 g |
| Calories from Fat ............... 11% | Saturated Fat .................... < 1 g | Cholesterol ......................... 22 mg | Protein .................................. 19 g | Sugars ...................................... 15 g |

## Popcorn Facts — True or False?

# Tip

*"Popcorn should be reserved as a snack and a snack only. It would be unhealthy to serve popcorn as the grain in your meal."*

**Answer:** FALSE!

Popcorn is corn, and corn is a healthy contribution to a meal, right? Corn is actually a grain (sorry, not a vegetable) and a grain or starch should be a major part of every meal. Who says potatoes, rice, pasta, and bread are the only grains allowed at mealtime? As long as your popcorn is healthfully prepared (including the truly low-fat versions of microwave), it's fine to include popcorn in a meal. My personal favorite combinations are beans and popcorn, and soup and popcorn!

# Speedy Minestrone with Rice

No idea what to have for dinner? How about this 10-minute soup?
It's as close to a homemade soup as a busy person gets. Enjoy!

**SERVES** | **MENU**

6

SPEEDY MINESTRONE
WITH RICE

POPCORN

SLICED FRUIT

FROZEN YOGURT

*Remember—
You want your
evening meal to be
the smallest meal
of the day!*

| | | |
|---|---|---|
| 2 cans | (14½ oz each) **chicken broth, ⅓ less sodium** | |
| 1 cup | **water** | |
| 2 cans | (14.5 oz) **stewed tomatoes** | |

In a large saucepan,
bring to a boil on medium-high heat.

| | |
|---|---|
| 1 cup | **instant whole-grain brown rice, uncooked** |
| 1 can | (15½ oz) **kidney beans, rinsed and drained** |
| 1 pkg | (10 oz) **frozen mixed vegetables** |
| ½ tsp | **dried oregano leaves** |
| ¼ tsp | **pepper** |

Stir in remaining ingredients. Return to boil.

Reduce heat to low, cover, and simmer 5 minutes.

Remove from heat and let stand 3 minutes while you set the table.

| | |
|---|---|
| 1 tsp | **Parmesan cheese** (per serving) |

Sprinkle servings with cheese if desired.

Serve with popcorn or whole-wheat crackers, and frozen yogurt
for dessert.

**EXCHANGE VALUES**

2 Starch — Meat 2 Veg. — Fruit — Milk — Fat

| Nutrition information for — about 2 cups | | | Preparation Time — 10 min. | |
|---|---|---|---|---|
| Calories .................................. 212 | Fat ............................... 2 g | Fiber .......................................... 7 g | Sodium ........................... 870 mg | Total Carbohydrate ............. 40 g |
| Calories from Fat ................. 7% | Saturated Fat ..................... .8 g | Cholesterol .......................... 2 mg | Protein ................................... 10 g | Sugars .................................... 12 g |

Speedy Minestrone with Rice                    *Lickety-Split Meals*

## True or False?

**Tip**

*"Air popping your popcorn is always better than oil popping."*

TRUE, with one exception. What do you put on top? Do you add melted butter or margarine to go on top? How much do you use? I bet you didn't know that if you're using 2 T or more of margarine to put on top, you'd be better off popping your corn in 1 T of OIL. (Because yes, oil is better for you than margarine.) 1 T oil in popping goes a lot further than does 1 T margarine dribbled on top.

**The solution:** Air-pop and use a product like *"I Can't Believe It's Not Butter"* spray, lightly on top, or oil pop ¼ cup of kernels in 1 T of canola or olive oil. (Serves 2 or more.)

# Quick Creamy Tomato Soup

| SERVES | MENU |
|---|---|

For those of you especially keen on the health benefits of soy, here's a surprisingly delicious way to sneak it in.

**4** — CREAMY TOMATO SOUP
TOSSED SALAD
POPCORN OR WHOLE-WHEAT GARLIC CHEESE TOAST
3 GINGERSNAP COOKIES

*Makes a great sauce over pasta or mashed potatoes.*

| 1 jar | (26 oz) **spaghetti sauce** |
|---|---|
| | (*Healthy Choice®*) |
| 6 oz | **silken soft tofu** |
| ¹/₂ tsp | **oregano, basil *or* Italian seasoning** |

| 1 can | (14¹/₂ oz) **chicken broth,** |
|---|---|
| | **¹/₃ less sodium** |

Combine in a food processor or blender and blend until creamy.

Add and blend again to thin the consistency.

Heat the desired amount in the microwave or over medium heat.

Serve with a salad & crackers or whole-wheat toast. Treat yourself to 3 gingersnap cookies for dessert.

---

**EXCHANGE VALUES**

— Starch    — Meat    3 Veg.    — Fruit    — Milk    — Fat

**Nutrition information for — about 1-1/2 cups**          **Preparation Time — 10 min.**

| | | | | |
|---|---|---|---|---|
| Calories .......... 110 | Fat .......... 2 g | Fiber .......... 3.5 g | Sodium .......... 620 mg | Total Carbohydrate .......... 18 g |
| Calories from Fat .......... 15% | Saturated Fat .......... < 1 g | Cholesterol .......... 2 mg | Protein .......... 6 g | Sugars .......... 12 g |

## Book Review—*Make the Connection* by Bob Greene and Oprah Winfrey

For an inspirational book on exercising and eating right, I highly recommend the book, *Make the Connection*, by Oprah Winfrey and Bob Greene (Oprah's personal trainer). You'll enjoy reading Oprah's personal journal entries about her years of battling weight and getting it right this time by "making the connection." That is, by changing your whole life to include regular exercise, eating right, and overcoming the use of food for comfort and stress. Bob Greene describes all the components of his program that have worked for Oprah to keep her weight off permanently.

Also of tremendous encouragement, the video, *Oprah: Make the Connection*. It will touch your heart and inspire you to new heights!

# Hearty Bean & Pasta Stew

| | | SERVES | MENU |
|---|---|---|---|

Have you always thought beans required some sort of meat for flavoring? This recipe is a good example of how beans can taste great without meat. You must try this!

**SERVES:** 12

**MENU**
HEARTY BEAN & PASTA STEW
TOSSED SALAD
WHOLE-GRAIN BREAD
BLUEBERRY BUCKLE (MAKE AHEAD)

| 2 medium | onions |
| 1 | green pepper |

Chop into pieces.

| 2 T | olive oil |
| 1 tsp | minced garlic (2 cloves) |

Heat in a large nonstick pot. Add onion and pepper. Sauté for 3 minutes on medium.

*This dish will keep in the frig. for up to 5 days and also freezes well.*

| 1 can | (14.5 oz) stewed tomatoes |
| 1 | (14.5 oz) chicken broth, 1/3 less sodium |
| 1 qt | low-sodium V-8® Juice |
| 2 cups | water |

Meanwhile… open cans and *V-8*® jar. Add to the pot.

| 1 can | (15 oz) each pinto beans, garbanzo beans, and kidney beans |

Open cans. Rinse and drain in colander. Add to the pot.

| 2 T | low-sodium chicken bouillon |
| 1 T | oregano |
| 2 tsp | basil |
| 1/4 tsp | red pepper flakes (optional) |
| 25 grinds | fresh ground pepper |

Add and mix thoroughly.

| 4 cups | small pasta shells, macaroni *or* corkscrew (preferably whole-wheat) |

Bring pot to a boil, then add. Set timer for 12 minutes. Make a salad and slice whole-grain bread. At the sound of the timer—it's time to eat!

| 12 T | reduced-fat shredded mozzarella cheese |
| 12 tsp | Parmesan cheese |

Sprinkle 1 T mozzarella and 1 tsp Parmesan cheese on top of individual servings.

Of course, a serving of *Blueberry Buckle* (page 154) is a perfect finish to this meal.

---

**EXCHANGE VALUES**

| 3 Starch | 1 Meat | 1 Veg. | — Fruit | — Milk | — Fat |
|---|---|---|---|---|---|

---

**Nutrition information for — 1 cup serving with mozzarella and Parmesan**

**Preparation Time — 35 min.**

| | | | |
|---|---|---|---|
| Calories ............................ 305 | Fat ......................... 5 g | Fiber ............................. 11 g | Sodium ........................ 540 mg | Total Carbohydrate ............ 52 g |
| Calories from Fat .............. 13% | Saturated Fat ........... 1.5 g | Cholesterol ..................... 4 mg | Protein ........................... 15 g | Sugars ............................. 10 g |

A slow-cooker (or crockery-cooker or *Crock-Pot®*) is simply a *must* for a busy family. Do you know that high stress, *just home from work, what's for dinner* chaos? Well, coming home to a house filled with a delicious aroma **completely** takes care of that!

The question is, where is your slow-cooker right now? Is it where it can be easily used each week? Or is it way back in some forgotten cupboard with an inch of dust on it?

Get ready to unearth it, because low-fat, easy-to-load recipes are all right here. When you thought slow-cooking "all tastes the same," or "only has high-fat recipes," this section comes to the rescue. If you don't own one yet, then check out the buying tips located within the chapter.

Since coming home to a nice stuffed slow-cooker makes for a completely stress-free easy dinner, I suggest Monday as your slow-cooker day. You can do the loading the night before (store it in the refrigerator) and simply plug it in on Monday morning for a complete "no cook" day!

It's time to get slow-cookin'. You're going to love coming home to the delicious aroma of dinner awaiting you!

Note: These recipes are designed for a 2-quart cooker.

# Slow-Cooking

# Tip

## Secrets to successful slow-cooked meat and vegetables

Some slow-cooker recipes recommend adding frozen meat to the crock, to help vegetables get a head start on cooking. This assures that the meat is tender but not overcooked when the vegetables are done.

Dense vegetables such as carrots, potatoes, and rutabagas take longer to cook than many meats. When combining ingredients in a slow-cooker, place root vegetables on the bottom of the pot; then add meats, seasonings, other vegetables, and liquid. This keeps vegetables moist during cooking, and cooks them more evenly.

# Turkey Vegetable Stew

Here's my favorite way to serve stew. Look for turkey tenderloins in the fresh poultry section of your grocery store. Freeze them when you get home. Add them frozen to the crockpot to prevent the meat from becoming overcooked before the vegetables are done.

**SERVES** | **MENU**

8 | TURKEY VEGETABLE STEW
CRUNCHY APPLE SALAD
WHOLE-WHEAT ROLLS

| | |
|---|---|
| 6 - 8 med | potatoes |

| | |
|---|---|
| 6 | carrots |
| 2 | onions |

| | |
|---|---|
| 2 | skinless, boneless, turkey tenderloins, frozen (about 1½ lbs)* |

| | |
|---|---|
| 1 cup | each of frozen peas and corn |
| 1 tsp | oregano |
| ½ tsp | hot pepper flakes |
| ½ jar | (about 13 oz) spaghetti sauce *(Healthy Choice®)* |
| 2 cups | water |

## 7 to 11 hours before serving:

Thoroughly wash and scrub, or peel if commercial potatoes. Quarter them and place into slow-cooker.

Peel and slice into chunks. Add to potatoes.

Place in slow-cooker while still frozen.

Place ingredients in slow-cooker in the order listed. Mix slightly.

Cook on HIGH for 7 hours, or on LOW for 10 to 11 hours.

## 8 minutes before serving:

Whip up a quick *Crunchy Apple Salad* (page 141) and serve with whole-wheat rolls.

**EXCHANGE VALUES**

2 Starch    2 Meat    2 Veg.    — Fruit    — Milk    — Fat

\* Chicken breasts can be substituted.

Nutrition information for — about 1-1/2 cups

Preparation Time — a.m. 12 min.

| | | | | |
|---|---|---|---|---|
| Calories .................... 270 | Fat ........................ 1.4 g | Fiber ...................... 6.5 | Sodium .................... 255 mg | Total Carbohydrate ........... 40 g |
| Calories from Fat ......... 4% | Saturated Fat ............. 0 g | Cholesterol ............. 40 mg | Protein ..................... 26 g | Sugars ........................... 8.5 g |

# Tip

## Who has time in the morning to load the slow-cooker?

If this is your attitude, try this 1-minute super-easy recipe. If that still seems like too much work, keep in mind that you can load the slow-cooker the night before (and simply store in the refrigerator overnight). And remember, a 1-minute investment now, means a GREAT reward later.

Come on! You can find 1 minute!

# Ravioli Stew

You can load the crockpot in less than a minute with this recipe! Popular with small kids, although you may want to serve the green beans on the side.

**MENU**

RAVIOLI STEW

GREEN BEANS

WHOLE-WHEAT GARLIC CHEESE TOAST

CANNED PEACHES

Kids' Favorite

| | | |
|---|---|---|
| 1 bag | **(25 oz) frozen cheese ravioli** | |
| 1 bag | **(16 oz) frozen cut green beans** | |
| 1 jar | **(26 oz) spaghetti sauce** *(Healthy Choice®)* | |
| ½ jar | **(13 oz) water** | |

**4 to 9 hours before serving:**

Place ingredients in slow-cooker in the order listed. Mix slightly.

Cook on HIGH for 4 hours or on LOW for 7 to 8 hours.

**5 minutes before serving:**

Serve with canned peaches and *Whole-Wheat Garlic Cheese Toast* (page 150).

---

**EXCHANGE VALUES**

| 2.5 Starch | 1 Meat | 2 Veg. | — Fruit | — Milk | — Fat |
|---|---|---|---|---|---|

**Nutrition information for — 8 ravioli**

Preparation Time — a.m. 1 min.

| | | | |
|---|---|---|---|
| Calories .................................. 290 | Fat ......................................... 6.5 g | Fiber ........................................ 5 g | Sodium ............................. 735 mg | Total Carbohydrate ............. 47 g |
| Calories from Fat ............... 19% | Saturated Fat ........................ 4 g | Cholesterol ........................ 13 mg | Protein ................................... 13 g | Sugars ..................................... 17 g |

Ravioli Stew

*Lickety-Split Meals*

# Tip

## Slow-cooker buying tips

**Size:** Slow-cookers range in size from 1 to 6 quarts, with the most common being the mid-range. It's up to you and depends on the size of your family and whether or not you enjoy leftovers. These recipes are designed for a 2-quart cooker.

**Removable inside crock:** I like this because it's easier to clean, prettier to serve and when you load it the night before, it fits in the refrigerator much more easily.

**Side versus bottom heating elements:** Most slow-cooking cookbooks use an appliance with the side element. In this design, the heat element stays on continuously, while the designs with a bottom element "cycle" on and off. My recipes have been tested with the side element type.

### Buffet Bonus

Slow-cookers are handy for buffets. Simply keep the pot on LOW and the food will be just as warm for the last guest as it was for the first.

# Mexican 5-Bean Soup

SERVES

MENU

Here's a delicious bean soup. I know what you're thinking—
"Can I just drink the beer with the soup, instead?"

10

MEXICAN 5-BEAN SOUP

CORNBREAD (MAKE AHEAD)
 OR CRACKERS

TOSSED SALAD

RASPBERRY SORBET

**5 to 10 hours before serving:**

| | |
|---|---|
| 1 can | (15 oz) **red kidney beans** |
| 1 can | (15 oz) **garbanzo beans** |
| 1 can | (15 oz) **navy beans** |
| 1 can | (15 oz) **black beans** |

Rinse and drain the beans
thoroughly in a colander.
Place in slow-cooker.

| | |
|---|---|
| 1 large | **onion** |
| 1 can | (4 oz) **green chilies** |

Dice and place in slow-cooker.

| | |
|---|---|
| 1 package | (9 oz) **frozen cut green beans** |
| 4 tsp | **chili powder** |
| 1½ tsp | **dried basil** |
| ½ tsp | **dried oregano** |
| ¼ tsp | **tabasco sauce** |
| 3 cups | **water** |
| 2 cans | (14.5 oz each) **chicken broth,** ⅓ **less sodium** |
| 1 can | (12 oz) **beer,** *or* **12 oz water** |

Place in slow-cooker and stir.

Cook on HIGH for 5 to 6 hours or on LOW for 9 to 10 hours.

**Just before serving:**

| | |
|---|---|
| 2 T | (per soup bowl) **reduced-fat shredded cheddar cheese** *or* **mozzarella cheese** |

Ladle into serving bowls.

Place on top of soup.

Serve with whole-wheat saltines or *Cornbread* (page 151)
and tossed salad.

---

**EXCHANGE VALUES**

2 Starch    1 Meat    1 Veg.    — Fruit    — Milk    — Fat

| Nutrition information for — about 1 cup | | | Preparation Time — a.m. 20 min. | |
|---|---|---|---|---|
| Calories ............................ 110 | Fat ............................... 2 g | Fiber ......................... 10 g | Sodium ..................... 735 mg | Total Carbohydrate ......... 35 g |
| Calories from Fat ............ 9% | Saturated Fat ............ < 1 g | Cholesterol .................. 2 mg | Protein ........................ 12 g | Sugars ........................ 6 g |

# Tip

**Beat the heat and save electricity!**

**A slow-cooker:**

Does not heat the kitchen like your oven does—a real bonus during summer months.

Saves energy by using very little electricity since the wattage is low.

**You may also like to know…**

The low-heat setting cooks foods in 8 to 10 hours, while the high-heat setting cooks foods in 5 to 6 hours.

Exact timing with slow-cooking is not critical. If you are working a little late or delayed in traffic, another hour of extra cooking time won't make a big difference to most recipes that are cooking on LOW.

# Split Pea Soup

Why is it that some people do not like split pea soup? This soup thickens as it cools, and I love it thick. Tasty, quick, and a good money saving recipe as well.

**SERVES** | **MENU**

10

SPLIT PEA SOUP

CORNBREAD (MAKE AHEAD) OR CRACKERS

TOSSED SALAD

FROZEN YOGURT

| | |
|---|---|
| 3¹/₂ cups | dried split peas |

**8 to 11 hours before serving:**

Rinse in a colander and place in slow-cooker.

| | |
|---|---|
| 3 ribs | celery |
| 3 | carrots |
| 1 large | onion |

Chop and place in slow-cooker.

| | |
|---|---|
| 4 cups | water |
| 2 cans | (14¹/₂ oz each) **chicken broth**, ¹/₃ less sodium |
| 1 tsp | poultry seasoning |
| 20 grinds | fresh ground pepper |

Place in slow-cooker and mix.

Cook on HIGH for 8 to 9 hours or on LOW for 10 to 11 hours.

**30 minutes before or just before serving:**

| | |
|---|---|
| 2 oz | lean ham (optional) |

Cut ham into small cubes. Add in the last hour of cooking.

Serve with crackers or *Cornbread* (page 151), tossed salad and low-fat frozen yogurt for dessert.

---

**EXCHANGE VALUES**

| 3 Starch | 2 Meat | — Veg. | — Fruit | — Milk | — Fat |
|---|---|---|---|---|---|

**Nutrition information for — about 1 cup**

**Preparation Time — a.m. 15 min.**

| | | | | | |
|---|---|---|---|---|---|
| Calories .................... 270 | Fat ........................ 1.5 g | Fiber ........................ 19 g | Sodium ..................... 325 mg | Total Carbohydrate ............. 46 g |
| Calories from Fat ............. 4% | Saturated Fat ............ 0 g | Cholesterol ............... 3 mg | Protein ...................... 20 g | Sugars ........................ 8 g |

# Tip

## No peeking allowed!

A slow-cooker makes foods moist and flavorful. Meat and vegetable juices blend together, creating a delicious combination of flavors.

Resist the temptation to lift the lid to take a quick peek or stir frequently. Slow-cooking depends on the heat that builds up in the crock itself and takes quite a bit of time to reheat. Stirring is not required unless noted in the recipe.

# Beef Barley Soup

Did you know barley has even more cholesterol-lowering powers than does oatbran?
Yes, we should eat more of it. And this soup, made with lean beef, is a great place to start.

| | |
|---|---|
| 1¹/₂ pounds | sirloin steak, well trimmed |

| | |
|---|---|
| 1 cup | thinly sliced carrots |
| 1 cup | sliced celery |
| 1 medium | onion, chopped |
| 1 | green pepper, chopped |

| | |
|---|---|
| 2 cans | (14¹/₂ oz each) beef broth |
| 1 can | (14.5 oz) stewed tomatoes |
| 1 cup | spaghetti sauce *(Healthy Choice®)* |
| ¹/₂ cup | quick-cooking or pearl barley |
| 1¹/₂ tsp | dried basil |
| ¹/₄ cup | fresh parsley, chopped |
| dash | pepper |

**4 to 12 hours before serving:**

Cut meat into 1" cubes. Place in slow-cooker.

Prep and place in slow-cooker.

Add to slow-cooker.

Cover and cook on HIGH for 4 to 5 hours
or on LOW for 10 to 12 hours.

**Just before serving:**

Skim off any fat.

Serve with crackers and lite fruit cocktail.

---

**EXCHANGE VALUES**

1 Starch   4 Meat   1 Veg.   — Fruit   — Milk   — Fat

**Nutrition information for — about 1-1/2 cups**

**Preparation Time — a.m. 25 min.**

| | | | | | |
|---|---|---|---|---|---|
| Calories ................................. 265 | Fat ........................................ 7 g | Fiber .................................... 4.5 g | Sodium ............................ 640 mg | Total Carbohydrate ............. 20 g |
| Calories from Fat ............... 24% | Saturated Fat .................... 2.7 g | Cholesterol ....................... 77 mg | Protein ................................. 30 g | Sugars ...................................... 7 g |

## Slow-cooker tips for dried beans

- They cook very well in the slow-cooker.
- Pre-soaking is usually not necessary.
- They cook best on the high-setting, and will require 4 to 6 hours of cooking.
- These are a great way to save money over buying canned beans.

# Gypsy Stew

A delicious way to cook dried beans in the crockpot. Choose from chicken, pork, or go meatless. The sweet potatoes and Spanish flavors are terrific together.

**8**

GYPSY STEW

BROCCOLI SALAD
WITH DRIED CHERRIES

FRENCH BREAD

| | |
|---|---|
| 1½ cups | dried garbanzo *or* navy beans |

| | |
|---|---|
| 1 box | (10 oz) frozen spinach |

| | |
|---|---|
| ¼ lb | pork tenderloin *or* skinless, boneless, chicken breast (optional) |
| 2 cans | (14½ oz each) chicken broth, ⅓ less sodium |
| 1 cup | water |
| 1 can | (14½ oz) stewed tomatoes |
| 1 large | sweet potato (peeled and cubed) |
| 1 | onion |
| 1 | red *or* yellow bell pepper |
| 2 tsp | paprika |
| 2 tsp | cumin |
| ¼ tsp | cinnamon |
| 1 tsp | dried basil |
| ½ tsp | salt |
| 8 grinds | fresh ground pepper |
| 8 dashes | cayenne (optional) |

**5 to 11 hours before serving:**

Sort and rinse beans, and place in a 3½ quart slow-cooker.

Place in a microwave-safe dish and defrost in microwave 3 minutes.

Cut meat into ½" cubes. Cut vegetables into wedges. Add all ingredients to slow-cooker.

Add thawed spinach to slow-cooker.

Cover and cook on LOW for 10 to 11 hours or on HIGH for 5 to 6 hours until beans are tender.

**Just before serving:**

For a delicious side dish, consider making *Broccoli Salad with Dried Cherries* (page 143).

Serve with whole-wheat french bread and applesauce for dessert.

Note:  Add 1 to 2 tsp sugar to smooth the flavors, if desired.

---

**EXCHANGE VALUES**

2 Starch    1 Meat    1 Veg.    — Fruit    — Milk    — Fat

---

**Nutrition information for — about 1-1/2 cup serving with pork**

**Preparation Time — a.m. 20 min.**

| | | | |
|---|---|---|---|
| Calories ................................... 230 | Fat ......................................... 3 g | Fiber ......................................... 9 g | Sodium ............................. 585 mg | Total Carbohydrate ............. 38 g |
| Calories from Fat ............... 12% | Saturated Fat ..................... < 1 g | Cholesterol ........................ 11 mg | Protein ................................. 15 g | Sugars ..................................... 11 g |

**Tip**

## Lessons learned from friends

It's amazing what you learn while living with friends. My husband and I had this opportunity for 6 weeks when the completion of our new home was taking longer than expected. In our friends' refrigerator, I couldn't help but notice on the upper shelf was this 8 x 4 inch glass relish plate. It would mysteriously be replenished daily with sliced peppers (green and red), carrots, cucumbers, or whatever was on hand. The plate would join the table during the preparation of every lunch and dinner (and sometimes breakfast too)! Everyone was invited to munch until the meal was served, in addition to throughout the meal. Talk about a super way to increase the family's vegetable consumption. It *really* worked!

—Lesson learned from
my friend, JAY JOHNSON, 33
(mother of 2 girls who **adore**
sliced red and green peppers)
practicing what she learned from
her mother Carita Rick, 72

# Crockpot® Fajitas

You want chicken fajitas—use chicken. You want beef fajitas—use beef!
Vegetarian? Got that covered too. These fajitas are a family favorite. OLÉ!

SERVES

6

MENU

FAJITAS

BAKED TOSTITOS®
AND SALSA

FRESH FRUIT

| | |
|---|---|
| 1 lb | beef flank steak *or* skinless, boneless, chicken breast *or* pork tenderloin *or* 2 cubes (12 oz each) tofu |

**4 to 8 hours before serving:**

Trim meat well and cut into 6 portions. Crumble or cube tofu. Place in slow-cooker.

| | |
|---|---|
| 1 | onion |
| 1 | green bell pepper |
| 1 | red bell pepper |
| 1 | yellow pepper |

Cut vegetables into strips and place in slow-cooker.

| | |
|---|---|
| 10 | jalepeno pepper rings from a jar |
| 1 tsp | minced garlic (2 cloves) |
| 1 tsp | ground cumin |
| 1 can | (15 oz) kidney *or* pinto *or* black beans, drained and rinsed |
| 1 pkt | (1.27 oz) fajita seasoning mix *(Lawry's®)* |

Add and mix well.

Cook on LOW for 7 to 8 hours or on HIGH for 4 to 5 hours.

**Just before serving:**

Remove meat from slow-cooker and shred.
Return the shredded meat to the pot and mix well.

| | |
|---|---|
| 12 | 8" flour tortillas |
| 3 | fresh tomatoes |
| 1 cup | lettuce |
| 12 T | light sour cream (1 T per fajita) |

Warm tortillas in the microwave. Chop tomatoes and lettuce.
Use a slotted spoon to remove contents from slow-cooker.
Assemble fajitas with the toppings of your choice.

Serve 2 fajitas per person with raw veggies and fruit for dessert.

---

**EXCHANGE VALUES**

4 Starch    2 Meat    1 Veg.    — Fruit    — Milk    — Fat

---

Nutrition information for — 2 fajitas using beef, with tomatoes, lettuce and sour cream          Preparation Time — a.m. 20 min.

| | | | | | |
|---|---|---|---|---|---|
| Calories ..... 505 | Fat ..... 14 g | Fiber ..... 9 g | Sodium ..... 1040 mg | Total Carbohydrate ..... 64 g |
| Calories from Fat ..... 25% | Saturated Fat ..... 5.5 g | Cholesterol ..... 40 g | Protein ..... 30 g | Sugars ..... 10 g |

## Encore! For Mexican Black Beans

Serve heated leftovers over rice or over a baked potato. Also superb as "nachos."

Pour hot beans over baked tortilla chips and top with low-fat cheese. Mmmm!

## Gourmet Taste Tip for Cumin Seed

Try "toasting" the cumin seed to intensify its flavor. Place cumin seed in a small dry saucepan over medium-high heat until toasty and the seeds begin to pop. Then add to the beans. This will take you less than 2 minutes to do and really boosts the flavor!

# Mexican Black Beans

SERVES    MENU

Thick, hearty, and awesome! By minimizing the liquid, we intensify the flavor. My thanks to Lynne DeMoor, M.S., R.D. for discovering this winner.

**8**

MEXICAN BLACK BEANS

CORNBREAD, CRACKERS OR BAKED TOSTITOS®

RAW VEGETABLES & DIP

SLICED BANANAS W/ CHOCOLATE SYRUP & NUTS

| | |
|---|---|
| 1 lb | dried black beans *or* 2¹/₂ cups |
| 6 cups | water |

### 4 to 13 hours before serving:

Place beans in a strainer 1 handful at a time, sorting out rocks. Rinse well. Put drained beans in slow-cooker with the 6 cups of water.

Cook on HIGH for 4 hours, or LOW for 12 to 13 hours.

**Note:** Recipe can be made on top of the stove in 2¹/₂ hours. Can also be doubled and freezes well.

| | |
|---|---|
| ¹/₂ | green pepper, chopped |
| ¹/₂ | yellow pepper, chopped |
| ¹/₂ | red pepper, chopped |
| 1 large | onion, chopped |
| 1 T | olive oil |
| 1 tsp | minced garlic (2 cloves) |

### 1 hour before serving:

Towards the end of the cooking time, prep vegetables and sauté about 5 minutes.

While veggies are sautéing, place a strainer over a bowl. Pour entire slow-cooker full of beans into strainer. Return beans to slow-cooker along with 1 cup only of bean water. (Discard remaining bean water or save for another use.)

Add sautéed vegetables to slow-cooker.

| | |
|---|---|
| 1 T | cumin seed (*or* 2 tsp ground cumin) |
| 1 T | oregano |
| ¹/₂ tsp | salt |
| 2 tsp | paprika |
| ¹/₄ tsp | cayenne pepper (optional) |
| 10 | hot pepper rings (from a jar), chopped |
| 1 can | (14.5 oz) stewed tomatoes |

Add and mix well. Allow to cook on HIGH 30 minutes to 1 hour longer. Use this time to make *Cornbread* (page 151) if you'd like.

Serve with crackers, *Baked Tostitos*® or *Cornbread* and crunchy raw veggies on the side.

Keep your servings small to save room for a quick dessert: sliced bananas w/ chocolate syrup and nuts!

### EXCHANGE VALUES
2 Starch    1 Meat    2 Veg.    — Fruit    — Milk    — Fat

| Nutrition information for — about 1-1/2 cups | | | Preparation Time — a.m. 2 min. — p.m. 20 min. | |
|---|---|---|---|---|
| Calories .................................. 240 | Fat ........................................ 2.5 g | Fiber ...................................... 10 g | Sodium ............................ 525 mg | Total Carbohydrate ............. 43 g |
| Calories from Fat .................. 9% | Saturated Fat ..................... < 1 g | Cholesterol ........................... 0 mg | Protein ..................................... 13 g | Sugars ........................................ 7 g |

## Low-Fat Slow-Cooking

When using meat in a slow-cooker, stick to the exceptionally lean choices such as skinless chicken and turkey, beef sirloin or round steak, pork tenderloin and lean ham, AND trim well. Otherwise, all the fat that cooks out of the meat ends up in the surrounding food and then on you!

# Tip

## After Dinner Exercisers — True or False

*"It is OK to exercise soon after eating dinner."*

TRUE!

You should be able to do mild exercise like walking without discomfort. If not, that "full stomach feeling" is telling you that you have eaten TOO MUCH. The difference lies in finishing your meal NOT when you are "full," but when you are "satisfied." This simple habit will do wonders for your evening energy level and for weight control! Remember that your EVENING meal should be your SMALLEST MEAL of the day!

# Beef Stroganoff over Noodles

Delicious down-home creamy taste. Hard to believe this finds a place on a healthy menu!

**SERVES** 8

**MENU**

BEEF STROGANOFF
OVER NOODLES

TOSSED SALAD

CHOCOLATE AMARETTO
CHEESECAKE

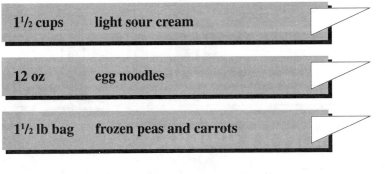

| | |
|---|---|
| 1 can | **(10.75 oz) cream of mushroom soup** |
| | *(Campbell's® Healthy Request®)* |
| 1 can | **(14¹/₂ oz) beef broth** |
| 1 can | **(4 oz) sliced mushrooms, drained** |
| 2 T | **quick-cooking tapioca** |
| ³/₄ tsp | **dried thyme** |
| ¹/₄ tsp | **garlic powder** |

**4¹/₂ to 10 hours before serving:**

Combine all together
in slow-cooker.

| | |
|---|---|
| 1 large | **onion, thinly sliced** |
| 2 lbs | **lean sirloin steak, trimmed of all fat** |

Add and slightly mix to cover meat in sauce.

Cover and cook on LOW for 9 to 10 hours
or on HIGH for 4¹/₂ to 5 hours.

**22 minutes before serving:**

| | |
|---|---|
| 1¹/₂ cups | **light sour cream** |

Place a large pot of water on to boil. Stir sour cream
into slow-cooker mixture. Beef should easily break apart.

| | |
|---|---|
| 12 oz | **egg noodles** |

Add to boiling water. Set timer for 9 minutes. Meanwhile…
see if you can find some raw salad fixings and set the table.

| | |
|---|---|
| 1¹/₂ lb bag | **frozen peas and carrots** |

When timer goes off, add to the bubbling noodles.
Set timer for 1 more minute.

Drain the noodles and vegetables. Serve the beef and mushroom
sauce over top, with a tossed salad on the side.

*Make up the Chocolate Amaretto Cheesecake the night before for a truly decadent meal!*

---

**EXCHANGE VALUES**

3 Starch   4 Meat   1 Veg.   — Fruit   — Milk   — Fat

---

Nutrition information for — 1 cup beef and sauce, 1-1/2 cups noodles & vegetables     Preparation Time — a.m. 15 min. — p.m. 22 min.

| | | | | | |
|---|---|---|---|---|---|
| Calories ...................... 485 | Fat ........................ 13 g | Fiber ..................... 5 g | Sodium ..................... 550 mg | Total Carbohydrate .......... 49 g |
| Calories from Fat ........ 24% | Saturated Fat ............ 6 g | Cholesterol ........... 131 mg | Protein ..................... 39 g | Sugars ....................... 11 g |

**Beef Stroganoff over Noodles**      *Lickety-Split Meals*

# Pork. "The Other White Meat®"

**Chicken. Chicken. Fish.**

**Chicken. Chicken. Fish.**

Many of you may feel you are about to grow feathers and gills. But did you know today's pork averages 31% less fat than it did 10 years ago? We can thank farmers for raising leaner hogs and butchers for trimming leaner cuts. The following cuts of pork have a slightly higher fat content than skinless chicken breast.

- Pork tenderloin
- Pork boneless sirloin chop or top loin chop
- Pork boneless loin roast or sirloin roast
- Pork loin chop
- Canadian bacon

As always trim well, and keep serving size to 3 - 4 ounces (the size of a deck of cards).

# Cranberry Pork Roast over Noodles

Guests will rave about this unique and tender roast! You'll love it because it's so simple.

**SERVES**

8

**MENU**

CRANBERRY PORK ROAST

NOODLES OR MASHED POTATOES

BROCCOLI AND CARROTS

TOSSED SALAD

| | |
|---|---|
| 2 lb | pork tenderloin, frozen (one long roast *or* cut into thick slices) |

**8 hours before serving:**

Place in slow-cooker.

| | |
|---|---|
| 1 can | (16 oz) jellied cranberry sauce |
| ½ cup | sugar |
| ½ cup | cranberry juice |
| 1 tsp | dry mustard |
| ¼ tsp | ground cloves |

In a medium bowl, mix together (mashing cranberry sauce). Pour over roast.

Cook on low for 8 hours.

| | |
|---|---|
| 1 bag | (16 oz) egg noodles (*or* 8 potatoes) |

**25 minutes before serving:**

Put a large pot of water on to boil. If you have the energy, peel potatoes for mashed potatoes or just boil noodles.

| | |
|---|---|
| 1 bunch | broccoli (2 *or* 3 stalks), cut into flowerets |
| 1 bag | (1 lb) baby carrots |
| 1 T | water |

Place in microwaveable dish, cover, and cook on high 7 minutes.

Drain 2 cups of juice from the roast. Skim off any fat (if there is any, pork tenderloin is so lean). Add water if necessary, to make 2 cups. Pour into a sauce pan. Bring to a boil over medium heat.

| | |
|---|---|
| 2 T | cornstarch |
| 2 T | water |

In a small cup, mix together and pour into boiling juice while whisking. Cook 1 minute until thick and bubbly.

Serve sauce over the sliced pork, potatoes or noodles, with vegetables on the side.

**EXCHANGE VALUES**

| 4 Starch | 4 Meat | 2 Veg. | 1 Fruit | — Milk | — Fat |
|---|---|---|---|---|---|

**Nutrition information for — 4 oz. pork, 1 cup noodles, 1/4 cup gravy, 1 cup broccoli & carrots**    **Preparation Time — a.m. 5 min. — p.m. 25 min.**

| | | | |
|---|---|---|---|
| Calories ..................... 580 | Fat ........................... 8 g | Fiber ........................ 4.7 g | Sodium ..................... 120 mg | Total Carbohydrate ........... 85 g |
| Calories from Fat .......... 13% | Saturated Fat .............. 25 g | Cholesterol ............... 143 mg | Protein ..................... 42 g | Sugars ....................... 35 g |

# Tip

## The Top 10 Sources of Calories in the U.S. Diet

1. White bread, rolls, crackers
2. Doughnuts, cookies, cakes
3. Alcoholic beverages
4. Whole milk
5. Hamburger, cheeseburgers
6. Beef steaks, roasts
7. Soft drinks
8. Hot dogs, ham, lunch meat
9. Eggs
10. French fries, potato chips

Source: The Food and Health of Western Man, J.L. Mount, 1975

# Chicken Cacciatore

Once again "Chicken Tonight®" comes to the rescue.

**SERVES**

6

**MENU**

CHICKEN CACCIATORE

CORKSCREW PASTA

TOSSED SALAD

APPLESAUCE DUMPLINGS OR
HOT FUDGE BROWNIE CAKE

| | | |
|---|---|---|
| 6 | chicken leg quarters (thigh & drumsticks), **skin removed** *or* | |
| 6 | **skinless, boneless, chicken breast** (halves) (still frozen is fine) | |

**4 to 11 hours before serving:**

Place in slow-cooker.

| | |
|---|---|
| 4 | zucchinis *or* **yellow crooked neck squash, cut in** ½ **lengthwise and sliced into 1" pieces** |
| 1 | **onion cut into wedges** |

Add to slow-cooker.

| | |
|---|---|
| 1 jar | (24 oz) cacciatore sauce (*Chicken Tonight®*) |

Pour over all.

Cook on HIGH 4 to 5 hours or on LOW 9 to 11 hours.

| | |
|---|---|
| 8 oz | **corkscrew** (or any shape) **pasta** (preferably whole-wheat) |

**15 minutes before serving:**

Put a large pot of water on to boil. Cook pasta 10 minutes.

Meanwhile… put together a salad.

Serve chicken over pasta with salad on the side.

Note: Stick with light portions and after an evening walk, enjoy *Applesauce Dumplings* (page 169) or *Hot Fudge Brownie Cake* (page 168).

---

**EXCHANGE VALUES**

| 2 Starch | 3 Meat | 3 Veg. | — Fruit | — Milk | — Fat |
|---|---|---|---|---|---|

**Nutrition information for — 1/6 of the recipe using chicken leg quarters over 2/3 cup pasta**    **Preparation Time — a.m. 15 min. — p.m. 15 min.**

| | | | | | |
|---|---|---|---|---|---|
| Calories .................... 410 | Fat ............................ 10 g | Fiber .................................. 6.5 g | Sodium ......................... 565 mg | Total Carbohydrate ............. 45 g |
| Calories from Fat .............. 22% | Saturated Fat .................... 2.4 g | Cholesterol ....................... 91 mg | Protein ............................... 36 g | Sugars ................................. 12 g |

# Tip

## 6 Keys to Your Lowest Blood Pressure Ever!

### Do YOU have high blood pressure?

1. **If you're at all overweight, lose weight.** Even losing just 5 or 10 pounds can have a very positive effect on your blood pressure.

2. **Enjoy regular exercise!** A lifestyle with regular exercise definitely helps lower your blood pressure. (As always, check with your doctor first!) See page 75 for suggestions.

3. **EAT MORE** foods high in potassium, calcium and magnesium. These work in opposition to sodium in the body, therefore lowering blood pressure. Include your 5 to 9 (or more!) fruits and vegetables per day, plus non-fat and low-fat dairy foods, whole-grains, and dried beans.

4. **Limit** your sodium intake to 2,000 mg or fewer per day. Keep in mind that the salt shaker is only 1/4 of the problem. The major culprit is processed foods—and not just the ones that taste salty. See pages 179 & 112 for more information.

5. **Avoid or limit alcohol.** There is increasing evidence of a link between high blood pressure and alcohol consumption.

6. **Find ways to relax and release stress** from your body. How about yoga? Also, always make time for your favorite hobbies that are relaxing.

# Sweet & Sour Chicken

You're gonna love this "Chicken Tonight®" sauce. Sometimes I omit the potatoes and make quick-cooking rice, just before dinner time, to serve with it instead.

**SERVES**

6

**MENU**

SWEET & SOUR CHICKEN
POTATOES OR RICE
CARROTS
SLICED APPLES & KIWI

| | |
|---|---|
| 6 medium | potatoes, cut into wedges |
| 24 | baby carrots, left whole |
| 1 large | green pepper, cut into 1" pieces |
| 1 medium | onion, cut into wedges |

**5 to 9 hours before serving:**

Add to slow-cooker in order given.

| | |
|---|---|
| 6 | skinless, boneless, chicken breasts |
| | (halves) (still frozen is fine) |

Stack on top.

| | |
|---|---|
| 1 jar | (24 oz) sweet & sour simmer sauce |
| | *(Chicken Tonight®)* |

Pour over all.

Cook on LOW 8 to 9 hours or on HIGH 5 to 6 hours.

**Just before serving:**

Slice apples and kiwi.

Serve with whole-grain rolls.

**EXCHANGE VALUES**

2 Starch    3 Meat    2 Veg.    1 Fruit    — Milk    — Fat

**Preparation Time — a.m. 10 min.**

| Nutrition information for — 1/6 of the recipe | | | |
|---|---|---|---|
| Calories ................................. 375 | Fat ....................................... 2 g | Fiber ......................................... 5 g | Sodium ............................. 390 mg | Total Carbohydrate ............. 57 g |
| Calories from Fat ................. 5% | Saturated Fat ..................... < 1 g | Cholesterol ......................... 70 mg | Protein ................................. 32 g | Sugars ..................................... 26 g |

# Salads & Sides

I've forgotten to mention…be SURE to eat LOTS and LOTS of isothiocyanates, indoles, dithiolthiones, limonene, allyl sulfides and saponins. Oh, and don't forget the caffeic acid, ellagic acid, ferulic acid and phytic acid.

What in the *world* am I talking about? These are just a few of the hundreds (perhaps thousands) of phyto-chemicals. (And you thought chemicals were bad?) While these sound like chemicals made in a lab, they are as natural as natural can be. They happen to be manufactured within the walls of plants, hence their name phyto (plant) chemicals. So what's the big deal about plant chemicals? They're big cancer fighters, that's what! New studies indicate that these compounds seem to play an important role in the production of enzymes that help dispose of potential carcinogens. For the past 20 years, scientists all over the world have consistently found that **people who eat greater amounts of fruits and vegetables have lower rates of most cancers.** Of course fruits and vegetables are already rich in life-saving folacin, vitamin C and beta carotene, but these newly discovered compounds now add even more gold to the pot.

This chapter is full of tasty ways to enjoy more fruits and vegetables! Many of these salads can be made ahead (like on the weekend) and enjoyed over the next several hectic weekdays.

# The Leafy Facts

## Tip

Many people eat an iceberg salad with a tomato fragment and think, ''I got my fiber in for the day!''

But just how nutritious is iceberg lettuce, compared to darker greens like romaine or spinach? Just as its color indicates, it **pales in comparison,** with less than half the fiber and valuable nutrients. To get more from your salads, try these suggestions:

1. Choose darker greens like romaine and spinach. Mix them 50-50 with iceberg until your family adjusts.

2. **Buy the ready-to-eat dark green salad mixes for a real timesaver.**

3. If you choose to buy the ''fresh'' lettuce and clean it yourself, buy a salad spinner. This allows you to wash and spin your lettuce dry in seconds.

4. Always chop as many vegetables as you can to go on top of the salad. The vegetables pack more nutrition and fiber than the greens do.

5. Or, just skip the lettuce altogether and hit the veggies hard, as in *Where's the Lettuce? Salad* (this page).

# Where's the Lettuce? Salad

SERVES

**TASTES GREAT WITH:**

Out of lettuce? No problem! All you need are vegetables and any combination of what you find in your refrigerator will do.

6

ANY MAINDISH THAT'S A LITTLE LOW ON VEGETABLES, LIKE RAVIOLI STEW, OR CHICKEN PAPRIKASH

This is a convenient recipe for later in the week, that "cleans" out your fridge.

**Scrounge through the refrigerator for whatever vegetables you can find.**

| 4 cups | **any of the following:** | |
|---|---|---|
| | • green, red *or* yellow peppers, chopped | Place in a medium-size bowl. |
| | • celery, chopped | |
| | • tomatoes, chopped | |
| | • onions, chopped | |
| | • fresh parsley, chopped fine | |
| | • carrots, sliced | |
| | • cauliflower, chopped | |
| | • broccoli, chopped | |

| 1 can | (15 oz) **Garbanzo beans, drained** (optional) | Add to bowl. |
|---|---|---|
| 1 can | (15 oz) **beets, drained** (optional) | |

| ⅓ cup | **low-fat dressing** *(Henri's® Private Blend TAS-TEE®) or* **light Thousand Island dressing** | Toss with dressing and serve, or let guests dress their own. |
|---|---|---|

**EXCHANGE VALUES**

| 1 Starch | — Meat | 3 Veg. | — Fruit | — Milk | .5 Fat |
|---|---|---|---|---|---|

**Nutrition information for — about 1-1/3 cups, including the Garbanzo beans and beets**

**Preparation Time — 10 min.**

| | | | | |
|---|---|---|---|---|
| Calories ..................... 145 | Fat .......................... 2.5 g | Fiber ......................... 7 g | Sodium ........................... 440 mg | Total Carbohydrate ............. 27 g |
| Calories from Fat ............... 14% | Saturated Fat .................... < 1 g | Cholesterol ......................... 0 mg | Protein ................................. 5 g | Sugars ...................................... 14 g |

# Tip

| | | |
|---|---|---|
| **Breakfast** | Cereal with 2 T raisins and 1 orange | 2 |
| **Snack** | 4 oz. juice diluted in 8 oz. water and ice (sparkling water is great!) | 1 |
| **Lunch** | ¼ of a cantaloupe | 1 |
| | 1 whole tomato (2 slices on my sandwich and I eat the rest) | 1 |
| | 6 baby carrots | 1 |
| **Snack** | 1 kiwi | 1 |
| | 4 more oz. juice diluted in 8 oz. water and ice | 1 |
| **Dinner** | 1½ cups mixed vegetables or stir-fry, or a huge green salad with lots of vegetables on top, or 1½ cups *Marinated Vegetable Salad* | <u>2-3</u> |

10-11 servings!

*Lickety-Split Meals*

# Marinated Vegetable Salad

A colorful dish to bring to potlucks and picnics.

| | |
|---|---|
| 3 | raw carrots, sliced diagonally |
| 2 cups | broccoli flowerettes |
| 2 cups | cauliflower flowerettes |

Clean and prep vegetables, and place in a microwave-safe dish with 2 tsp water. Cover and microwave for 4 minutes, or until vegetables just begin to get tender. Transfer to a colander and rinse with cold water to halt the cooking process.

| | |
|---|---|
| ½ each | green, red and yellow pepper |
| 2 | green onions |
| ½ cup | light *or* fat-free Italian dressing |
| 1 tsp | dried oregano |

Cut peppers into 1" slices and chop onions.
Combine everything with cooked vegetables and toss.

Allow to marinate for 1 to 3 hours and serve.

Note: This salad does not keep longer than 1 day. The vegetables begin to wilt, due to the salt in the dressing.

Canned sliced beets, drained, are also nice in this salad.

---

**EXCHANGE VALUES**

— Starch — Meat 2 Veg. — Fruit — Milk .5 Fat

**Nutrition information for — about 1 cup**　　　　**Preparation Time — 10 min.**

| | | | | |
|---|---|---|---|---|
| Calories .................. 60 | Fat .......................... 2 g | Fiber ..................................... 3.6 g | Sodium ............................ 190 mg | Total Carbohydrate .............. 9 g |
| Calories from Fat .............. 30% | Saturated Fat .................... < 1 g | Cholesterol ......................... 1 mg | Protein ...................................... 2 g | Sugars ...................................... 5 g |

## Tip

### Food Coloring

Let's talk food colorings: reds, oranges, yellows, purples, and greens. I'm not talking about the dyes made in a lab, but the natural colors produced by plant cells. How colorful is your diet? In addition to the fine vitamins and minerals present in vegetables and fruits, the colors alone (called bioflavonoids) of peppers, carrots, sweet potatoes, etc., nourish your cells with powerful agents to fight disease (and brighten your menu.)

How often do you serve carrot-raisin salad? I'm warning you that once you make this, your family will want it on the menu 30 times a year!

# Sunshine Carrot-Raisin Salad

This salad is a great way to get loads of beta-carotene and tastes like candy! Toss this together 30 minutes before your main dish is done.

**SERVES**

6

**TASTES GREAT WITH:**

TURKEY JOES OR
BROILED ORANGE ROUGHY

Kids' Favorite

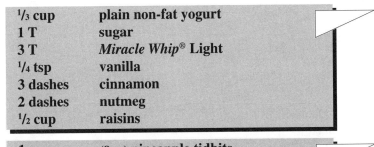

| | |
|---|---|
| ¹/₃ cup | plain non-fat yogurt |
| 1 T | sugar |
| 3 T | *Miracle Whip*® Light |
| ¹/₄ tsp | vanilla |
| 3 dashes | cinnamon |
| 2 dashes | nutmeg |
| ¹/₂ cup | raisins |

In a medium-size bowl, mix together to form the dressing.

| | |
|---|---|
| 1 can | (8 oz) pineapple tidbits, in its own juice, drained |

Reserve juice for another use. Mix pineapple into dressing.

| | |
|---|---|
| 3 cups | finely shredded carrots (about 5 medium *or* 45 baby carrots) |

Use a food processor to shred carrots. Stir into dressing. Chill salad until ready to serve.

**Optional Additions:**

| | |
|---|---|
| 2 T | shredded coconut (remains less than 2.2 grams of fat per serving) |
| | *or* |
| 1 T | peanut butter |

For a nice variation, add 1 of these as an option.

**EXCHANGE VALUES**

— Starch　— Meat　2 Veg.　1 Fruit　— Milk　— Fat

**Nutrition information for — about 2/3 cup without optional additions**

**Preparation Time — 10 min.**

| | | | | |
|---|---|---|---|---|
| Calories .................... 110 | Fat ........................... 1.7 g | Fiber ................................. 2.5 g | Sodium ........................... 91 mg | Total Carbohydrate ........... 23 g |
| Calories from Fat ........... 13% | Saturated Fat ................. 0 g | Cholesterol ...................... 0 mg | Protein ............................. 2 g | Sugars ................................. 18 g |

# Pineapple juice works like lemon juice

Did you know that pineapple juice works just as well as lemon juice to keep sliced apples from turning brown? Remember this the next time you make a fresh fruit salad with sliced apples or pears. (We call this a *Fruit Explosion.*) Simply stir in a can of pineapple chunks, along with the juice, to prevent browning (and also to avoid that tart lemon taste)!

# Crunchy Apple Salad

**SERVES** | **TASTES GREAT WITH:**

Do you have apples in your fruit bowl that are, well, shall we say, "past their prime?" Let this recipe resuscitate them back to life. It only takes about 8 minutes to put this together.

4 | POLYNESIAN PIZZA OR TURKEY VEGETABLE STEW

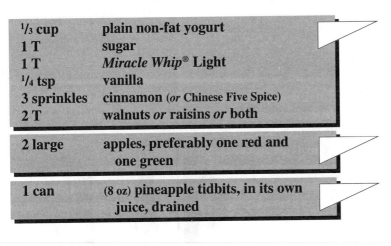

| ¹/₃ cup | plain non-fat yogurt |
| 1 T | sugar |
| 1 T | *Miracle Whip®* Light |
| ¹/₄ tsp | vanilla |
| 3 sprinkles | cinnamon (*or* Chinese Five Spice) |
| 2 T | walnuts *or* raisins *or* both |

Mix ingredients together in a medium-size bowl.

| 2 large | apples, preferably one red and one green |

Slice, core, and cut into chunks. Add to bowl.

| 1 can | (8 oz) pineapple tidbits, in its own juice, drained |

Drain pineapple, reserving juice for another use. Add to the bowl and toss gently.

Chill salad until ready to serve.

---

**EXCHANGE VALUES**

— Starch    — Meat    — Veg.    2 Fruit    — Milk    .5 Fat

| Nutrition information for — about 1 cup | | | Preparation Time — 8 min. | |
|---|---|---|---|---|
| Calories ................. 160 | Fat ......................... 3.5 g | Fiber ..................... 4.5 g | Sodium ........................ 45 mg | Total Carbohydrate ........... 32 g |
| Calories from Fat ........... 19% | Saturated Fat ............. < 1 g | Cholesterol ............ 0 mg | Protein ...................... 2.5 g | Sugars ........................ 27 g |

# Tip

## 5-a-day (at least!) for better health

So what about the "5-a-day" campaign? I recommend aiming for 5-a-day *without* counting juice servings, since juice does not contain important fiber. Also, if you can achieve 5-a-day and then drink 8 ounces of juice a day (2 fruit servings), this will get you up to 7 servings. Double your "token" portion of vegetables at dinner and you're up again. Think of fruit at every snack time. While it may seem tough at first, just take it one meal and one snack at a time. You'll get better and better at remembering to include fruit and or vegetables with every meal!

So, how does your plate rate? Americans in general average 2.1 servings per day of fruits and vegetables *combined*. The Center for Science in the Public Interest recommends 5-9 servings per day. The American Cancer Institute is so convinced about the cancer-fighting abilities of fruits and vegetables, that it is considering raising the recommendation to 9-11 servings each day! And you thought 5-a-day was a lot!

# Veggie Pasta Salad

This recipe relies on my favorite dressing, Henri's® Private Blend TAS-TEE® low-fat dressing. It not only makes this taste great, but easy, too. Keep it in mind for lunch, dinner, and potlucks! **Please Note:** This is an intentionally large batch, as it will keep for 3 days for quick meals throughout the week.

| SERVES | TASTES GREAT WITH: |
|---|---|
| 8 AS A MAIN DISH | SOUP OR SLICED FRUIT |

**Put a large pot of water on to boil.**

| | |
|---|---|
| 1 box | (16 oz) **dry pasta of your choice** |

Begin boiling water for pasta. While you wait for water to boil, begin steps below. As soon as water is ready, add pasta and follow directions on box.

| | |
|---|---|
| 2 cups | **carrots** |
| 1 large | **bunch broccoli** |
| 1 each | **red, yellow and green pepper** |
| ¾ cup | **Henri's® Private Blend TAS-TEE® low-fat dressing** (or a light coleslaw dressing) |

Cut carrots diagonally. Cut broccoli into bite-sized flowerettes. Seed and cut peppers into small chunks.

At the sound of the timer, quickly toss carrots and broccoli into boiling water with pasta. Set timer for 1 minute. When timer goes off again, quickly drain and rinse in cold water to halt the cooking process. (This step brightens the vegetables while taking the edge off their rawness.)

Transfer pasta into a large bowl that has a tight-fitting lid. Add peppers and dressing. Mix.

| | |
|---|---|
| 2 | **tomatoes*** |

Chop tomatoes. Prepare dishes for immediate serving. Add chopped tomato and serve.

\* Adding chopped tomato to the large batch in this recipe will not allow it to be kept for 3 days. Each time you are ready to serve the dish, just add more freshly chopped tomato.

**EXCHANGE VALUES**

| 3 Starch | — Meat | 3 Veg. | — Fruit | — Milk | 1 Fat |
|---|---|---|---|---|---|

**Nutrition information for — about 2 cups**

**Preparation Time — 30 min.**

| Calories | 305 | Fat | 3 g | Fiber | 5.3 g | Sodium | 200 mg | Total Carbohydrate | 62 g |
|---|---|---|---|---|---|---|---|---|---|
| Calories from Fat | 8% | Saturated Fat | < 1 g | Cholesterol | 0 mg | Protein | 10 g | Sugars | 15 g |

Veggie Pasta Salad

**Salads & Sides**
142

*Lickety-Split Meals*

# Tip

Try this "golden rule" for eating 7-9 servings of fruit and vegetables a day

**Eat at least one fruit and/or vegetable with every meal and every snack (without counting juices).**

Once you do this, THEN add in the juice servings you drink, and you will hit the mark with little effort. This really works!

# Broccoli Salad with Dried Cherries

I bet you're surprised to see such a high-fat salad in my book. I figure the price of the pecans and dried cherries will assure that you make it on special occasions only. As I always say, "With moderation and balance, all foods can fit!"

**SERVES**

8

**TASTES GREAT WITH:**

SLOW-COOKED DISHES LIKE:
RAVIOLI STEW OR
GYPSY STEW

| | |
|---|---|
| 1 bunch | broccoli, cut into bite sized pieces |
| 1/2 | red onion, thinly sliced, then chopped |
| 1/2 cup | chopped pecans |
| 1 cup | dried cherries |

Combine in a large attractive serving bowl .

| | |
|---|---|
| 1/2 cup | *Miracle Whip*® Light |
| 1/2 cup | plain non-fat yogurt |
| 1/4 cup | Parmesan cheese |
| 1 T | sugar |
| 1 T | vinegar (cider *or* any variety) |
| 1/2 tsp | cinnamon |

Combine in a small bowl.
Pour over broccoli mixture, toss gently and serve.

**EXCHANGE VALUES**

— Starch    — Meat    2 Veg.    1 Fruit    — Milk    2 Fat

| Nutrition information for — 1/8 of the recipe | | | Preparation Time — 8 min. | |
|---|---|---|---|---|
| Calories ..................... 185 | Fat ............................. 9 g | Fiber ........................... 3 g | Sodium ....................... 190 mg | Total Carbohydrate ............. 24 g |
| Calories from Fat ............... 40% | Saturated Fat ................... < 1 g | Cholesterol ..................... 2 mg | Protein ....................... 4.5 g | Sugars ................................. 15 g |

# Hunger versus thirst

Many people mistake feelings of mild thirst for hunger. (Confusing these feelings is especially common if you are fatigued.) Eating when you are thirsty can put on unwanted pounds. If weight control is important to you, drink a glass of water first before nibbling.

# Cranberry Salad

A festive and popular holiday and potluck favorite.
Simple, low calorie, and delicious.

8

THANKSGIVING DINNER OR
EVERYDAY SANDWICHES

Make 4 to 12 hours ahead

| 1 large pkg | (0.6 oz) sugar-free strawberry gelatin |
| 2 cups | boiling water |

Place gelatin into a decorative serving bowl.
Dissolve with water.

| 1½ cups | cold water |
| 1 | apple, cored and chopped |
| 2 cans | (8 oz each) pineapple tidbits, in its own juice, undrained |
| ⅓ cup | chopped pecans *or* walnuts |

Add and stir.

| 1 package | (12 oz) fresh cranberries (can be frozen *or* partially thawed) |

Place in a food processor and process until partly chunky, mostly smooth. Add to salad and stir well.

Refrigerate at least 4 hours before serving.

---

**EXCHANGE VALUES**

— Starch   — Meat   — Veg.   1 Fruit   — Milk   .5 Fat

| Nutrition information for — 1/8 of the recipe | | | Preparation Time — 8 min. | |
|---|---|---|---|---|
| Calories .......... 90 | Fat .......... 2.6 g | Fiber .......... 3 g | Sodium .......... 4 mg | Total Carbohydrate .......... 16 g |
| Calories from Fat .......... 24% | Saturated Fat .......... < 1 g | Cholesterol .......... 0 mg | Protein .......... 2 g | Sugars .......... 9 g |

# Which picnic would your heart rather have?

**Typical Picnic "A"**

1 oz potato chips

1 charbroiled bratwurst on a bun

$^1/_2$ cup traditional coleslaw

1 cup traditional potato salad

Another 1 oz potato chips

2 chocolate brownies

*Or ...*

**Picnic "B"**

4 carrot sticks

$^1/_2$ skinless chicken breast

2 T BBQ sauce

Whole-wheat bun

$^1/_2$ cup reduced-fat coleslaw

1 cup *5-Bean Salad*

Fresh fruit for dessert

---

**This meal contains 1,485 calories and 90 grams of fat!**

**That's equal to 6 tablespoons (over $^1/_3$ cup) of shortening or lard!**

---

**This meal contains 700 calories, and 12.5 grams of fat! What a BIG FAT DIFFERENCE!!**

*The choice is yours!*

*Lickety-Split Meals*

# Potato Salad

Here that delicious Henri's® Private Blend TAS-TEE® low-fat dressing is the secret ingredient again. Traditional tasting potato salad with a nice twist!

| SERVES | TASTES GREAT WITH: |
|---|---|
| 16 | TURKEY OR SALMON BURGERS |

**Put both a large and small pot of water on to boil.**

| | |
|---|---|
| 8 medium | redskin potatoes, scrubbed clean and cubed |

Add to large pot of boiling water.

| | |
|---|---|
| 4 | eggs |

Add to small pot of boiling water. Set timer for 10 minutes.

| | |
|---|---|
| 1 small | red or yellow onion, minced |
| 3 ribs | celery, diced (optional) |

Meanwhile… chop. Place in a large serving bowl.

When timer sounds, drain eggs and rinse with cold water. Set timer for 20 additional minutes (to finish potatoes). Crack and peel eggs. Chop and add to bowl.

When timer sounds, drain potatoes and cool slightly before adding to bowl.

| | |
|---|---|
| ½ cup | *Henri's® Private Blend TAS-TEE® low-fat dressing®* (or light coleslaw dressing) |
| ¼ cup | *Miracle Whip®* Light |
| 10 grinds | fresh ground pepper |
| ¼ tsp | salt (optional) |
| 2 T | mustard (plain *or* Dijon) |

Gently mix with potatoes.

| | |
|---|---|
| 2 | fresh tomatoes (optional) |

Garnish with tomato wedges.

---

**EXCHANGE VALUES**

1 Starch — Meat — Veg. — Fruit — Milk .5 Fat

| Nutrition information for — about 1/2 cup with 1 tomato wedge | | | Preparation Time — 45 min. | |
|---|---|---|---|---|
| Calories .......... 105 | Fat .......... 3 g | Fiber .......... 1.6 g | Sodium .......... 174 mg | Total Carbohydrate .......... 17 g |
| Calories from Fat .......... 23% | Saturated Fat .......... < 1 g | Cholesterol .......... 53 mg | Protein .......... 3.5 g | Sugars .......... 3 g |

## Tip

### Trying to lower your cholesterol?

In addition to making the low-fat, high fiber recipes in this book, be sure to:

1. Choose several (2 to 4) bean recipes each week.

2. Eat oatmeal or oat bran cereal and muffins as often as possible.

3. Limit saturated fats even more by selecting cheeses that are fat-free instead of low-fat.

4. Cook with as much garlic as possible and or consider a garlic supplement.

5. Include soy products as much as possible.

6. Choose fish 2 to 3 times per week.

Following these steps will lead to your absolute best cholesterol level ever!

# 5-Bean Salad

Why stop at 3 bean salad? This has triple the cholesterol-lowering power of 3-bean salad, and a lot less oil. This makes a big batch, so plan on enjoying it **all** week long.

Why stop at 3 bean salad? This has triple the cholesterol-lowering power of 3-bean salad, and a lot less oil. This makes a big batch, so plan on enjoying it **all** week long.

**SERVES**

10

**TASTES GREAT WITH:**

GRILLED CHICKEN
OR FISH

*If you wish to make only 1/2 this batch, simply reserve 1/2 the beans for an upcoming batch of chili.*

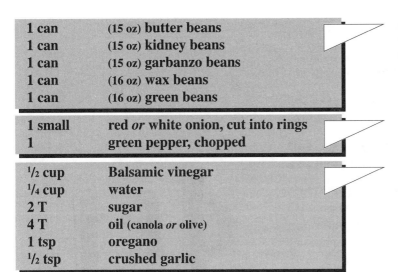

| | | |
|---|---|---|
| 1 can | (15 oz) **butter beans** | |
| 1 can | (15 oz) **kidney beans** | |
| 1 can | (15 oz) **garbanzo beans** | |
| 1 can | (16 oz) **wax beans** | |
| 1 can | (16 oz) **green beans** | |

Open cans and rinse and drain beans thoroughly. Transfer to a large bowl with a tight-fitting lid.

| | |
|---|---|
| 1 small | **red *or* white onion, cut into rings** |
| 1 | **green pepper, chopped** |

Add to beans.

| | |
|---|---|
| ½ cup | **Balsamic vinegar** |
| ¼ cup | **water** |
| 2 T | **sugar** |
| 4 T | **oil (canola *or* olive)** |
| 1 tsp | **oregano** |
| ½ tsp | **crushed garlic** |

Mix together in a 2 cup measuring cup. Pour over beans and toss to coat.

Best if allowed to marinate 4 or more hours.

**EXCHANGE VALUES**

| 1 Starch | — Meat | 2 Veg. | — Fruit | — Milk | 1 Fat |
|---|---|---|---|---|---|

| Nutrition information for — about 1 cup | | | | Preparation Time — 10 min. | | |
|---|---|---|---|---|---|---|
| Calories ................................. 195 | Fat ........................................ 6.5 g | Fiber ............................................ 7 g | Sodium ............................. 672 mg | Total Carbohydrate ............. 30 g |
| Calories from Fat ............... 29% | Saturated Fat ..................... < 1 g | Cholesterol ......................... 0 mg | Protein ........................................ 7 g | Sugars .................................... 12 g |

## Attention ladies:
## Exercise helps prevent breast cancer

Researchers at the University of Southern California* found that **1 to 3 hours of exercise** per week during the reproductive years cuts breast cancer risk **by 30%**.

**4 or more hours** of exercise each week **cuts risk by 60%!**

*How many hours have you gotten in so far this week?*

\* Bernstein, L; Henderson, BE; Hanisch, R; Sullivan-Halley, J; Ross, RK. *Physical exercise and reduced risk of breast cancer in young women.* J Natl Cancer Inst 1994;86:1403-08.

# Creamy Tuna Twist

Tired of sandwiches in your lunch box? Try this! A batch of this will provide a family with lunches for 3 days. Great for picnics and potlucks.

**Put a medium-size pot of water on to boil.**

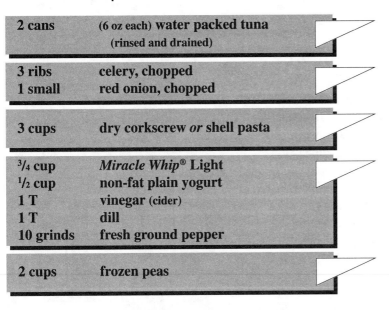

| | |
|---|---|
| 2 cans | (6 oz each) **water packed tuna** (rinsed and drained) |

Open cans and place in a large bowl which has a tight-fitting lid.

| | |
|---|---|
| 3 ribs | **celery, chopped** |
| 1 small | **red onion, chopped** |

Chop onions and celery and mix with the tuna.

| | |
|---|---|
| 3 cups | **dry corkscrew *or* shell pasta** |

When water is boiling, add pasta. Set timer for 8 minutes.

| | |
|---|---|
| ³/₄ cup | *Miracle Whip*® **Light** |
| ¹/₂ cup | **non-fat plain yogurt** |
| 1 T | **vinegar** (cider) |
| 1 T | **dill** |
| 10 grinds | **fresh ground pepper** |

Mix together in a 2 cup measuring cup. Mix with tuna.

| | |
|---|---|
| 2 cups | **frozen peas** |

When timer sounds, add peas to boiling pasta.
Set timer for 2 minutes.

When timer sounds, quickly drain and rinse both pasta and peas in cold water. Toss with the tuna mixture. Serve chilled.

---

**EXCHANGE VALUES**

| 1 Starch | 1 Meat | 1 Veg. | — Fruit | — Milk | 1 Fat |
|---|---|---|---|---|---|

**Nutrition information for — about 2/3 cup**

**Preparation Time — 25 min.**

| | | | | |
|---|---|---|---|---|
| Calories ................... 175 | Fat ............................ 4 g | Fiber ......................... 2 g | Sodium ........................ 255 mg | Total Carbohydrate ............ 22 g |
| Calories from Fat ........ 20% | Saturated Fat ............ 0 g | Cholesterol ................ 9 mg | Protein .......................... 12 g | Sugars .................................... 5 g |

# Tip

## The wonder of cruciferous vegetables

How often do you eat cabbage? Brussels sprouts? Kale? Important studies show cruciferous vegetables (the cabbage family) appear to protect you against colorectal, stomach, and respiratory cancers. Cruciferous vegetables include **broccoli, Brussels sprouts, cabbage, cauliflower, collards, kale, kohlrabi, mustard greens, bok choy, rutabaga, turnip greens, and turnips.**

Please take a hard look at this list. How many of these cabbage family vegetables do you eat in a week? How can you increase that number? You guessed it! Pasta slaw comes to the rescue. It's both low calorie and full of cancer fighters. Enjoy!

## Produce Shopping the European Way

The Europeans make it an afterwork ritual to stop at a corner produce market so they can enjoy the freshest ingredients for dinner. Have you considered this habit for your family? If you find huge grocery stores too overwhelming, maybe it's time to break out of your grocery store rut and find a more intimate place to shop.

# Pasta Slaw

You know how salads are great for helping you lose weight? Well, so is this. I make this up whenever my clothes are fitting snug. I then include a serving with lunch and dinner. Just think of it as a negative calorie food!

| | SERVES |
|---|---|
| | 8 |

**TASTES GREAT WITH:**

GRILLED CHICKEN
OR FISH

**Put a medium-size pot of water on to boil.**

| 2 cups | shredded cabbage |
| 2 cups | shredded carrots |

Buy already shredded, or shred using a food processor.
Place in a large serving bowl.

| 2 oz | dry spaghetti pasta (1 cup cooked) |

When water is boiling, add pasta. Set timer for 10 minutes.

| 1 | green pepper, chopped |
| 1 | red pepper, chopped |
| ½ | red onion, *or* 4 green onions, chopped |

Add to cabbage and carrots.

| 1 T | lemon juice (preferably fresh squeezed) |
| 2 T | Balsamic vinegar (*or* red wine) |
| ½ tsp | salt |
| ½ tsp | oregano |
| 1 T | oil (olive *or* canola) |
| ½ tsp | crushed garlic |
| dash | pepper (to taste) |

Mix together in a small bowl.

At sound of timer, drain pasta and add to vegetables while still hot.

Toss all together with dressing. Serve warm or chilled.

**EXCHANGE VALUES**

| .5 Starch | — Meat | 2 Veg. | — Fruit | — Milk | .5 Fat |
|---|---|---|---|---|---|

**Nutrition information for — about 1 cup**

**Preparation Time — 20 min.**

| Calories | 100 | Fat | 2 g | Fiber | 3 g | Sodium | 220 mg | Total Carbohydrate | 18 g |
|---|---|---|---|---|---|---|---|---|---|
| Calories from Fat | 18% | Saturated Fat | < 1 g | Cholesterol | 0 mg | Protein | 3 g | Sugars | 6 g |

# Anti-oxidants

You've been hearing this word a lot lately. What is it again? The best example is to slice an apple and watch what happens. In only a few minutes the milky white flesh turns brown. This is "oxidation." Every good cook knows that lemon juice will slow the browning process. The vitamin C in the lemon juice is the "anti-oxidant." Here are some examples of oxidation in the human body:

**Cataracts:** Eye fluids normally contain large amounts of vitamin C, but with aging, these levels decline. As that happens, proteins in the lens oxidize, making the lens more susceptible to clouding and the development of cataracts.

**Heart disease:** Scientists are now concerned not only with the presence of "bad" LDL (low density lipoprotein) cholesterol in the blood stream, but at what rate it oxidizes with the artery wall to create plaque.

**Cancer:** Many scientists believe that some cancers result from oxidative damage to cells, therefore reducing their resistance to carcinogens.

Therefore, eating a diet high in antioxidants becomes increasingly important to fight the onset of common diseases.

*Cinnamon Butternut Squash* is LOADED with the powerful anti-oxidant, beta carotene, as well as tons of phytochemicals. Make it often!

# Cinnamon Butternut Squash

Train yourself to make this delicious side dish frequently.
Winter squash is one of the best anti-aging foods around!

**Preheat oven to 375°.**

| | |
|---|---|
| 2 medium | butternut squash |
| 10 sprinkles | cinnamon |

Slice squash in $^1/_2$ lengthwise, and scoop out the seeds.

Sprinkle cinnamon into the squash.

Place **cut side down** on a cookie sheet and add about $^1/_2$ cup of water to the pan. (This helps keep it moist without having to add butter to the squash.)

Bake 1 hour.

Scoop squash out and into a bowl. Mash with a fork. Sprinkle with additional cinnamon if desired.

(Brown sugar can be added, but taste it first. Sometimes the squash is so naturally sweet it doesn't need it!)

---

**EXCHANGE VALUES**

— Starch    — Meat    2 Veg.    — Fruit    — Milk    — Fat

| Nutrition information for — about 1/2 cup mashed squash | | Preparation Time — 5 min. | Oven Time — 1 hour |
|---|---|---|---|
| Calories ...... 50 | Fat ...... 0 g | Fiber ...... 1 g | Sodium ...... 10 mg | Total Carbohydrate ...... 10 g |
| Calories from Fat ...... 0% | Saturated Fat ...... 0 g | Cholesterol ...... 0 mg | Protein ...... 0 g | Sugars ...... 3 g |

# Tip

## When to serve bread, garlic toast, or rolls at your meal

Why is it that some meals get bread and some don't? While it often just depends on "what goes well together," each meal really should have 2 or 3 servings of starch (high complex carbohydrate).

A slice of bread, garlic toast, or roll is best included when the meal has just one starch serving, such as: broiled fish, broccoli and a baked potato, or a pasta dish. Examples of meals containing 2 starch servings are: potatoes and corn, or rice and beans. It's up to you if you'd like a third starch. Active individuals who burn a great deal of calories, and most men, need the third serving of carbohydrate calories. So let them eat bread at every meal!

Remember, if a substantial dessert is planned, weight conscious individuals and people with diabetes will want to forego the bread or some of the potatoes or rice, to "save up" for a small serving of dessert.

# Whole-Wheat Garlic Cheese Toast

| | SERVES | TASTES GREAT WITH: |
|---|---|---|
| Throughout my recipes, I call for serving dishes with garlic toast. Here's what I make that's healthy and fast. | 4 | SOUPS<br>ANY PASTA DISH INCLUDING LAZONYA |

**Turn oven on to broil. Remember to leave the door ajar.**

| | |
|---|---|
| 4 slices | whole-wheat bread (*Brownberry®* or *Koepplingers®*) |
| 16 sprays | *I Can't Believe It's Not Butter®* spray |

Place bread on a cookie sheet. Spray bread with 4 sprays each slice.

| | |
|---|---|
| 4 dashes | oregano (as desired) |
| 4 dashes | garlic powder (as desired) |
| 4 dashes | Parmesan cheese (as desired) |

Sprinkle on bread.

Broil 1 to 2 minutes. Set the timer, they can burn quickly! I usually just broil one side, but flip the bread and toast another minute if desired.

For serving, cut toast diagonally in each direction to make 4 triangles per slice.

---

**EXCHANGE VALUES**

| 1 Starch | — Meat | — Veg. | — Fruit | — Milk | — Fat |
|---|---|---|---|---|---|

**Nutrition information for — 4 triangles (1 slice of bread)**          **Preparation Time — 5 min.**

| | | | |
|---|---|---|---|
| Calories ...... 75 | Fat ...... 1.5 g | Fiber ...... 2 g | Sodium ...... 171 mg | Total Carbohydrate ...... 13 g |
| Calories from Fat ...... 18% | Saturated Fat ...... .5 g | Cholesterol ...... 0 mg | Protein ...... 3 g | Sugars ...... 1 g |

# Margarine vs. butter, the slippery debate

Thinking butter is "natural" and therefore better for you than margarine? Think again. Butter is more saturated than LARD. You are better off putting lard on your bread than butter!

Margarine on the other hand, is not picture perfect either. It's "hydrogenated" (which makes it thick and spreadable) and contains troublesome "trans-fatty acids."

What should you do?

1. At breakfast, opt for low-sugar jams, jellies, apple butter, honey and/or natural peanut butter, instead of habitually spreading on margarine.

2. When sautéing use nonstick spray or 1 T of oil, instead of butter or margarine.

3. When making grilled cheese sandwiches or garlic toast, lightly brush on oil instead of spreading on margarine.

4. In baking, use applesauce or other mashed fruit, and use small amounts of oil when necessary.

5. Use a product like *I Can't Believe It's Not Butter*® spray for popcorn and baked potatoes.

6. Buy a small tub of light margarine. Store it in the back of your refrigerator and use it rarely. (Following steps 1-5, you should not need to use it more than twice a week.)

P.S. Try honey on this cornbread instead of the "habitual" margarine!

# Cornbread

| | SERVES | TASTES GREAT WITH: |
|---|---|---|
| Even as a child, I loved cornbread. I can mix this up in 5 minutes and pop it in the oven for 20 minutes. This gives me time to whip up a main dish. Remember to make a double batch while you're at it! This recipe uses oil instead of shortening and less of it. | 10 | CHILI<br>LENTIL SPINACH SOUP<br>HEARTY BEAN & PASTA STEW |

**Preheat oven to 425°.**
**Thoroughly spray a 9" pie plate or an 8" x 8" pan**
**with nonstick cooking spray.**

| 1 cup | cornmeal |
|---|---|
| 1 cup | flour (whole-wheat pastry flour if you like) |
| ½ cup | sugar |
| 1 T | baking powder |

Mix together in a bowl using a fork.
Be sure baking powder is well distributed.

| 1 cup + 2 T | skim milk |
|---|---|
| 1 T | canola oil |
| 2 | egg whites *or* 1 egg |

Add to dry ingredients and mix until blended.

Pour into the sprayed baking pan. If you prefer muffins, spray 8 muffin cups with nonstick cooking spray and pour in the batter.

Bake for 20 minutes or until a toothpick comes out clean.
Bake muffins 16 to 17 minutes.

**EXCHANGE VALUES**

2 Starch — Meat — Veg. — Fruit — Milk — Fat

| Nutrition information for — 1/10 of a piece | | Preparation Time — 10 min. | Oven Time — 20 min. |
|---|---|---|---|
| Calories ..................................... 155 | Fat ......................................... 2 g | Fiber ...................................... 2.5 g | Sodium ............................. 145 mg | Total Carbohydrate ............. 31 g |
| Calories from Fat ................ 11% | Saturated Fat ..................... < 1 g | Cholesterol .......................... 0 mg | Protein ...................................... 4 g | Sugars ...................................... 11 g |

# Sweet Treats

## Dessert before dinner anyone?

Have you ever wished that a scrumptious dessert could be so good for you that you could actually justify eating it before dinner? How about eating it for breakfast? Well look no further. Desserts from a well-devised recipe, like the ones in this chapter, can actually provide as much nutrition as a healthy snack or breakfast!

Sure, you can save time and buy commercially made fat-free cookies and cakes, but they are generally loaded with sugar and made with few, *if any*, whole grains. Of course consuming these is fine *in moderation*. But if you'd like to have dessert more often (and who doesn't?) then check out the recipes in this chapter!

A low-fat, high-fiber diet is much easier to stick with when there are frequent desserts on the menu. And these desserts are truly "crime without punishment." Enjoy!

# Tip

## Do you suffer from sweet cravings?

How much fruit have you been eating? Chances are, you've been missing the mark. Your brain requires simple carbohydrates. Fruit is very high in simple carbohydrates. When you don't get enough, your brain sends you a fruit craving. The problem is you *misinterpret* the signal as "sweets" or "chocolate" cravings!

**Solution:** Eat 3 to 4 pieces of fruit every day and notice the difference!

P.S. A slice of this scrumptious pie counts as 1 fruit serving!

# Simple Summer Fresh Fruit Pie

Here's a simply gorgeous (and easy!) dessert. One summer weekend at the lake, my husband suggested we eat the pie first, since it looked so good. Everyone agreed. It was so light and delicious, we all had another piece afterwards!

| | |
|---|---|
| 1 large pkg | **(0.6 oz) sugar-free strawberry gelatin** |
| 2 cups | **boiling water (as called for on box)** |

Place gelatin in a medium bowl, add boiling water, and stir to dissolve. (You *will not* be adding the cold water step.)

| | |
|---|---|
| 1 large pkg | **(5.1 oz) instant vanilla pudding** |
| 1½ cups | **skim milk (instead of 3 cups called for on package)** |

In a large bowl, mix together with an electric mixer. It will be thicker than usual. Add the dissolved gelatin and mix until smooth.

| | |
|---|---|
| 2 | **graham cracker crusts, regular *or* chocolate (I use the 9 oz. crust for the larger 10 serving pie)** |
| 1 quart | **fresh strawberries, cleaned and left whole** |
| 2 | **bananas, sliced** |
| 4 | **fresh peaches *or* nectarines, sliced into wedges** |
| 1 pint | **fresh blueberries, washed and drained** |

Place the fruit attractively to fill the crust, using the order listed.

Pour ½ of the jello/pudding mix over each pie.
The jello/pudding mix will seep between each piece of fruit.

Refrigerate until firm, about 2 hours.

Serve proudly and prepare for rave reviews.

---

**EXCHANGE VALUES**

| 1 Starch | — Meat | — Veg. | 1 Fruit | — Milk | 1 Fat |
|---|---|---|---|---|---|

**Nutrition information for — 1/8 of one pie**

**Preparation Time — 25 min.**

| | | | | | |
|---|---|---|---|---|---|
| Calories ................................. 170 | Fat ............................. 4 g | Fiber ...................................... 2.5 g | Sodium ............................ 250 mg | Total Carbohydrate ............. 31 g |
| Calories from Fat ............... 21% | Saturated Fat ....................... 1 g | Cholesterol ...................... < 1 mg | Protein ......................................... 3 g | Sugars ....................................... 13 g |

# Tip

## A tasty whole-grain secret

In many of the recipes, you will see that I've called for "whole-wheat pastry flour." This flour is different from the "whole-wheat flour" you commonly find in grocery stores. "Whole-wheat pastry flour," sometimes called "whole-grain flour," is very nutritious because it is a "whole grain" flour, yet is very light and cakey in texture, similar to that of white flour. It can be used in equal amounts to replace all-purpose flour in any "non-yeast" recipe. It makes wonderfully light cookies, cakes, muffins, and quick breads, and the best part is: only you will know that you used "healthy" flour!

Yeast recipes, on the other hand, require gluten for structure and whole-wheat pastry flour has very little. This is where the common "whole-wheat flour" referred to as "bread" flour (that you find commonly

in stores) is required. Just remember, if the recipe calls for baking powder or baking soda, it will work fine with whole-wheat pastry flour. If it uses yeast, it will not.

**Now, where do you find it?** Be aware, that you will probably not find it in the standard flour section of your grocery store. It is considered specialty flour and may be found in the health food section among special brands like *Arrowhead Mills* or *Bob's Red Mill*. If you do not find it, request it from your grocer. I buy it in bulk quantities at natural food stores or co-ops. Please look for it. It really is worth the effort. Until you find it, you can substitute for each cup of whole-wheat pastry flour: 1/2 cup all-purpose and 1/2 cup whole-wheat flour, or (as a last resort) use 1 cup of all-purpose flour.

# Blueberry Buckle

This recipe, amazingly, contains no fat. It's super easy to make and delicious. Don't feel guilty eating it for breakfast either. It's just as nutritious as toast with jam and fruit!

**Preheat oven to 375°.**
**Spray a 9" x 13" pan with nonstick cooking spray.**

| | |
|---|---|
| 2 bags | (12 oz each) **frozen blueberries** *or* **2 pints fresh blueberries** |
| 3 T | **sugar** |
| ½ cup | **orange juice** |

| | |
|---|---|
| 1 cup | **whole-wheat pastry flour\*** |
| ½ cup | **sugar** |
| 1 tsp | **baking powder** |
| 3 | **egg whites** |
| ¼ tsp | **lemon, orange** *or* **almond extract** (optional) |

| | |
|---|---|
| 1 T | **sugar** |

### Berry Bottom

Place blueberries in baking dish. Sprinkle sugar on top, then add juice.

### Cake Topping

Mix together in a medium-sized bowl. Drop 8 equal spoonfuls of dough on top of the blueberries in 2 rows of 4.

Sprinkle sugar over the dough. Bake for 35 minutes or until cake is lightly browned.

Take out of oven. Serve warm with a scoop of fat-free vanilla ice cream or yogurt. Yummm!

---

**EXCHANGE VALUES**

1.5 Starch — Meat — Veg. 1 Fruit — Milk — Fat

**\* If you don't have whole-wheat pastry flour, you can substitute with ½ cup whole-wheat flour and ½ cup all-purpose flour.**

| Nutrition information for — 1/8 of the recipe, without ice cream | | Preparation Time — 15 min. | Oven Time — 35 min. |
|---|---|---|---|
| Calories ........ 165 | Fat ........ < 1 g | Fiber ........ 4 g | Sodium ........ 72 mg | Total Carbohydrate ........ 39 g |
| Calories from Fat ........ 4% | Saturated Fat ........ 0 g | Cholesterol ........ 0 mg | Protein ........ 3 g | Sugars ........ 26 g |

# Tip

## What's it like being married to a nutritionist?

*"Most awesome."*

—My husband,
SCOTT FOCO, 34
Maintaining a
20 pound weight loss,
since 3 months after we met.

# Chocolate-Amaretto Cheesecake

When invited over to friends for dinner, I love bringing this dessert. They can't believe a "dietitian" could bring anything so good. This is truly "Crime without Punishment!"

**Preheat oven to 300°.**

Note: This recipe requires 8 hours of chilling. Make this the day before or morning of the day you plan to serve it.

| | |
|---|---|
| 12 | chocolate wafers *or* |
| | 6 graham cracker squares |

**8 hours or day before serving:**

Finely crush and sprinkle into bottom of 8" springform pan.[†] Set aside.

| | |
|---|---|
| 1 cup | light cream cheese |
| 1 cup | sugar |
| 1½ cup | low-fat cottage cheese |
| 6 T | unsweetened baking cocoa |
| ¼ cup | all purpose flour |
| ¼ cup | Amaretto* |
| 1 tsp | vanilla extract |

Position knife blade in food processor bowl. Add ingredients, processing until smooth.

| | |
|---|---|
| 1 | egg |

Add and process just until blended.

Pour mixture over crumbs in pan.

| | |
|---|---|
| 2 T | semi-sweet chocolate mini-morsels |

Sprinkle on top of mixture.

Bake for 45 to 50 minutes or until cheesecake is set. Let cool in pan on wire rack. Once cheesecake is cool, cover and chill at least 8 hours. Remove sides of pan and serve.

| | |
|---|---|
| 1 - 2 cups | clean whole raspberries *or* |
| | sliced strawberries |

Place in a bowl and serve alongside the cheesecake platter. Invite guests to top their cake as desired.

---

**EXCHANGE VALUES**

| 2 Starch | 1 Meat | — Veg. | — Fruit | — Milk | — Fat |
|---|---|---|---|---|---|

\* **Chocolate-mint Cheesecake:** Substitute ¼ cup Creme de Menthe for the Amaretto.
† An 8-inch round pan can be used, but it's more difficult to remove a slice neatly.

---

**Nutrition information for — 1 slice (1/12) topped with 3 to 6 berries** — Preparation Time — 25 min. — Oven Time — 45-50 min.

| | | | |
|---|---|---|---|
| Calories ..................... 215 | Fat ............................. 6 g | Fiber ......................... 2 g | Sodium ..................... 256 mg | Total Carbohydrate ............. 30 g |
| Calories from Fat ............... 26% | Saturated Fat ................ 3 g | Cholesterol .................. 29 mg | Protein ......................... 8 g | Sugars ....................... 24 g |

**Super Time Saving Tip:**

Buy shredded carrots from your grocer. I tested the matchstick cut carrots and they turned out very tender in this recipe.

## Tip

### An argument FOR desserts

Many nutrition professionals suggest NOT getting in the habit of dessert every night. I certainly work with many clients who blame their "dessert after every meal" upbringing for their weight problems. On the other hand, clients who grew up never being allowed dessert, now have the strong tendency to overeat them. Many studies clearly suggest that deprivation is a major contributor to overeating forbidden foods. **The solution is to include something satisfyingly sweet in moderation.**

# Creamy Frosted Carrot Cake

Did you know traditional carrot cake uses 1 cup of oil? Add the cream cheese frosting and you're looking at 50 to 60 grams of fat per slice! Well, throw out that old recipe and replace it with this delicious treat. No one will know, I promise.

**Preheat oven to 350°.**

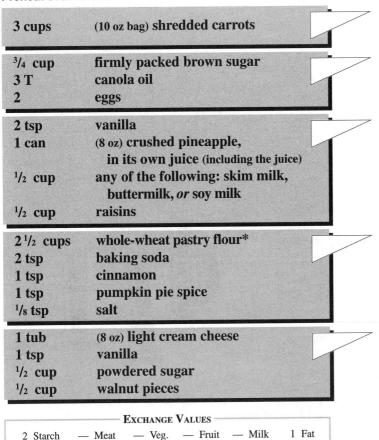

| | |
|---|---|
| 3 cups | (10 oz bag) **shredded carrots** |

Buy pre-shredded carrots or use a food processor to shred. Set aside 3 cups for this recipe. Use any leftovers in your next salad.

| | |
|---|---|
| ³/₄ cup | **firmly packed brown sugar** |
| 3 T | **canola oil** |
| 2 | **eggs** |

In a large bowl, mix well with a wire whisk.

| | |
|---|---|
| 2 tsp | **vanilla** |
| 1 can | (8 oz) **crushed pineapple, in its own juice** (including the juice) |
| ¹/₂ cup | **any of the following: skim milk, buttermilk,** *or* **soy milk** |
| ¹/₂ cup | **raisins** |

Stir in the large bowl.

| | |
|---|---|
| 2 ¹/₂ cups | **whole-wheat pastry flour*** |
| 2 tsp | **baking soda** |
| 1 tsp | **cinnamon** |
| 1 tsp | **pumpkin pie spice** |
| ¹/₈ tsp | **salt** |

Mix in a medium-size bowl. Add mix, a little at a time, into the large bowl and mix well. Add carrots to mix.

Spray a 9" x 13" pan or (2) 8" round pans with nonstick cooking spray. Pour batter into pan(s). Bake 28 to 30 minutes.

| | |
|---|---|
| 1 tub | (8 oz) **light cream cheese** |
| 1 tsp | **vanilla** |
| ¹/₂ cup | **powdered sugar** |
| ¹/₂ cup | **walnut pieces** |

Allow the cream cheese to soften on the counter while the cake is baking. When the cake comes out of the oven, mix ingredients together in a bowl. Once cake has cooled, frost it. (If using round pans, frosting will only cover tops of cakes, not the sides.)

**EXCHANGE VALUES**

| 2 Starch | — Meat | — Veg. | — Fruit | — Milk | 1 Fat |
|---|---|---|---|---|---|

\* If you don't have whole-wheat pastry flour, you can substitute with 1¹/₄ cups whole-wheat flour and 1¹/₄ cups all-purpose flour.

**Nutrition information for — 1 slice (1/18) with frosting**          Preparation Time — 25 min.          Oven Time — 28-30 min.

| Calories ..................... 195 | Fat .......................... 7 g | Fiber ....................... 2 g | Sodium ..................... 235 mg | Total Carbohydrate ............ 30 g |
|---|---|---|---|---|
| Calories from Fat ............... 31% | Saturated Fat ............... 1.9 g | Cholesterol ................... 30 mg | Protein ........................ 5 g | Sugars ........................... 18 g |

# How much dessert is TOO much?

First, take a look at the recommended serving size. Use this as a guide, but most importantly, listen to your body. It will tell you when you've had enough. Never eat dessert when you are "full." Always SAVE ROOM FOR DESSERT.

*Lickety-Split Meals*

# Chewy Multi-Grain Bars

These mock *Kellogg® NutriGrain Bars* make a fabulous snack, dessert, or lunchbox treat. They're even nutritious enough for breakfast along with a glass of milk or yogurt and a piece of fruit. You can freeze half of the bars in *Ziplock®* bags for future use.

**Preheat oven to 350°.**

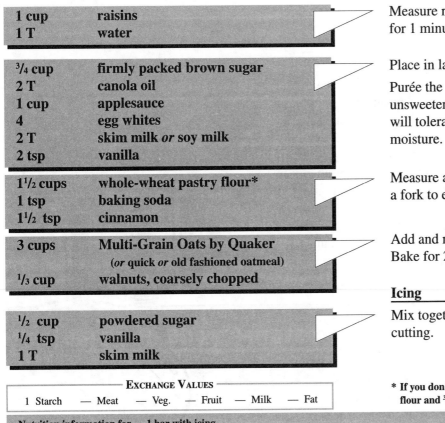

| 1 cup | raisins |
|---|---|
| 1 T | water |

Measure raisins into a glass measuring cup. Add water and microwave for 1 minute on high. Allow to soak.

| ³/₄ cup | firmly packed brown sugar |
|---|---|
| 2 T | canola oil |
| 1 cup | applesauce |
| 4 | egg whites |
| 2 T | skim milk *or* soy milk |
| 2 tsp | vanilla |

Place in large bowl and mix thoroughly.

Purée the soaking raisins in a food processor. Add to the large bowl, unsweetened, and mix thoroughly. (People who don't care for raisins will tolerate them better puréed. Puréeing increases sweetness and moisture. Raisins can be added without puréeing if you prefer.)

| 1¹/₂ cups | whole-wheat pastry flour* |
|---|---|
| 1 tsp | baking soda |
| 1¹/₂ tsp | cinnamon |

Measure and sift into the large bowl (or combine in another bowl using a fork to evenly distribute soda and cinnamon).

| 3 cups | Multi-Grain Oats by Quaker |
|---|---|
| | (*or* quick *or* old fashioned oatmeal) |
| ¹/₃ cup | walnuts, coarsely chopped |

Add and mix. Spread dough into an ungreased 9" x 13" baking pan. Bake for 23 minutes. Cool and cut into 32 bars.

### Icing

| ¹/₂ cup | powdered sugar |
|---|---|
| ¹/₄ tsp | vanilla |
| 1 T | skim milk |

Mix together in a small bowl. Drizzle over cooled bars before or after cutting.

***EXCHANGE VALUES***

| 1 Starch | — Meat | — Veg. | — Fruit | — Milk | — Fat |
|---|---|---|---|---|---|

* If you don't have whole-wheat pastry flour, you can substitute with ³/₄ cup whole-wheat flour and ³/₄ cup all-purpose flour.

**Nutrition information for — 1 bar with icing**

Preparation Time — 30 min.    Oven Time — 23 min.

| Calories .................. 100 | Fat .......................... 2 g | Fiber ..................... 1.5 g | Sodium ...................... 50 mg | Total Carbohydrate ............. 19 g |
|---|---|---|---|---|
| Calories from Fat .............. 18% | Saturated Fat ............... < 1 g | Cholesterol .................... 0 mg | Protein ........................ 3 g | Sugars ........................ 9 g |

# Who has time to bake anymore?

Even the busiest people can find themselves in the middle of a rainy weekend, hankering for some fun in the kitchen. Besides, the stress-reducing power of tinkering in the kitchen, sending heavenly aroma throughout the house, is excellent therapy. That these recipes are simple to put together, makes this "therapy session" easy. And to double the benefits of your efforts, make a double batch and freeze.

# Chocolate Chip Bar Cookies

My thanks to Registered Dietitian, Lori Hunt, for this delicious guilt-free chocolate chip cookie recipe. The instant pudding and applesauce replaces the shortening entirely. (Use chocolate pudding for chocolate chocolate chip cookies.) Since these cookies are so moist, I suggest storing them in the refrigerator or freezer. They freeze wonderfully.

**Preheat oven to 350°.**

| 2 Doz. | 4 Doz. | |
|---|---|---|
| 1 c | 2 c | applesauce, unsweetened |
| ¾ c | 1½ c | firmly packed brown sugar |
| 2 tsp | 1T+1tsp | vanilla |
| 4 | 8 | egg whites |

Using a fork, mix well in a large bowl.

| | | |
|---|---|---|
| 1 lg pkg | 2 lg pkg | (5.1 oz) **instant vanilla** *or* (5.9 oz) **chocolate pudding** |
| 1 tsp | 2 tsp | baking soda |
| 1 tsp | 2 tsp | baking powder |
| 2 c | 4 c | whole-wheat pastry flour* |

In a medium-sized bowl, mix with a fork. Then add to the liquid ingredients. Using a large wooden spoon, stir well.

| | | |
|---|---|---|
| 1 c | 2 c | dry oats (quick-cooking *or* old fashioned) |

Add and mix.

| | | |
|---|---|---|
| ½ pkg | 1 pkg | (12 oz) **semi-sweet chocolate chips** |

Add and mix. Let dough sit about 10 minutes. Spray (1 or 2) 9" x 13" pans with nonstick spray. Place dough in pan(s). Lay a sheet of wax paper on top. Press dough out. Remove wax paper.

Bake 25 minutes. When you take the cookies out of the oven, they will look lightly browned on top and will be soft to the touch. They will firm up as they cool. Then cut each pan into 24 small, equal size bars. If keeping past 2 days, store cookies in refrigerator or freezer.

\* If you don't have whole-wheat pastry flour, you can substitute with 1 cup whole-wheat flour and 1 cup all-purpose flour, or for the large recipe, 2 cups whole-wheat flour and 2 cups all-purpose flour.

### EXCHANGE VALUES

2 Starch — Meat — Veg. — Fruit — Milk — Fat

| Nutrition information for — 1 bar cookie | | Preparation Time — 35 min. | Oven Time — 25 min. |
|---|---|---|---|
| Calories .................... 125 | Fat ............................ 2 g | Fiber .................................. 1.5 g Sodium ............................ 170 mg | Total Carbohydrate ............. 26 g |
| Calories from Fat ............... 14% | Saturated Fat ...................... 1 g | Cholesterol .......................... 0 mg Protein ..................................... 3 g | Sugars .................................. 10 g |

# EXERCISE: A new way to get your quota

## Tip

**Long gone are the days that you MUST exercise 30-40 minutes NON-STOP to receive the benefits. Studies show that** breaking your 30 to 40 minute exercise into 3 or 4 separate 10-minute segments, has the same cardiovascular AND weight-loss benefits.

Now there is additional good news from the University of Pittsburgh, where researchers determined that at the end of 6 months, women on the short-bout program exercised 30 more minutes per week than the long-bout exercisers. That's an extra day's worth! They also lost 2 pounds more, on average. Obviously 10 minutes here and there is easier to stick to!

**Is short-bout exercise the answer for you?**

- Frequent 10 minute breaks will do wonders for alleviating stress!

**Also keep in mind:**

- 10 minutes doesn't work up enough of a sweat to require a shower.

# Oatmeal Cookies

This recipe was inspired by one of Evelyn Tribole's recipe makeovers in *Shape* magazine. I found that the sugar could come down further. The cream cheese works nicely for both flavor and moistness. As I love to say, 3 of these with milk and an orange are nutritious enough for breakfast!

**Preheat oven to 350°.**

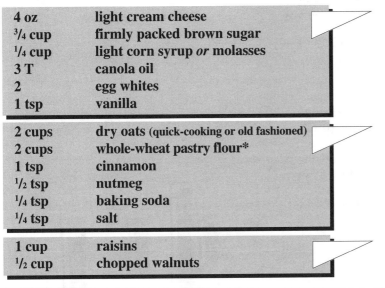

| | |
|---|---|
| 4 oz | **light cream cheese** |
| ³/₄ cup | **firmly packed brown sugar** |
| ¹/₄ cup | **light corn syrup *or* molasses** |
| 3 T | **canola oil** |
| 2 | **egg whites** |
| 1 tsp | **vanilla** |

In a large mixing bowl, use an electric mixer to beat together. Set aside.

| | |
|---|---|
| 2 cups | **dry oats (quick-cooking or old fashioned)** |
| 2 cups | **whole-wheat pastry flour\*** |
| 1 tsp | **cinnamon** |
| ¹/₂ tsp | **nutmeg** |
| ¹/₄ tsp | **baking soda** |
| ¹/₄ tsp | **salt** |

In a medium-size bowl, mix together with a fork until soda and salt are well distributed. Add to liquid mixture and mix well.

| | |
|---|---|
| 1 cup | **raisins** |
| ¹/₂ cup | **chopped walnuts** |

Mix in.

With a knife, cut dough into 3 equal sections. (Use this as a guide to make 3 dozen cookies.) Drop by slightly heaping tablespoons. Flatten each cookie with the back of your spoon. (Option: a reader tells me she places 3 chocolate chips firmly on top of each cookie. This doesn't add too much fat and calories, and her family raves!)

Bake for 10 minutes.

---

**EXCHANGE VALUES**

| 1 Starch | — Meat | — Veg. | — Fruit | — Milk | — Fat |
|---|---|---|---|---|---|

**\* If you don't have whole-wheat pastry flour, you can substitute with 1 cup whole-wheat flour and 1 cup all-purpose flour.**

| Nutrition information for — 1 cookie | | | Preparation Time — 30 min. | Oven Time —10 min. |
|---|---|---|---|---|
| Calories .................................. 100 | Fat ........................................ 3 g | Fiber ........................................ 1 g | Sodium ............................. 50 mg | Total Carbohydrate ............. 16 g |
| Calories from Fat ............... 26% | Saturated Fat ........................ .6 g | Cholesterol ......................... 1 mg | Protein ................................. 2.5 g | Sugars ..................................... 8 g |

# Chocoholics unite!

The following are a few of my favorite "healthier" ways to lick a chocolate craving:

- Cup of hot cocoa

- Glass of chocolate milk (bottle of chocolate syrup comes in handy)

- Sliced banana drizzled with chocolate syrup

- Frozen cherries (defrosted slightly) drizzled with chocolate syrup

- Low-fat chocolate chip granola bar

- *Chocolate No-Bakes* (this page!)

- *Cocoa Lava Kisses* (page 161)

- *Chocolate Chip Cookie Bars* (page 158)

# Chocolate No-Bakes

The same wonderful cookie from my childhood with only ¹/₂ the fat!

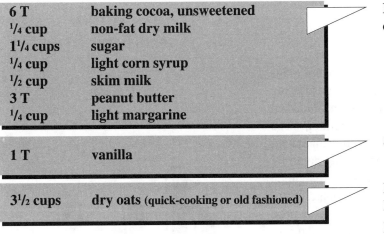

| | |
|---|---|
| 6 T | baking cocoa, unsweetened |
| ¹/₄ cup | non-fat dry milk |
| 1¹/₄ cups | sugar |
| ¹/₄ cup | light corn syrup |
| ¹/₂ cup | skim milk |
| 3 T | peanut butter |
| ¹/₄ cup | light margarine |

In a medium saucepan, bring to a boil and continue to boil 1 to 2 minutes. Remove from heat.

| | |
|---|---|
| 1 T | vanilla |

Stir in.

| | |
|---|---|
| 3¹/₂ cups | dry oats (quick-cooking or old fashioned) |

Measure into a medium-sized bowl.
Pour hot mixture over oats and mix well.

Drop by spoonfuls onto waxed paper and allow to cool. Be sure to make 36 cookies if you want the nutrition information to be accurate.

Transfer to a *Tupperware*® container and refrigerate. (Because these have less saturated fat, they do not set up "solid" at room temperature like the traditional No-Bakes. Expect them to be gooey and good.)

---

**EXCHANGE VALUES**

1 Starch — Meat — Veg. — Fruit — Milk — Fat

| Nutrition information for — 1 cookie | | Preparation Time — 20 min. | |
|---|---|---|---|
| Calories .......................... 85 | Fat .............................. 2 g | Fiber .......................... 1 g | Sodium .......................... 20 mg | Total Carbohydrate ............. 15 g |
| Calories from Fat ............... 20% | Saturated Fat ..................... .5 g | Cholesterol .................. < 1 mg | Protein ............................ 2 g | Sugars .................................... 8 g |

## Tip

### Chocolate facts: Did you know?

Chocolate is basically a creamy mixture of 3 ingredients: cocoa, sugar, and fat. Studies have shown that this combination of ingredients creates the impulsive, addictive, "lack of control" behavior, with fat being the key culprit. The fat provides the creamy smoothness, dulling the sweetness slightly, so you don't tire of the teaspoons upon teaspoons of sugar that you are consuming. The fat combined with the sugar makes the calories soar.

But say you get smart and use the cocoa and sugar, but not the fat? Could you gain chocolate satisfaction with fewer calories and more control to stop at a few? Try this strategy in these *Cocoa Lava Kisses*. You'll be surprised at the satisfaction you'll feel with fewer bites.

# Cocoa Lava Kisses

These heavenly clouds of sweet chocolate work great to take care of a chocolate craving. Unbelievably, they're fat-free! They are intensely sweet, which will make it easier to stop at 3, which is only 75 calories!

**Preheat oven to 250°.**
**Line 2 cookie sheets with wax paper.**

*These freeze well, making them convenient for future chocolate cravings!*

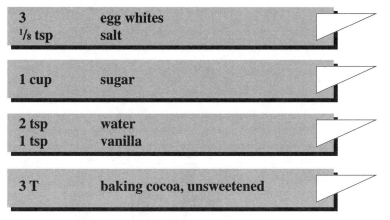

| | |
|---|---|
| **3** | **egg whites** |
| **¹/₈ tsp** | **salt** |

Place in medium-size bowl. Whip with an electric mixer until soft peaks form.

| | |
|---|---|
| **1 cup** | **sugar** |

Gradually add ¹/₂ cup of the sugar to egg whites while constantly whipping.

| | |
|---|---|
| **2 tsp** | **water** |
| **1 tsp** | **vanilla** |

Combine in a cup. Add to mix, a few drops at a time, alternating with the remaining ¹/₂ cup sugar while constantly whipping.

| | |
|---|---|
| **3 T** | **baking cocoa, unsweetened** |

Flake cocoa with a fork to break clumps. Sift if necessary. Fold into mix.

Place bite-size rounded **teaspoons** (*not* tablespoons) of mix onto the wax paper on a cookie sheet.

Bake approximately 30 minutes. They will be dry on the outside, but moist and lava-like on the inside. They will retain their shape. (If they become completely dry like styrofoam, they are overbaked.)

While kisses are still hot, remove from wax paper and place on a wire rack so they will not stick.

After cooling, store kisses in an airtight container.

---

**EXCHANGE VALUES**

.5 Starch — Meat — Veg. — Fruit — Milk — Fat

| Nutrition information for — 1 cookie | | | Preparation Time — 30 min. | Oven Time — 30 min. |
|---|---|---|---|---|
| Calories ..................................... 25 | Fat ............................................ 0 g | Fiber ........................................ 0 g | Sodium ............................. 16 mg | Total Carbohydrate ............... 6 g |
| Calories from Fat .................. 0% | Saturated Fat ........................ 0 g | Cholesterol ............................. 0 g | Protein ...................................... 0 g | Sugars ..................................... 5 g |

## Tip

## Banana buying and ripening tips

1. Buy a few yellow and a few green, for "just in time" bananas all week.

2. Once your bananas reach their desired ripeness, place them in the refrigerator to halt the ripening process for a few days. Don't be alarmed when the skins turn black. They will still be perfect on the inside.

3. If your bananas have reached the banana bread stage, but you don't have the 30 minutes to mix this up, simply peel them and slip them into *Ziplock*® bags for the freezer. They can be thawed and used another time for *Nana bread*, page 162; *Banana Nut Cake*, page 166; or *Smoothies*, page 16.

# 'Nana Bread

Who doesn't love banana bread? Every household needs a banana bread recipe for those bananas that peter out before the family can get around to eating them all. And the recipe needs to be without all the fat, yet so moist that each slice can be eaten as is! Ask no more, it's all right here!

**Preheat oven to 350°.**

*In this recipe, applesauce completely replaces the shortening or margarine!*

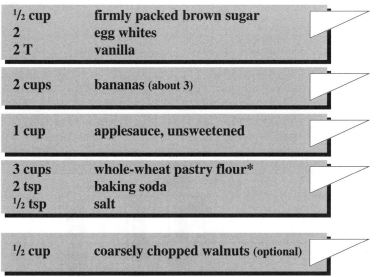

| | |
|---|---|
| ½ cup | firmly packed brown sugar |
| 2 | egg whites |
| 2 T | vanilla |

Mix together in a large mixing bowl.

| | |
|---|---|
| 2 cups | bananas (about 3) |

Mash. (I use a food processsor). Stir into mix.

| | |
|---|---|
| 1 cup | applesauce, unsweetened |

Add to mix and stir.

| | |
|---|---|
| 3 cups | whole-wheat pastry flour* |
| 2 tsp | baking soda |
| ½ tsp | salt |

Place in a sifter and sift into the mix (or place in a separate bowl and use a fork to equally distribute the salt and soda). Stir together thoroughly with the wet ingredients.

| | |
|---|---|
| ½ cup | coarsely chopped walnuts (optional) |

Add to mix.

Spray loaf pans with nonstick cooking spray.

Divide batter evenly into each pan (loafs will not be high).

Bake for 45 minutes, or until a toothpick comes out with no batter sticking to it.

---

**EXCHANGE VALUES**

| 1 Starch | — Meat | — Veg. | — Fruit | — Milk | — Fat |
|---|---|---|---|---|---|

\* If you don't have whole-wheat pastry flour, you can substitute with 1½ cups whole-wheat and 1½ cups all-purpose flour.

| Nutrition information for — 1 slice (1/12 of one loaf) | | | Preparation Time — 15 min. | Oven Time — 45 min. |
|---|---|---|---|---|
| Calories .................................. 90 | Fat .......................................... 2 g | Fiber ........................................ 2 g | Sodium ............................ 160 mg | Total Carbohydrate ............. 17 g |
| Calories from Fat ............... 16% | Saturated Fat ..................... < 1 g | Cholesterol ......................... 0 mg | Protein ................................. 2.6 g | Sugars ...................................... 6 g |

**Tip**

## What's moderation?

I am often asked, ''Zon, do you ever eat full-fat foods?'' My answer is, ''Sure! But not real often.'' Of course the next question is, ''How often is often?''

My answer is the ''80-20 rule.'' All foods can fit when your base diet is healthfully selected 80% of the time. That's 80% of all your breakfasts, lunches, dinners, and snacks being healthy low-fat choices. The remaining 20% leaves room for the special occasions, holidays, and ''treats.'' The sweet treats in this chapter can be considered more like the ''80%'' instead of the ''20%,'' since they are low in fat and offer good nutritional value.

# Enlightened Zucchini Bread

Toss out that old recipe that called for 1 cup of oil, because now you have a much healthier alternative, without sacrificing taste! My thanks to Ann Jones, MS, RD and her daughter for this great find.

MAKES 1 OR 2 LOAVES
12 SLICES PER LOAF

| 1 loaf | 2 loaves | |
|---|---|---|
| | | **Preheat oven at 350°.** |
| 1 ½ c | 3 c | whole-wheat pastry flour* |
| ½ tsp | 1 tsp | baking soda |
| ¼ tsp | ½ tsp | baking powder |
| 1 tsp | 2 tsp | cinnamon |
| ¼ tsp | ½ tsp | each, cloves and nutmeg |

Mix together in a small bowl.

| 1 loaf | 2 loaves | |
|---|---|---|
| ¾ c | 1 ½ c | sugar |
| 2 | 4 | egg whites |
| ¼ c | ½ c | skim milk *or* non-fat plain yogurt |
| 1 tsp | 2 tsp | vanilla |
| 1 T | 2 T | lemon juice |
| ¼ tsp | ½ tsp | lemon extract |

Beat together in a separate medium-size bowl.

| 1 loaf | 2 loaves | |
|---|---|---|
| 1 c | 2 c | shredded zucchini, unpeeled |

Stir into liquid mix in the medium bowl.

| 1 loaf | 2 loaves | |
|---|---|---|
| ½ c | 1 c | nuts *or* raisins |

Stir flour mix into zucchini mix.
Add optional nuts and/or raisins and stir.

Spray loaf pan(s) with nonstick cooking spray.
Pour batter into pan(s). Bake 45 to 55 minutes.

**EXCHANGE VALUES**

| 1.5 Starch | — Meat | 1 Veg. | — Fruit | — Milk | .5 Fat |
|---|---|---|---|---|---|

\* If you don't have whole-wheat pastry flour, you can substitute with ¾ cup whole-wheat flour and ¾ cup all-purpose flour, OR for the large recipe, 1½ cup whole-wheat flour and 1½ cup all-purpose flour.

**Nutrition information for — 1 slice (1/12 of one loaf)** — Preparation Time — 30 min. — Oven Time — 45-55 min.

| | | |
|---|---|---|
| Calories ................................. 125 | Fat ......................................... 3 g | Fiber ...................................... 1.5 g | Sodium ............................... 73 mg | Total Carbohydrate ............. 22 g |
| Calories from Fat ............... 22% | Saturated Fat ...................... 0 g | Cholesterol .......................... 0 mg | Protein ................................... 3.5 g | Sugars ................................... 13 g |

## True or False?

**"People with diabetes cannot eat foods containing sugar."**

**Answer:** FALSE.

People with diabetes need to control the number of carbohydrates they consume at every meal and snack. Eating foods high in sugar makes this very difficult to do, since high sugar foods contain high amounts of carbohydrates. On the other hand, they *can include foods containing sugar when done in the following way:*

1. Know how many carbohydrates the serving of food contains (by reading the nutrition facts).

2. Choose recipes using less sugar and more whole grains (like the ones in this book). The less sugar a dessert contains, the more generous the portion can be.

3. "Make room" for the dessert by cutting back equally on other carbo-hydrate containing foods like bread, rice, potatoes, or pasta. Cutting back exactly 30 grams of carbohydrate to enjoy a 30 gram carbohydrate dessert, means a controlled blood sugar level.

People with diabetes must remember that eating a diet that is low in fat and high in fiber is also of **KEY** importance for success in the control of their health.

# Surprise Pumpkin Pie

"Surprise" because it makes its own crust. What a time and fat saver! This pie is so fast that you can have it in the oven in less than 10 minutes. It's delicious **and** beta-carotene rich. Why not serve it all year round?

**Preheat the oven to 350°.**

| | |
|---|---|
| 2 | eggs *or* 4 egg whites *or* ¹/₂ cup egg beaters |
| ³/₄ cup | sugar |
| ¹/₂ cup | reduced-fat *Bisquick*® mix |
| 1¹/₂ cups | pumpkin, canned |
| 2 tsp | pumpkin pie spice (*or* 1 tsp cinnamon, ¹/₂ tsp ginger, ¹/₄ tsp cloves, and ¹/₄ tsp nutmeg) |
| ¹/₄ tsp | salt |
| 1 can | (13 oz) evaporated skim milk |

Mix all ingredients in a blender or food processor for 2 minutes.

Spray a 9" pie plate (preferably glass) with nonstick cooking spray. Pour in the batter.

Bake at 350º for 50 to 60 minutes, or until firm.

Cool completely before cutting. Serve with fat-free ice cream or yogurt, if desired.

---

**EXCHANGE VALUES**

2 Starch — Meat 1 Veg. — Fruit — Milk — Fat

* This recipe makes either (1) 9" deep dish (4 cup volume) or (2) shallow dish (2 cup volume) pies. If making the (2) shallow pies, adjust baking time to 35 to 45 minutes. Nutrition information per slice will be ¹/₂ of what is listed below.

| Nutrition information for — 1 slice (1/8) | | | Preparation Time — 10 min. | Oven Time — 50-60 min. |
|---|---|---|---|---|
| Calories ..................................... 175 | Fat ........................................... 2 g | Fiber ....................................... 1.4 g | Sodium ............................. 240 mg | Total Carbohydrate ............. 34 g |
| Calories from Fat .................. 9% | Saturated Fat .................... < 1 g | Cholesterol ....................... 55 mg | Protein ................................. 6.5 g | Sugars ...................................... 20 g |

## Tip

## Coffee: the diuretic

Did you know that chances are, you wake up in the morning dehydrated? You haven't consumed any liquids for 8 hours or longer. Charging off to work with 2 cups of coffee makes matters worse. A cup of caffeinated coffee works like a diuretic. For every cup, you excrete a cup and a half. No wonder so many people get headaches by mid-afternoon, which is a classic sign of dehydration. Coupled with fatigue, this means you're definitely not operating at your optimal level.

**Solution:**

Make it a goal to drink a glass of water or diluted juice FIRST THING in the morning. In fact, you may find it convenient to just open up in the shower! (Think about it! There isn't anything weird about using your showerhead as a drinking fountain. *Try it!*)

# Pumpkin Oatbran Bread or Muffins

A super way to eat beta carotene loaded pumpkin. This makes a large batch, so freeze the muffins for another busy time, especially breakfast!

MAKES 3 LOAVES OR
1 LOAF AND 24 MUFFINS

**Preheat oven to 350°.**

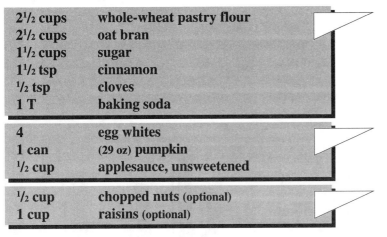

| | |
|---|---|
| 2¹/₂ cups | whole-wheat pastry flour |
| 2¹/₂ cups | oat bran |
| 1¹/₂ cups | sugar |
| 1¹/₂ tsp | cinnamon |
| ¹/₂ tsp | cloves |
| 1 T | baking soda |

Mix dry ingredients in a large bowl.

Make a well in the center of the mix.

| | |
|---|---|
| 4 | egg whites |
| 1 can | (29 oz) pumpkin |
| ¹/₂ cup | applesauce, unsweetened |

Add to the well in the dry mix. Stir just until moistened.

| | |
|---|---|
| ¹/₂ cup | chopped nuts (optional) |
| 1 cup | raisins (optional) |

Stir in.

Spray loaf pans or muffin tins with nonstick cooking spray.

Pour in batter.

Bake loaf 45 minutes; muffins 30–35 minutes or until toothpick inserted in center comes out clean.

---

**EXCHANGE VALUES**

1 Starch — Meat — Veg. .5 Fruit — Milk — Fat

| Nutrition information for — 1 slice (1/12 of one loaf) or 1 muffin | | | Preparation Time — 15 min. | Oven Time — 30-45 min. |
|---|---|---|---|---|
| Calories .................................. 120 | Fat ............................................. 2 g | Fiber ............................................. 3 g | Sodium ............................... 110 mg | Total Carbohydrate ............. 23 g |
| Calories from Fat ............... 13% | Saturated Fat .................... < 1 g | Cholesterol .......................... 0 mg | Protein ....................................... 4 g | Sugars ....................................... 12 g |

# Tip

## "I'd like the non-adhesive muffin papers, please."

Have you ever noticed how low-fat or fat-free muffin recipes tend to make muffin papers stick to the muffin? Peeling the paper down takes half the muffin with it. Until they invent edible muffin papers, try this:

Lightly spray the inside of each muffin paper with nonstick cooking spray. Your muffin papers will now peel off easily, leaving the muffin unscathed!

# Banana Nut Cake or Muffins

This recipe is somewhat similar to the 'Nana Bread recipe. It's whole-grain, no added fats, and delicious.

**Preheat oven to 350°.**
**Spray pan(s)† with nonstick spray.**

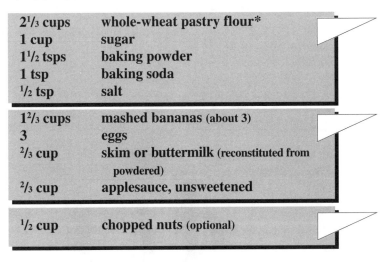

| | |
|---|---|
| 2⅓ cups | **whole-wheat pastry flour*** |
| 1 cup | **sugar** |
| 1½ tsps | **baking powder** |
| 1 tsp | **baking soda** |
| ½ tsp | **salt** |

Using a fork, mix dry ingredients in a large bowl.
Be certain the baking powder and soda are well distributed.

| | |
|---|---|
| 1⅔ cups | **mashed bananas** (about 3) |
| 3 | **eggs** |
| ⅔ cup | **skim or buttermilk** (reconstituted from powdered) |
| ⅔ cup | **applesauce, unsweetened** |

Mash bananas in a food processor or in a separate bowl by hand.
Add liquids and bananas to dry ingredients and mix.

| | |
|---|---|
| ½ cup | **chopped nuts** (optional) |

Mix in.

Pour batter into prepared pan(s). Bake until wooden pick inserted in center comes out clean; rectangle 40 minutes, rounds 35 minutes.

Cool and cut into 18 squares and serve as a snacking cake.

Note:  If it's someone's birthday, I'll frost with Snackwell's frosting.

† **Attention muffin lovers:** Makes great muffins. Adjust baking time to 22 to 25 minutes.
* If you don't have whole-wheat pastry flour, you can substitute with 1 cup whole-wheat flour and 1⅓ cups all-purpose flour.

---

EXCHANGE VALUES

| 1 Starch | — Meat | — Veg. | 1 Fruit | — Milk | .5 Fat |
|---|---|---|---|---|---|

| Nutrition information for — 1 piece (1/18 slice of the cake) | | | Preparation Time — 25 min. | Oven Time — 40 min. |
|---|---|---|---|---|

| | | | | |
|---|---|---|---|---|
| Calories .................................. 140 | Fat ............................................ 3 g | Fiber ........................................ 2 g | Sodium ............................ 185 mg | Total Carbohydrate ............. 26 g |
| Calories from Fat ............... 19% | Saturated Fat ...................... .4 g | Cholesterol ....................... 35 mg | Protein ...................................... 4 g | Sugars ..................................... 14 g |

## Flaming tips:

- Turn lights down to enjoy the flame.

- Try this recipe outdoors, using your grill as your heat source.

- Try it after dark.

- Use caution. The flames may rise 2 feet.

- Be aware that flaming does not remove all the alcohol.

# Flaming Bananas Foster

I learned to make this when I was 15 years old, after dining at "Brennans" in New Orleans.
It's my absolute favorite dessert for entertaining. Talk about fun, fast, tasty, and impressive!

Delegate
Someone to:
Find the matches
and scoop ice cream
(1/2 cup each
serving)

| | |
|---|---|
| **3 T** | **light margarine** |
| **⅓ cup** | **firmly packed brown sugar** |

Melt brown sugar and margarine
in a nonstick sauté pan over medium heat.

| | |
|---|---|
| **3** | **bananas, peeled, diagonally sliced ¼" thick** |
| **6 dashes** | **cinnamon** |

Add bananas and cinnamon, and sauté until tender,
turning once. (Use this time to find your matches!)

| | |
|---|---|
| **⅓ cup** | **white rum** |
| **3 T** | **banana liqueur** |

Combine in a cup. With matches ready, pour over bananas, stand back
and attempt to "touch" the liquid with your lit match. Be sure to yell
"everybody now… OOMPA!" as it lights. (The louder the OOMPAs,
the better it will taste!)

Continue to simmer dish over medium heat throughout flaming process
(about 20 seconds).

| | |
|---|---|
| **6 scoops** | **(½ cup each) vanilla fat-free ice cream** *or* **yogurt** |

Once flame goes out on its own, serve immediately over ice cream.

### EXCHANGE VALUES

| 2 Starch | — Meat | — Veg. | 1 Fruit | .5 Milk | — Fat |
|---|---|---|---|---|---|

**Nutrition information for — 1/6 of the recipe over 1/2 cup frozen yogurt**  **Preparation Time — 15 min.**

| | | | | |
|---|---|---|---|---|
| Calories ........................ 270 | Fat .............................. 3 g | Fiber ............................... 1 g | Sodium ...................... 100 mg | Total Carbohydrate ............ 48 g |
| Calories from Fat ............... 10% | Saturated Fat .............. < 1 g | Cholesterol ..................... 0 mg | Protein .......................... 4.5 g | Sugars .............................. 35 g |

# Save room for dessert

It is customary in this country to eat until full and **then** eat dessert. This makes the dessert COMPLETELY fattening! Yes, even if it is fat free! Thin people eat dessert, but they "save room" for it. When you know you'll be having dessert, plan ahead by eating $\frac{1}{2}$ of your potato or skip the bread.

# Hot Fudge Brownie Cake

A quick way to bake up a super chocolate treat. The hot water poured over the top will turn into a yummy hot fudge.

**Preheat oven to 350°.**

| | |
|---|---|
| 1 cup | flour |
| ½ cup | sugar |
| 2 T | baking cocoa, unsweetened |
| 2 tsp | baking powder |
| ¼ tsp | salt |

In a medium bowl, combine with a fork until well distributed.

| | |
|---|---|
| ½ cup | skim milk |
| 2 T | oil (canola) |
| 1 tsp | vanilla |

Stir in until smooth. Spread into an ungreased 9" square baking pan.

| | |
|---|---|
| ½ cup | firmly packed brown sugar |
| ¾ cup | chopped nuts |
| ¼ cup | baking cocoa, unsweetened |

Sprinkle each over batter.

| | |
|---|---|
| 1½ cup | hot water |

Pour over all and do not stir. (This is not a mistake!) Bake for 35 to 40 minutes. Allow to stand for 10 minutes. Serve warm with a scoop of low-fat frozen yogurt.

---

**EXCHANGE VALUES**

| 3 Starch | — Meat | — Veg. | — Fruit | — Milk | 2 Fat |
|---|---|---|---|---|---|

| Nutrition information for — 1/9 of the recipe, without frozen yogurt | | | Preparation Time — 15 min. | Oven Time — 35-40 min. |
|---|---|---|---|---|
| Calories .................................. 270 | Fat ........................................ 9.5 g | Fiber ............................................ 1 g | Sodium .............................. 210 mg | Total Carbohydrate ............. 43 g |
| Calories from Fat .............. 31% | Saturated Fat .................... < 1 g | Cholesterol ....................... < 1 mg | Protein ................................. 5.5 g | Sugars .................................... 22 g |

## Tips on sugar

My recipes contain somewhere around ¹/₂ the sugar of other dessert recipes. The nutrition information provided in this book includes grams of "sugar" (lower right, under carbohydrates). **Every 4 grams of sugar you see equals 1 teaspoon of sugar.** Up to 3 teaspoons (or 12 grams) of sugar is an acceptable amount for a dessert. You can easily flip through the recipes and see which recipes have the most and least amounts of sugar.

P.S. Understanding "grams of sugar" also helps you evaluate breakfast cereals, telling you which ones have a lot of sugar and which ones don't. Check it out!

# Applesauce Dumplings

Hungry for something sweet and there's nothing in the house? Try this simple-to-whip-up apple dessert that requires no apple peeling! My thanks to Grandma Minnie for this neat find.

| | |
|---|---|
| 3 cups | applesauce, unsweetened |
| 1/2 cup | water |
| 1 tsp | cinnamon |

Place in a wide mouth non-stick pan and turn on medium heat.

| | |
|---|---|
| 1 cup | reduced-fat *Bisquick*® |
| 1/4 c | sugar |
| 1/2 cup | skim milk |

In a medium bowl, combine just until moistened.

Applesauce should be boiling by now. Remove from heat and drop 6 even dumplings onto applesauce.

Cover and return to heat. Simmer 12 minutes. Serve warm.

| | |
|---|---|
| 6 scoops | (1/2 cup each) **vanilla fat-free ice cream *or* yogurt** |

Top each with a scoop.

## EXCHANGE VALUES

2 Starch — Meat — Veg. 1 Fruit .5 Milk — Fat

Nutrition information for — 1 dumpling, 1/2 cup sauce, 1/2 cup frozen yogurt — Preparation Time — 10 min. — Cook time — 12 min.

| | | | | | |
|---|---|---|---|---|---|
| Calories ................................... 260 | Fat ........................................ 1 g | Fiber ...................................... 1.5 g | Sodium ............................ 308 mg | Total Carbohydrate ............. 56 g |
| Calories from Fat ................. 4% | Saturated Fat .................... < 1 g | Cholesterol .......................... 0 mg | Protein ...................................... 6 g | Sugars ................................... 10 g |

# Tip

## Great ideas from people like you!

*"For many years now I have loved the 'Peanut Buster Parfait' at Dairy Queen. With my new commitment to healthy eating, I decided to substitute fat-free frozen yogurt for the ice cream and chocolate syrup for the hot fudge. I also order the small instead of the medium. The result: I am just as satisfied without feeling at all deprived."*

—STACEY W., 26, celebrating the 6th month of her new healthy lifestyle.

**Congratulations, Stacey!** You've successfully saved 200 calories and 25 grams of fat, while not feeling deprived. This is what it's all about!

# Brownie Banana Split

This recipe utilizes the convenience of the new low-fat box mixes, and adds nutrition via wheat-germ and fresh fruit! This simple dessert ends up with nutritional value to go along with the sugar. Its heavenly appearance makes it a favorite for entertaining.

**Preheat oven according to box directions.**

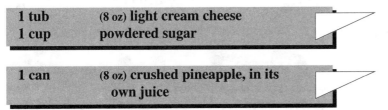

| 1 box | low-fat brownie mix |
| 1/3 cup | toasted wheat-germ (optional) |

Pour brownie mix in a bowl. Add water as listed on box. Add wheat germ. Mix well. Bake as directed in a well-greased 9" x 13" pan.

When finished baking, invert entire brownie cake onto a serving platter. Let cake cool.*

| 1 tub | (8 oz) light cream cheese |
| 1 cup | powdered sugar |

Mix together. Spread onto the cooled brownie cake.

### Just before serving:

| 1 can | (8 oz) crushed pineapple, in its own juice |

Drain pineapple well, reserving juice for another use. Sprinkle pineapple on top of the cream cheese frosting.

| 2 | fresh bananas |
| 12 to 15 | fresh strawberries |

Slice, then place on top of the pineapple.

| 1/4 cup | chocolate syrup (squeeze bottle kind) |

Just before serving, drizzle syrup over entire brownie. Enjoy!

---

**EXCHANGE VALUES**

| 3 Starch | — Meat | — Veg. | 1 Fruit | — Milk | 1 Fat |

\* If you have 6 or fewer guests, cut cake in 1/2 and only top 1/2 now. Do the other 1/2 another day, since the fresh appearance does not keep overnight.

**Nutrition information for — 1 square (1/12)**

**Preparation Time — 30 min.**

| Calories .................... 275 | Fat ............................ 6 g | Fiber ........................ 3 g | Sodium ...................... 200 mg | Total Carbohydrate ........... 50 g |
| Calories from Fat .......... 19% | Saturated Fat ............. 2.7 g | Cholesterol ............... 9 mg | Protein ......................... 5 g | Sugars ............................. 40 g |

# Grocery List

# Lickety-Split List
## SHOPPING SOLUTION!

This list includes every ingredient necessary to make any recipe in *Lickety-Split Meals for Health Conscious People on the Go!* This list is designed to (1) guide you in "stocking your larder" so you can make any Lickety-Split recipe you wish, and (2) make weekly re-stocking a snap. Gone are the days of not having everything you need when you need it. And NO more tedious list making! Each week your list is organized, neatly typed with brand name recommendations.

## Here's how it works:

**STEP #1**

### Inventory Your Larder & Customize Your List

While at home, use the list to guide you through your refrigerator, freezer, and all your cupboards. Using a pencil, check-mark any item that you don't already have, or is so old it needs replacing. (This is a good time to "clean and toss" to make space for all the new items you'll be bringing home.)

The "par stock" column is the number I suggest you keep on hand for each item.

This number is based on a family of four. You will need to adjust for your family size and preferences. The "re-stock" column is for check-marking the quantity you need in order to achieve the "par stock" level.

For an ingredient that you question you will ever use, look at the "for use in" column to see what the item is used for. If the item is perishable, and for a recipe that you do not plan to make this week, skip it. If it doesn't sound appetizing, skip it. In fact, for any item that you know you will never use, simply draw a line through it with a pencil.

Finally, use the blank lines in the back to write in items that you commonly use, which aren't on the list. (Every family has their own favorites!) Now your list is customized, and ready for your first big "stocking" trip!

*Lickety-Split Meals*

## STEP #2 — *Embark on Your First Big "Stocking" Trip*

This initial trip will require extra time, energy, and money. But I promise, you will enjoy having every thing you need, and each subsequent trip will be super quick, easy, and much less expensive! Pick a time when you are fresh and energized. Eat before you go. Consider enlisting someone to go with you for help. Find a sitter for small children. Be prepared to read some labels, however, you'll be glad to know that most times, I've given you brand name recommendations just to save you time.

## STEP #3 — *Organize and Train the Family*

Once home with your fresh supply, try to refrain from "shoving stuff any old place." Take time to group all the like canned items together, like freezer items together, and so on. These minutes spent now will save you hours in the coming weeks! Consider cleaning and cutting raw vegetables for easy snacking during the week.

Now, erase the "re-stock" column of your Lickety-Split grocery guide and return the book to its counter top position. Next, call all family members into the kitchen. Explain the shopping you have done. Point out the newly organized cupboards and brainstorm for simple strategies to keep them that way. And most importantly, explain that whenever someone discovers an item is "almost used up, or all used up," they check-mark it on the list. Point out how the list is organized, and how to use it.

Be prepared to spend the next few weeks reminding family members of this important new habit.

Assuming your education session is successful, when it's time to go shopping again, your list will be already made! All neatly typed and organized according to stock sections and with brand name recommendations. Even Dad won't mind picking up the groceries once in a while! Now this is living!

## What equals a fruit or vegetable serving?

| | |
|---|---|
| 1 | Small apple, pear, orange, nectarine, kiwi, etc. |
| 2 | plums |
| 4 | apricots |
| 1 cup | berries or melon |
| 15 | grapes |
| 2 T | raisins |
| 4 | dried apricots |
| ½ cup | applesauce (unsweetened) |
| ½ cup | canned fruit (own juice, drained) |
| ½ cup | cooked vegetables |
| 1 cup | raw vegetables |
| 6 | baby carrots |

# How to calculate your "Family FRUIT Quota" for 1 WEEK

**Tip**

Decide if your goal is 1, 2, 3 or 4 pieces per person each day. Keep in mind that the American Institute for Cancer Research says that 2 servings is the minimum and MORE is better!

Yes, canned fruit in its own juice, applesauce, and dried fruit can be substituted! (See page 175 to find out why juice is not recommended as one of your minimum servings.)

| # in family | 1 | 2 | 3 | 4 | 5 | 6 |
|---|---|---|---|---|---|---|
| **pieces per person per day** | | | | | | |
| 1 | 7 | **14** | 21 | 28 | 35 | 42 |
| 2 | 14 | **28** | 42 | 56 | 70 | 84 |
| 3 | 21 | **42** | 63 | 84 | 105 | 126 |
| 4 | 28 | **56** | 84 | 112 | 140 | 168 |

**I see your eyes popping out!!!** I know this seems like WAY too much, but the facts are the FACTS!

**Tips:** If you have a large family, to prevent spoilage, buy ½ now and shop for the rest mid-week.

- Buy some bananas green and some yellow, for "just in time" bananas all week.
- Likewise, buy some hard and some soft peaches, pears, and kiwis.
- Store ripe, ready-to-eat fruit in the refrigerator and the rest at room temperature.
- A fruit bowl on your kitchen counter helps everyone remember to snack on fruit!

**What about the cost?**

To generate "fruit" money, spend LESS in other departments:

1. Refrain from buying soda pop and beer. It's amazing how much more affordable water is!
2. Instead of buying products like instant scalloped potatoes and Rice-a-Roni®, stick with the less expensive versions: raw potatoes and rice.
3. Serve smaller portions of meat and serve more vegetarian meals like beans and rice or pasta. Examples include: *Veggie Sghetti, 3-Bean Chili*, meatless stir-fry, and bean burritos.

**Presto!** Money to fuel your new stepped-up fruit habit!

*Lickety-Split Meals*

# Grocery List

| Restock | Par Stock | Item and size | For use in ... |
|---|---|---|---|

## Fresh Fruit

*(Choose from seasonal selections. Adjust the amount your family needs using the chart above. The par-stock numbers below are a guide for 2 people for one week.)*

| Restock | Par Stock | Item and size | For use in ... |
|---|---|---|---|
| _____ | 8 | Bananas | **Breakfasts & Snacking** *Banana Bread/Cake/Muffins* *Banana Pancakes* *Summer Fresh Fruit Pie* |
| _____ | 8 | Oranges | **Breakfasts & Snacking** |
| _____ | 8 | Apples | **Snacking** *Scrumptious Swiss Oats ...* *Crunchy Apple Salad* |
| _____ | 1 | Grapes (bunch) | **Snacking** *Ambrosia Breakfast Rice* *Almond Chicken Salad* |
| _____ | 1 | Cantaloupe | **Breakfasts & Snacking** |
| _____ | 0-1 | Strawberries (qt) | **Breakfasts & Snacking** *Scrumptious Swiss Oats ...* *Summer Fresh Fruit Pie* |
| _____ | 0-1 | Blueberries (pt) | **Breakfasts & Snacking** *Scrumptious Swiss Oats ...* *Summer Fresh Fruit Pie* |

| Restock | Par Stock | Item and size | For use in ... |
|---|---|---|---|
| _____ | 0-1 | Raspberries (pt) | **Breakfasts & Snacking** *Scrumptious Swiss Oats ...* *Summer Fresh Fruit Pie* |
| _____ | 0-8 | Nectarines | **Breakfasts & Snacking** *Summer Fresh Fruit Pie* |
| _____ | 0-8 | Peaches | **Breakfasts & Snacking** *Summer Fresh Fruit Pie* |
| _____ | 4-8 | Pears | **Breakfasts & Snacking** |
| _____ | 4-6 | Grapefruit | **Breakfasts & Snacking** |
| _____ | 4 | Kiwi | **Breakfasts & Snacking** *Scrumptious Swiss Oats ...* |
| _____ | 1-2 | Lemon | **Flavoring ice water** **Recipes with fish** *Pasta Slaw* *Lentil Spinach Soup* *Curried Chickpeas ...* *Broiled Orange Roughy* *Tzatziki* |
| _____ | optional | Pineapple | **Snacking** *Marinated Sesame Chicken ...* |

**Tip**

# How to get your "Family VEGGIE Quota" for 1 WEEK

Do this math:

____ # of people in your family x 3 servings per day (minimum) x 7 days a week = ____

For a family of 4 x 7 days, that equals **84 servings!**

Here's an example of how to fuel your family for 1 week.
**Adjust** according to your preferences:

| Produce | Servings |
|---|---|
| 2 bundles of fresh broccoli | 16 |
| ½ head of fresh cauliflower (buy one head and serve ½ this week and ½ the next) | 5 |
| 2 lbs. baby carrots | 12 |
| 1 bag (10 oz. each) salad greens | 4 |
| 2 cucumbers | 4 |
| 5 tomatoes | 5 |
| 6 green/red peppers | 12 |
| 8 med. potatoes | 8 |
| 2 large sweet potatoes | 4 |
| 2 cans of vegetable soup, corn, or beets | 4 |
| 2 bags (1 lb. each) frozen veggies | 10 |
| **Total servings per week !!!** | **84** |

**Tips**

1. If your cart doesn't look anything like this, increase gradually!
2. If you have a large family, to prevent spoilage, buy ½ now and shop for the rest mid-week.
3. Instruct the whole family to think of "vegetables" for snacks.
4. Use your fresh produce early in the week and use frozen or canned later in the week.
5. Double the "token spoonful" of vegetables you may have grown up with.
6. Consider single serving cans of V-8® juice for lunches and snacks.
7. Try vegetable soup and a weekly stir-fry to help meet your weekly quota.

# Grocery List

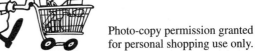

Photo-copy permission granted
for personal shopping use only.

| Restock | Par Stock | Item and size | For use in ... |
|---------|-----------|---------------|----------------|

## Fresh Veggies

*Each week purchase as needed to have on hand:*

| Restock | Par Stock | Item and size | For use in ... |
|---------|-----------|---------------|----------------|
| _____ | 1 | **Potatoes (bag)** regular or redskin | **Baked Potatoes** *Oven Fries* *Potato Salad* |
| _____ | 4+ | **Sweet potatoes or yams** Don't forget these! | **Baked Sweet Potatoes** *Gypsy Soup* |
| _____ | 1 | **Onions (bag)** | **Used regularly** |
| _____ | optional | **Green onions (bunch)** | **Salads** *South of the Border Roll-ups* *Herbed Salmon Spread* *Oklahoma Bean Dip* *7-Layer Bean Dip* *Beanito Bean Dip and Burritos* *Great Northern Tuna Salad ...* *Chicken Dijon Stuffed ...* *Gingered Black Beans ...* *Oriental Noodle Toss ...* |
| _____ | 1+ | **Broccoli** 2 heads are better than 1! | **Used regularly** |
| _____ | 1+ | **Cauliflower (heads)** | **Used regularly** |

| Restock | Par Stock | Item and size | For use in ... |
|---------|-----------|---------------|----------------|
| _____ | 1+ | **Baby carrots (Lg. bag)** | **Used regularly** |
| _____ | 1 | **Celery (bunch)** | **Snacking** **Salads** *Miracle Soup* *Potato Salad* |
| _____ | 3+ | **Green peppers** | **Used regularly** |
| _____ | 1+ | **Red pepper** | **Used regularly** |
| _____ | 1+ | **Yellow pepper** | **Used regularly** |
| _____ | 4+ | **Tomatoes** | **Used regularly** |
| _____ | 1+ | **Cucumbers** | **Snacking** **Salad** *Tzatziki* |
| _____ | 1+ | **Lettuce (dark greens)** If desired, pre-bagged, ready to eat | **Instant tossed salads** |
| _____ | optional | **Shredded carrots (bag)** | *Carrot Cake* *Carrot Raisin Salad* |
| _____ | 0-2 | **Shredded cabbage (bags)** | *Miracle Soup* *Pasta Slaw* |

# Tofu Buying Tips

You will find tofu in the produce section of your grocery store. Here's a summary of your options:

*Fresh:* packed in a small tub of water, must be refrigerated (usually a 7-10 day shelf life).

*Vacuum packaged:* does not require refrigeration, and offers the luxury of a 6 or more month shelf life (looks like juice boxes).

*Low-fat tofu:* available in the vacuum packaged varieties (Nori Nu brand).

*Soft, firm, extra firm and silken:* refers to the texture and will have a huge effect on your recipe.

### My recommendations:

The vacuum packaged is definitely the most convenient, but I've found even the "firm" variety is more "silken" and does not provide the meaty texture my recipes need. I therefore buy fresh tofu. The brand names available in the Detroit area are: *China Rose®, Soyplant®* or *Panda®.*

*Tip:* Changing the water every day will extend the freshness of the product a week or two past the stamped date.

While you might assume low-fat is the best choice, I've only found it available in the "silken" variety, which does not provide the meaty texture my recipes seek. Don't worry, regular tofu has only a small amount of soybean oil (healthy) and when balanced against the rest of the meal (potatoes, corn, bread, etc.) it calculates to a healthy percent of calories from fat. Because of this natural soybean oil, I use a nonstick spray with tofu recipes rather than the oil I usually call for with dishes using chicken breast and ground turkey meat.

See page 50 for information about what tofu is and its benefits.

*Lickety-Split Meals*

# Grocery List

Photo-copy permission granted for personal shopping use only.

| Restock | Par Stock | Item and size | For use in ... |
|---|---|---|---|

## Fresh Veggies (continued)

*Each week choose 2 or 3 for variety:*

| Restock | Par Stock | Item and size | For use in ... |
|---|---|---|---|
| _____ | 0-1 | Green beans (bunch) | *Crispy Chicken Dijon* <br> *Hungarian Chicken Paprikash* |
| _____ | 0-1 | Asparagus (bunch) <br> Buy frozen if you prefer | *Salmon Patties* <br> *Chicken Dijon Stuffed ...* <br> *Creamy Chicken Dijon* |
| _____ | 0-4 | Zucchini (sm) | *Ratatouille* <br> *Chicken Cacciatore* <br> *Veggie Sghetti* <br> *Southwest Chicken Pizza* <br> *Easy Pepper Steak Stir-Fry* |
| _____ | 0-2 | Yellow crooked-neck squash (sm) | *Ratatouille* |
| _____ | 0-20 | Mushrooms | *Ratatouille* <br> *Marinated Sesame Chicken ...* |
| _____ | 0-1 | Eggplant (med) | *Ratatouille* |
| _____ | 0-1 | Butternut squash (2) | *Cinnamon Butternut Squash* |
| _____ | optional | Alfalfa sprouts | **Salads** <br> *Mediterranean Lavash ...* |
| _____ | 0-20 | Cherry tomatoes | *Marinated Sesame Chicken ...* |

## Miscellaneous Produce

| Restock | Par Stock | Item and size | For use in ... |
|---|---|---|---|
| _____ | 1 | Garlic, minced in a jar or head of fresh cloves | **Basic supply** |
| _____ | 1 | Gingerroot, minced in a jar or a 4" fresh root | **Basic supply** |
| _____ | optional | Parsley (bunch) <br> Will keep for 3 weeks in fridge | *Curried Chickpeas ...* |
| _____ | optional | Cilantro (bunch) <br> Will keep for 3 weeks in fridge | *Tofu Fiesta* <br> *7 Layer Bean Dip* |
| _____ | 0-2 | Tofu, firm (6 oz) <br> (see buying tips above) | *Scrambled Tofu* <br> *Tofu Bites* <br> *Tofu Fiesta* <br> *Fajitas* <br> *Sweet & Sour Stir-Fry* <br> *Eggless Salad Sandwiches* |
| _____ | 0-2 | Tofu, soft (6 oz) | *Creamy Tomato Soup* |
| _____ | 0-1 | Fresh salsa | **Snacking** <br> *Black Bean & Corn Salad* |
| _____ | 0-2 | Cranberries <br> Fresh are available in the fall. <br> Buy several and freeze to have on hand. | *Cranberry Salad* |

# Tip

## Buying everything on this list is going to cost me a fortune!

True, you will be writing out a big check and going home with a car full of groceries on your first "stock-up" trip. But this is "bringing the grocery store to you," so you will *always* have what you need. How much is that worth to you? To *always* have what you need. (Listen to the sound of that word again!) You're not really

spending more, you're just spending it earlier. And think, with all the time you'll be saving by not making extra trips to the store mid-week, and making your own pizza instead of having it delivered, you will recover that up-front investment **in no time at all!**

### What is hummus and tabouli?

For information see page 48.

# Grocery List

Photo-copy permission granted for personal shopping use only.

| Restock | Par Stock | Item and size | For use in ... |
|---------|-----------|---------------|----------------|

## Miscellaneous Produce (continued)

| Restock | Par Stock | Item and size | For use in ... |
|---------|-----------|---------------|----------------|
| _____ | 0-1 | Tabouli | *Mediterranean Lavash Roll-ups* |
| _____ | 0-1 | Pumpkin (medium) A special Autumn treat! | *Jack in the Pumpkin* |
| _____ | 0-1 | Hummus I recommend the roasted red pepper or hummus with spinach | Snacking *Mediterranean Lavash Roll-ups* *1 Minute Mini-Meals* |

## Dried Fruit

| Restock | Par Stock | Item and size | For use in ... |
|---------|-----------|---------------|----------------|
| _____ | 1 | Raisins (box) | Cereal Baking Snacking |
| _____ | 0-1 | Dried cherries (tub) | *Broccoli & Dried Cherry Salad* *Scrumptious Swiss Oats ...* |
| _____ | optional | Craisins (tub) (dried cranberries) | Salad toppings *Scrumptious Swiss Oats ...* |
| _____ | 0-1 | Apricots (box) | Snacking Office pick-me-up *Scrumptious Swiss Oats ...* |

## Dried Beans and Grains

| Restock | Par Stock | Item and size | For use in ... |
|---------|-----------|---------------|----------------|
| _____ | 1 | Lentils, dried (16 oz) | *Lentil Spinach Soup* *Baked Lentils & Rice* |
| _____ | 1 | Black beans, dried (16 oz) | *Mexican Black Beans* |
| _____ | 1 | Garbanzo beans, dried (16 oz) | *Gyspy Soup* |
| _____ | 1 | Split peas, dried (16 oz) | *Split Pea Soup* |
| _____ | 2 | Instant whole-grain brown rice, *Minute®* | Numerous quick meals |
| _____ | 1 | Brown rice I highly recommend the flavor Basmati | *Baked Lentils and Rice* *Jack in the Pumpkin* |
| _____ | optional | Wild rice | *Jack in the Pumpkin* |
| _____ | 1 | Barley, quick-cooking | *Beef Barley Soup* |

*Lickety-Split Meals*

Misc. Produce (Cont.) / Dried Fruit / Dried Beans and Grains

Grocery List
175

## Storage Tip

I store my pasta in clear decorative jars on top of my cupboards. This saves me space INSIDE my cupboards and reminds me to cook pasta weekly.

# Tip

## Try to buy whole-wheat pasta whenever possible.

If you do not find whole-wheat pasta in the pasta section, try the natural or health food section, or better yet, a natural food store. Remember, the nutritional benefit is worth the extra effort!

A brand of pasta I highly recommend, is *Eden*®. They make high quality whole-wheat pasta, including an ingenious alternative, 50-50 pasta, which is made with ¹/₂ whole-wheat and ¹/₂ sifted flour. This is a great way for kids (or anyone) to "warm up" slowly to whole-wheat pasta.

# Grocery List

Photo-copy permission granted
for personal shopping use only.

| Restock | Par Stock | Item and size | For use in ... |
|---|---|---|---|

## Pasta

*The following is a recommended selection of pasta shapes to keep on hand:*

| Restock | Par Stock | Item and size | For use in ... |
|---|---|---|---|
| _____ | 2 | **Spaghetti (16 oz)** | *Veggie Sghetti* |
| _____ | 1 | **Angel hair (16 oz)** | *Parmesan Turkey Cutlets* <br> *Oriental Noodle Toss* |
| _____ | 1 | **Corkscrews (16 oz)** | *Southwest Chili Pasta* |
| _____ | 1 | **Macaroni (16 oz)** | *Herbed Italian Sausage* |
| _____ | 1 | **Shells, medium (16 oz)** | *Hearty Bean & Pasta Stew* |
| _____ | 1 | **Penne (16 oz)** | *White Beans & Penne Pasta* |
| _____ | 2 | **Lasagna noodles (16 oz)** <br> Buy 4 to make a <br> double batch | *LaZonya* |
| _____ | 1 | **Egg noodles, wide (16 oz)** <br> *No-Yolks*® are preferred | *Creamy Chicken Dijon* <br> *Hungarian Chicken ...* <br> *Cranberry Pork Roast* |

## Soups

| Restock | Par Stock | Item and size | For use in ... |
|---|---|---|---|
| _____ | optional | **Chicken bouillon** <br> **granules, low-sodium (sm)** | Basic supply |
| _____ | optional | **Beef bouillon granules,** <br> **low-sodium (sm)** | Basic supply |
| _____ | 4 | **Chicken broth,** <br> *Swanson Natural* <br> *Goodness* **100% fat-free,** <br> **1/3 less sodium (14.5 oz)** | Basic supply |
| _____ | 2 | **Beef broth (14.5 oz)** <br> reduced-sodium, if available | Basic supply |
| _____ | 2 | **Cream of mushroom** <br> **soup,** *Campbell's*® <br> *Healthy Request*® **(10.5 oz)** | *Tuna Noodle Salad* <br> *Beef Stroganoff* |
| _____ | 1 | **Cream of chicken soup,** <br> *Campbell's*® *Healthy* <br> *Request*® **(10.5 oz)** | *Creamy Chicken Enchiladas* |
| _____ | 1 | **Dry vegetable soup mix,** <br> *Knorr*® or *Mrs. Grass*® <br> **(pkg)** | *Spinach Dip* <br> *Miracle Soup* |

*Lickety-Split Meals*

**Pasta / Soups**

Grocery List
176

# Tip

## Do you know about Eden® beans?

I highly recommend them! These are absolutely delicious, supreme quality, low sodium, and organic beans. They come both plain and flavored and taste great straight from the can. (Perfect for a 1-minute mini-meal right out of your briefcase!) They are available in 15 oz. cans or in single serving 8 oz. "pull-top" cans.

This is THE marriage of convenience, health, and taste that we've all been waiting for!

**My favorites:**

- *Eden® Black Beans with Ginger and Lemon* (8 oz. pull-tops for mini-meals & two 15 oz. size for the *Gingered Black Beans and Squash*, page 60)

- *Eden® Spicy Pintos* (8 oz. pull-tops)

- *Eden® Lentil with Sweet Onion and Bay Leaf* (8 oz. pull-tops)

- *Eden® Baked Beans, with Sorghum & Mustard* (8 oz. pull-tops & 15 oz. size)

- *Eden® Chili Beans* (8 oz. pull-tops and 2 of the 15 oz. size for the *Chili Cornbread Pie*, page 92)

- *Eden® Garbanzo Beans* (8 oz. pull-tops, perfect for topping a salad)

**Find these at finer food stores like** Whole Foods Market.

**You can also order by calling:**
Whole Foods at 1-800-780-FOOD
*or*
Eden Foods at 1-888-424-EDEN

# Grocery List

Photo-copy permission granted for personal shopping use only.

| Restock | Par Stock | Item and size | For use in ... |
|---|---|---|---|

## Canned Fruit

| Restock | Par Stock | Item and size | For use in ... |
|---|---|---|---|
| _____ | 2 | Peaches, lite (16 oz) | **Serve with meals** |
| _____ | 2 | Pears, lite (16 oz) | **Serve with meals** |
| _____ | 1 | Apricots, lite (16 oz) | **Serve with meals** |
| _____ | 1 | Fruit cocktail, lite (16 oz) | **Serve with meals** |
| _____ | 1 | Mandarin oranges (15 oz) | *Ambrosia Breakfast Rice* *Almond Chicken Salad* |
| _____ | 6 | Pineapple tidbits, unsweetened (8 oz) | *Crunchy Apple Salad* *Sunshine Raisin Salad* *Cranberry Salad* *Ambrosia Breakfast Rice* |
| _____ | 1 | Pineapple crushed, unsweetened (8 oz) | *Carrot Cake* |
| _____ | 2 | Applesauce, unsweetened (large jar) | **Numerous desserts** **Serve with meals** |
| _____ | 1 | Cranberry sauce, jellied (16 oz) | *Cranberry Pork Roast* |

## Canned Vegetables and Beans

| Restock | Par Stock | Item and size | For use in ... |
|---|---|---|---|
| _____ | 2 | Corn (16 oz) | *Black Bean & Corn Salad* |
| _____ | optional | Cream style corn (16 oz) | **Serve with meals** |
| _____ | 1 | Wax beans (15 oz) | *5-Bean Salad* |
| _____ | 1 | Green beans (15 oz) | *5-Bean Salad* |
| _____ | 1 | Butter beans (15 oz) | *5-Bean Salad* |
| _____ | 1 | Pumpkin (29 oz) | *Pumpkin Surprise Pie* *Pumpkin Oatbran Bread ...* |
| _____ | 4 | Mushrooms, sliced (7 oz) | **Numerous maindishes** |
| _____ | 2 | Beets, sliced (15 oz) | **Serve with meals** **Great in salads** |
| _____ | 6 | Stewed tomatoes (14.5 oz) | **Numerous entrée's** |
| _____ | 1 | Tomato sauce or purée, low-sodium (16 oz) | *Mexican LaZonya* |
| _____ | 2 | Black beans (16 oz) | *Black Bean & Corn Salad* *Curried Chickpeas ...* *3 Bean Chili* *Mexican 5-Bean Soup* *Oriental Noodle Toss* |

# Hitting the Sauce

The following are selected samples of spaghetti sauces which meet the recommended criteria of **5 or fewer grams of fat and 800 mg or less of sodium** *per cup*.

| Per 1 cup of sauce | Fat (g) | Sodium (mg) |
|---|---|---|
| *Eden® Organic, no salt added** | 5 | 20 |
| *Colavita® (average of 4 flavors)* | 5 | 490 |
| *Classico® Spicy Red Pepper* | 5 | 540 |
| *Mama Rizzo's® (average of 4 flavors)* | 3 | 510 |
| *Healthy Choice®** or Ragu® Light*** | 1 | 780 |

*This is "salt to YOUR taste." Adding up to a ¼ tsp. of salt to each cup of sauce (500 mg of sodium) would still be within the recommended guideline for sodium.

**Average for the entire line.**

| For Comparison | | |
|---|---|---|
| *Newman's Own®* | 4 | 1,400 |
| *Progresso® Spaghetti Sauce* | 9 | 1,240 |
| *Barilla®* | 8 | 1,130 |

(Thirsty yet? With either one, you just consumed around ½ to ⅔ tsp of salt! Yuk!)

*Lickety-Split Meals*

# Grocery List

Photo-copy permission granted for personal shopping use only.

| Restock | Par Stock | Item and size | For use in ... |
|---|---|---|---|

## Canned Vegetables and Beans (continued)

| Restock | Par Stock | Item and size | For use in ... |
|---|---|---|---|
| _____ | 2 | **Pinto beans (48 oz jar)** | *Beanito Bean Dip* <br> *7-Layer Bean Dip* <br> *Burritos* |
| _____ | 1 | **Navy beans (15 oz)** | *Mexican 5-Bean Soup* |
| _____ | 2 | **Great Northern beans (24 oz jar)** | *Great Northern Tuna ...* <br> *White Beans & Penne Pasta* |
| _____ | 2 | **Kidney beans (15½ oz)** | *3-Bean Chili* <br> *Mexican 5-Bean Soup* <br> *Crockpot Fajitas* |
| _____ | 2 | **Garbanzo beans (15½ oz)** | *Curried Chickpeas ...* <br> *Oklahoma Bean Dip* |
| _____ | 1 | **Black-eyed peas (15½ oz)** | *Oklahoma Bean Dip* |
| _____ | 2 | **Chili beans (15 oz)** | *Chili Cornbread Pie* |
| _____ | 2 | **Baked beans (15 oz)** (vegetarian if possible) | *1 Minute Mini-Meals* |

## Canned Sauces

| Restock | Par Stock | Item and size | For use in ... |
|---|---|---|---|
| _____ | 4 | **Spaghetti sauce (28 oz)** *Healthy Choice®* (or see above) | **Numerous Pasta** <br> **Numerous Pizza** <br> **Numerous Stews** |
| _____ | 2 | **Sloppy Joe sauce (16 oz)** *Manwich®* | *Turkey Joes* |
| _____ | 1 | **Cacciatore sauce (24 oz)** *Chicken Tonight®* | *Chicken Cacciatore* |
| _____ | 1 | **Sweet and Sour (24 oz)** *Chicken Tonight®* | *Sweet & Sour Chicken* <br> **Stir-fry dinners** |

# Tip

## Sodium Alert!

While most of my recipes have less than 800 mg of sodium per entrée, some are higher. Eating an occasional entrée that is higher in sodium is not a problem for most people. However, for people who have been instructed to follow a "low-sodium diet," I recommend substituting sodium-free products for the reduced-sodium products whenever possible.

### For added sodium-reduction:

1. Use no salt added stewed tomatoes.

2. Use no salt added spaghetti sauce (see page 178 for suggestions).

3. Use no salt added canned beans instead of the conventional brands. While rinsing and draining beans reduces sodium by about ¹/₃, this can still leave a recipe too high in sodium. (Use the *Eden®* brand which has no salt added and you'll save 700-800 mg of sodium per can.)

4. Use no salt added canned chicken broth. (Use *Pritikin®* or *Health Valley®* instead of the ¹/₃ less sodium and you'll save about 400-700 mg of sodium per can.)

5. Buy reduced-sodium salsa. Often fresh salsa is lower in sodium than salsa in a jar. Check the label for less than 120 mg per 2 T. (Use *Gourmet Jose® Fresh Salsa* instead of *Pace® Picante* from a jar, and you'll save 280 mg per ¹/₄ cup.)

6. My recipes do not call for salt unless the recipe is particularly low in sodium and needs it for flavor. However, you can use a reduced-sodium salt (for instance *Morton's® Lite-Salt*) or complete salt substitute (like *No-Salt®*) or eliminate the salt I've called for altogether.

# Grocery List

Photo-copy permission granted
for personal shopping use only.

| Restock | Par Stock | Item and size | For use in ... |
|---------|-----------|---------------|----------------|

## Canned Meat

| Restock | Par Stock | Item and size | For use in ... |
|---------|-----------|---------------|----------------|
| _____ | 4 | Tuna, water packed (6 oz) | *Great Northern Tuna...* *Tuna Noodle Casserole* |
| _____ | 1 | Tuna, water packed (6 pack of 2 oz pull-tops) | **Desk drawer lunches** *1-Minute Mini-Meal* |
| _____ | 2 | Salmon, red or pink water packed (15+ oz) | *Salmon Burgers* *Herbed Salmon Spread...* |
| _____ | 4 | Chicken, white meat water packed (10 oz) | **1-Minute Mini-Meals** *Simple Baked Chicken...* *Almond Chicken Salad* *Chicken Dijon Stuffed...* *Eggless Salad Sandwiches* |
| _____ | optional | Sardines in mustard sauce (3+ oz) | **1-Minute Mini-Meals** |
| _____ | 1 | Crabmeat (6 oz) | *Crab Dip* |

## Condiments

| Restock | Par Stock | Item and size | For use in ... |
|---------|-----------|---------------|----------------|
| _____ | 1 | Ketchup | **Basic supply** |
| _____ | 1 | Mustard, regular | **Basic supply** |
| _____ | 1 | Dijon mustard *Grey Poupon®* | *Chicken Dijon Stuffed...* *Creamy Chicken Dijon* *Crispy Chicken Dijon* *Kickin' Chicken* *Potato Salad* |
| _____ | 1 | Honeycup mustard or other spicy flavor of your choice | **Turkey & tuna sandwiches** *Turkey & Hot Mustard ...* |
| _____ | optional | Pimentos, chopped (2 oz) | *Salmon Burgers* *Oven Baked Lentils and Rice* |
| _____ | 2 | Black olives, sliced (2.25 oz) | *Creamy Enchiladas* *Mexican Pizza* |
| _____ | 1 | Hot pepper rings or Jalepeño rings (12 oz jar) | *Mexican Black Beans* *Hot & Spicy Pizza* *3 Bean Chili* |
| _____ | 1 | Tabasco sauce | **Basic supply** |

## *Miracle Whip® Light*

While I'm aware that fat-free mayonnaise is available, I've found that for taste, many people prefer *Miracle Whip®* Light. Therefore, this is what I call for throughout the book. You are welcome to substitute fat-free if you wish, and you will save more fat grams if you do.

## What kind of oil is best?

For the answer, see page 9.

## What is chutney?

Chutney is the relish that traditionally accompanies Indian food and is made of chopped fruits and spices like ginger, allspice, cinnamon, garlic, vinegar, and hot pepper. Look for it in the specialty section of your grocery store. Trust me, it's a delicious spicy-sweet dynamo.

# Grocery List

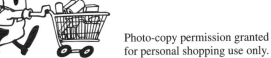

Photo-copy permission granted for personal shopping use only.

| Restock | Par Stock | Item and size | For use in ... |
|---|---|---|---|

## Condiments (continued)

| | | | |
|---|---|---|---|
| _____ | 1 | *Miracle Whip®* Light | **Basic supply** |
| _____ | 1 | **Thousand Island dressing, light or fat-free** | **Basic supply** |
| _____ | 1 | **Italian dressing, light or fat-free** | *Oklahoma Bean Dip*<br>*Chicken & Vegetables...*<br>*Marinated Vegetable Salad* |
| _____ | 1 | *Henri's® Light TAS-TEE® Private Blend* **or any light coleslaw dressing** | *Pasta & Potato Salad* |
| _____ | 1 | **Chutney, mango, pineapple or peach (8 oz) Gourmet specialty section** | *Chicken Chutney Pizza* |
| _____ | 1 | **Barbecue sauce** | *Chicken & Vegetables...*<br>*Polynesian Pizza* |
| _____ | 1 | **Seafood cocktail sauce (8 oz)** | *Shrimp Pizza & Crab Dip* |
| _____ | 1 | **Vinegar, balsamic** | **Basic supply** |
| _____ | 1 | **Vinegar, cider** | **Basic supply** |
| _____ | 1 | **Marsala wine** cooking wine | *Chicken Marsala* |

## Cooking Oils

*You can get by with nonstick spray and Canola oil for everything if you wish.*

| | | | |
|---|---|---|---|
| _____ | 1 | **Nonstick cooking spray** | **Basic supply** |
| _____ | 1 | **Canola oil (small)** | **Basic Supply**<br>**Desserts** |
| _____ | 1 | **Olive oil (small)** | **Italian dishes** |
| _____ | 1 | **Sesame oil (very small)** Toasted tastes best. | **Stir-fry dinners**<br>**Marinade**<br>*Oriental Noodle Toss* |

## Baking Supplies

| | | | |
|---|---|---|---|
| _____ | 1 | **Sugar (5-10 lb)** | **Basic supply** |
| _____ | 1 | **Brown sugar (2 lb)** | **Basic supply** |
| _____ | 1 | **Powdered sugar (2 lb)** | *Carrot Cake*<br>*Brownie Banana Split*<br>*Chewy Multi-Grain Bars* |
| _____ | 2 | **Honey (1 honey-bear and 1 re-fill jar)** | **Use on toast**<br>**instead of margarine**<br>*Breakfast in a Cookie* |

## Tip

# What is whole-wheat pastry flour?

"Whole-wheat pastry flour," sometimes called "whole-grain pastry flour," is very nutritious because it is a "whole grain" flour, yet is very light and cakey in texture, similar to that of white flour. It can be used in equal amounts to replace all-purpose flour in any "non-yeast" recipe. It makes wonderfully light cookies, cakes, muffins, and quick breads, and the best part is: only you will know that you used "healthy" flour!

**Where do you find it?**

Be aware that you will probably not find it in the standard flour section of your grocery store. It is considered specialty flour and may be found in the health food section among special brands like *Arrowhead Mills* or *Bob's Red Mill*. If you do not find it, request it from your grocer. I buy it in bulk quantities at finer food stores or co-ops. Please look for it. It really is worth the effort!

# Grocery List

| Restock | Par Stock | Item and size | For use in ... |
|---------|-----------|---------------|----------------|

## Baking Supplies (continued)

| Restock | Par Stock | Item and size | For use in ... |
|---------|-----------|---------------|----------------|
| _____ | 1 | Corn syrup (light vs dark) | *Cinnamon Nut Buns* *Oatmeal Cookies* *Chocolate No-Bakes* |
| _____ | 1 | Pancake syrup (light) | Basic supply |
| _____ | optional | Molasses | Basic supply |
| _____ | 1 | All-purpose flour (5 lbs) | Basic supply |
| _____ | 1 | Whole-wheat pastry flour (10 lbs) | Basic supply (see above) |
| _____ | 1 | Cornmeal, yellow (sm. canister) | Basic supply |
| _____ | 1 | *Bisquick®*, reduced-fat | *Pumpkin Pie Surprise* *Applesauce Dumplings* |
| _____ | 1 | Brownie mix, reduced-fat | *Brownie Banana Split* |
| _____ | 1 | Oatbran (1 lb. box) uncooked, similar to the way you buy *Cream of Wheat®* | *Breakfast in a Cookie* *Ambrosia Breakfast Rice* *Pumpkin Oatbran Bread* *Oatbran Muffins* |

| Restock | Par Stock | Item and size | For use in ... |
|---------|-----------|---------------|----------------|
| _____ | 1 | Oats, quick-cooking or old-fashioned (lg. canister) | *Scrumptious Swiss Oats...* *Banana Oat Pancakes* *Breakfast in a Cookie* *Chocolate No-Bakes* *Oatmeal Cookies* *Chocolate Chip Cookies* |
| _____ | optional | Multi-grain oatmeal (sm. canister) | *Multi-Grain Bars* |
| _____ | 1 | Non-fat dry milk (small) | *Breakfast in a Cookie* *Chocolate No-Bakes* |
| _____ | optional | Non-fat dry buttermilk | *Banana Nut Cake ...* |
| _____ | 1 | Evaporated skim milk (12 oz) | *Pasta Primavera* *Pumpkin Surprise Pie* |
| _____ | 1 | Baking powder | Basic supply |
| _____ | 1 | Baking soda | Basic supply |
| _____ | 1 | Cornstarch | Basic supply |
| _____ | 1 | Cocoa, unsweetened powder for baking | *Chocolate No-Bakes* *Chocolate Amaretto ...* |

## Tip

**Will I need to add on a second kitchen?**
**This *Lickety-Split* list is HUGE!**

Negative on the second kitchen, but you will need to do some cupboard cleaning. For instance, throw out the 5-year-old pudding boxes and cake decorating icing that you know it's time to toss. Bingo, a new shelf. You may even want to open up a couple of shelves in your laundry room to store extra canned items. What good is that broken flashlight anyway? Can't half of this stuff go in the garage? Two more new shelves. And yes, give up that junk drawer full of pens that don't write, old glasses you will never wear, and keys to what locks? I'm sure you can find another place

for these precious items, like the dumpster. If the thought of this is too much to bear, simply transfer the gems to a cardboard box and place them in the basement as a safe purgatory.

And lastly, what about that drawer full of the kids' crayons, coloring books, shoe-strings, and a yo-yo? If it doesn't help you cook, get it out of there! Presto! You now have two open drawers and 3 open pantry shelves for the extra *Lickety-Split* cooking supplies you will need!

# Grocery List

Photo-copy permission granted
for personal shopping use only.

## Baking Supplies (continued)

| Restock | Par Stock | Item and size | For use in ... |
| --- | --- | --- | --- |
| _____ | 1 | Tapioca, quick cooking<br>for thickening slow-cooker<br>recipes | Basic supply |
| _____ | 2 | Vanilla pudding, instant<br>(5.1 oz) | *Fresh Fruit Pie*<br>*Chocolate Chip Cookies* |
| _____ | 2 | Chocolate pudding<br>instant (5.9 oz) | *Chocolate-Chocolate Chip...* |
| _____ | 2 | Strawberry gelatin<br>sugarfree (0.6 oz) | *Fresh Fruit Pie*<br>*Cranberry Salad* |
| _____ | 1 | Marshmallows | **Hot chocolate**<br>**Fat-free snack** |
| _____ | 1 | Chocolate chips<br>store in freezer | *Chocolate Chip Cookies* |
| _____ | 1 | Chocolate chips<br>mini-morsels<br>Store in freezer. | *Choc. Amaretto Cheesecake* |
| _____ | 2 | Graham cracker crusts<br>regular or chocolate<br>(9 oz. deep dish size) | *Summer Fresh Fruit Pie* |

## Peanut Butter & Nuts

*(store nuts in freezer)*

| Restock | Par Stock | Item and size | For use in ... |
| --- | --- | --- | --- |
| _____ | 1 | Peanut butter<br>preferably natural<br>(sm. or lg.) | *Chocolate No-Bakes*<br>*Snacking* |
| _____ | 1 | Chopped walnuts (8 oz) | **Cookies**<br>**Stir-fries**<br>**Pancakes**<br>*Banana Nut Cake*<br>*Bread and Muffins* |
| _____ | 1 | Chopped pecans (8 oz) | *Ambrosia Breakfast Rice*<br>*Cinnamon Nut Buns*<br>*Dried Cherry and Broccoli...* |
| _____ | 1 | Slivered almonds (8 oz) | **Stir-fry dinners**<br>*Almond Chicken Salad* |

# Tip

## Money saving tip for buying spices

If your spices are over 3 years old, empty out the jars and head to your local bulk food store, health food store, or co-op, where you can purchase spices *by the ounce* (the staff will show you how). You can purchase as little as 1 tablespoon, if that's all you want to try. This would cost you less than 10 cents. You buy only what you know you'll need and replenish your supply with fresh after that. No more paying $3 for a jar of spice that you'll only use a little of!

# Grocery List

Photo-copy permission granted for personal shopping use only.

| Restock | Par Stock | Item and size | For use in ... |
|---------|-----------|---------------|----------------|

## Spices and Flavorings

| Restock | Par Stock | Item and size | For use in ... |
|---------|-----------|---------------|----------------|
| _____ | 1 | Vanilla (lg) | Basic supply |
| _____ | 1 | Lemon extract (sm) | Basic supply |
| _____ | 1 | Almond extract (sm) | Basic supply |
| _____ | 1 | Basil | Basic supply |
| _____ | 1 | Cayenne pepper | Basic supply |
| _____ | 1 | Chili powder (lg) | Basic supply |
| _____ | optional | Chinese Five Spice | Basic supply |
| _____ | 1 | Cinnamon (lg) | Basic supply |
| _____ | 1 | Cloves | Basic supply |
| _____ | 1 | Crushed red pepper flakes | Basic supply |
| _____ | optional | Coriander | Basic supply |
| _____ | 1 | Cumin, ground (lg) | Basic supply |
| _____ | optional | Cumin Seed | Basic supply |
| _____ | 1 | Curry powder | Basic supply |
| _____ | 1 | Dill | Basic supply |
| _____ | 1 | Garlic powder | Basic supply |

| Restock | Par Stock | Item and size | For use in ... |
|---------|-----------|---------------|----------------|
| _____ | 1 | Marjoram | *Creamy Cauliflower Soup* |
| _____ | 1 | Dried mustard | Basic supply |
| _____ | 1 | Oregano (lg) | Basic supply |
| _____ | 1 | Onion flakes | Basic supply |
| _____ | 1 | Paprika (Lg.) | Basic supply |
| _____ | 1 | Pepper corns, whole black | Basic supply |
| _____ | 1 | Poultry seasoning | Basic supply |
| _____ | 1 | Pumpkin Pie Spice | Basic supply |
| _____ | 1 | Rosemary | Basic supply |
| _____ | 1 | Sage | Basic supply |
| _____ | 1 | Salt | Basic supply |
| _____ | 1 | Savory | *Creamy Cauliflower Soup* |
| _____ | 1 | Sesame seeds | Basic supply |
| _____ | 1 | Salt (consider lite or salt sub.) | Basic supply |
| _____ | 1 | Thyme | Basic supply |
| _____ | 1 | Mrs. Dash or Spike | Basic supply |
| _____ | 1 | Taco seasoning (pkt) | Basic supply |
| _____ | 1 | Fajita seasoning (pkt) | Basic supply |

# What is tamari?

For information, see page 101.

# Iron Fortified Cereals: The good and not so good

While 100% fortification of the RDA of iron is great for people who run low in iron (like heavily menstruating women or recent blood donors), it may not be so good for others who are not low in iron. Recent concerns are based on the understanding that iron is a pro-oxidant which can be harmful in excess. Many health profession-als suggest iron only be supplemented when a person is in need of it. Therefore, you may prefer to choose cereals that have been fortified with no more than 25% of iron.

P.S. It's smart to use iron fortified cereals or iron supplements for 4 weeks after donating blood.

## Cereal Selection Tips

For healthy cereal, follow these label-reading criteria:

1. **Fat:** 2 grams of fat or less per serving. (Keep in mind that whole grains, including oats, have up to 2 grams of naturally occurring fat. The goal is to avoid cereals with "added fats.")

2. **Fiber:** 4 or more grams of fiber per serving is ideal.

3. **Sugars:** Less than 10 grams of sugar. (The lower the better.) Every 4 grams equals 1 teaspoon of sugar.

# Grocery List

Photo-copy permission granted
for personal shopping use only.

| Restock | Par Stock | Item and size | For use in ... |
|---------|-----------|---------------|----------------|

## Cereal

*The following is a few of my favorite cereals,
meeting my criteria for fat, fiber and taste.*

| Restock | Par Stock | Item and size | For use in ... |
|---------|-----------|---------------|----------------|
| _____ | | **Wheat germ** <br> Tastes best toasted. | **Sprinkle on cereal** <br> **Use in brownies** <br> ***Whole-Grain Pancakes*** |
| _____ | | ***Grapenuts*®** | **Breakfast** |
| _____ | | **Shredded Wheat with Bran** | **Breakfast** |
| _____ | | **Frosted Shredded Wheat** | |
| | | | **Breakfast and finger snack** |
| _____ | | ***Quaker*® Oat Bran (hexagon chex in the red box)** | **Breakfast and finger snack** |
| _____ | | ***Quaker*® Oat Squares** | **Breakfast and finger snack** |
| | | **Corn Bran** | **Breakfast and finger snack** |
| _____ | | ***Wheaties*®** | **Breakfast** |
| _____ | | **Bran Flakes** | **Breakfast** |

## Ethnic Foods

| Restock | Par Stock | Item and size | For use in ... |
|---------|-----------|---------------|----------------|
| _____ | 2 | **Refried beans, fat-free (16 oz)** | **Quick burritos** <br> ***Chicken & Bean Enchiladas*** |
| _____ | 1 | **Enchilada sauce** <br> ***Old El Paso*® (10 oz)** | ***Chicken & Bean Enchiladas*** |
| _____ | 2 | **Green chilies, chopped (4 oz)** | ***Creamy Enchiladas*** <br> ***Southwest Pizza*** <br> ***South of the Border Roll-ups*** <br> ***Mexican 5-Bean Soup*** |
| _____ | 2 | **Waterchestnuts, sliced (8 oz)** | ***Spinach Dip*** <br> ***Saucy Almond Chicken...*** |
| _____ | 3 | **Salsa, hot, medium or mild (16 oz)** | **Numerous entrées** <br> **Snacking** |
| _____ | 1 | **Soy sauce reduced-sodium (lg)** | **Numerous entrées** <br> **"Appeteasers"** |
| _____ optional | | **Tamari sauce reduced-sodium (sm)** | ***Marinated Sesame Chicken*** <br> ***Kabobs*** <br> ***Simple Tofu Bites*** |
| _____ | *2* | **Sweet n' sour sauce** <br> ***LaChoy*® (10 oz)** | ***Easiest Stir-Fry Ever*** |

(See page 186 for more selection suggestions!)

# Nutrients lost when whole-wheat is refined

| 86% | Vitamin E | 75% | Fiber |
| 81% | Niacin* | 70% | Vitamin B-6 |
| 80% | Riboflavin* | 67% | Folic Acid |
| 77% | Thiamin* | 50% | Pantothenic acid |

* Replaced commercially after refinement as required by law.

***Now you know WHY I make all the fuss about whole-wheat flour!***

## Why buy Lavash?

For information, see page 47.

*Lickety-Split Meals*

# Grocery List

Photo-copy permission granted for personal shopping use only.

| Restock | Par Stock | Item and size | For use in … |
|---|---|---|---|

## Bread Products

*Buy according to your family's needs, all breads freeze well!*

| Restock | Par Stock | Item and size | For use in … |
|---|---|---|---|
| _____ | 1-4 | 100% whole-wheat bread, *Brownberry®*, *Koepplinger's®*, *Healthy Choice®*, *Roman Meal®* | Sandwiches Toast |
| _____ | 0-1 | Rye or Pumpernickel bread, round loaf | *Spinach Dip in …* |
| _____ | 0-6 | Pita bread, whole-wheat | Pita sandwiches *Pita Pizza* |
| _____ | 0-6 | Hamburger buns, whole-wheat if possible | *Salmon Burgers* |
| _____ | 0-12 | Rolls, whole-wheat or nine-grain | Serve with meals |
| _____ | 0-6 | English muffins, whole-grain if possible | Breakfasts |

| Restock | Par Stock | Item and size | For use in … |
|---|---|---|---|
| _____ | 1-12 | Bagels, whole-grain if possible | Breakfasts Snacking *1 Minute Mini-Meals* |
| _____ | 1 | Flour tortillas, 8" (pkg of 10) fat-free, no lard | *South of the Border Roll-ups* *Burritos* *Chicken Enchiladas* *Crockpot® Fajitas* *Mexican LaZonya*    Option for corn tortillas |
| _____ | 1 | Corn tortillas (pkg of 10) These freeze well. | *Mexican LaZonya* |
| _____ | 1-2 | Lavash, flat breads (pkg of 6) | Roll-up sandwiches Appeteasers |
| _____ | 1-4 | Pizza crusts, ready-made *Boboli®* or *Oliveri®* | Friday night pizza's |
| _____ | 1-4 | Rice cakes popcorn cakes (pkg) | Snacking *1 Minute Mini-Meals* |
| _____ | 1 | Bread crumbs unseasoned (canister) | *Tantalizing Turkey Loaf* *Crispy Chicken Dijon* |

# Tip

## Tips for selecting a "healthy" commercial stir-fry sauce

Comparing the labels for stir-fry sauces can be quite confusing. Sometimes the serving size is 1 T, sometimes it's 1/2 cup! What should be the appropriate serving size? I find 1/4 cup works nicely, and an 8-ounce jar serves 4 very well. In the sweet and sour type sauces, fat is not an issue but sodium is. Take a look at the following to get an idea of what's out there. I've adjusted all the portions to 1/4 cup. (That's 4 tablespoons.)

Sodium per 1/4 cup

| | |
|---|---|
| *Chicken Tonight® Sweet & Sour Sauce* | 170 mg |
| *LaChoy® Sweet and Sour Sauce* | 210 mg |
| *Kraft® Sweet 'n Sour Sauce* | 250 mg |
| *Kikkoman® Sweet & Sour Sauce* | 380 mg |
| *LaChoy® Stir-Fry Vegetables 'n Sauce* | 410 mg |
| *Lawry's® Stir-Fry Oriental Style Cooking Sauce* | 1,320 mg |
| *Kame® Szechuan Sauce* | 1,640 mg |

As you can see, some are a salt mine!

**Your goal is 250 mg or less per 1/4 cup.**

# Grocery List

| Restock | Par Stock | Item and size | For use in ... |
|---------|-----------|---------------|----------------|

## Snacks

| Restock | Par Stock | Item and size | For use in ... |
|---------|-----------|---------------|----------------|
| _____ | 1 | **Chocolate syrup** *Hershey's®* (squeeze bottle kind) | **Chocolate milk** **Drizzling over fruit** *Brownie Banana Split* |
| _____ | 1 | **Hot cocoa mix** | **Snacking** |
| _____ | 1-2 | **Baked tortilla chips** *Tostitos®* | *Guiltless Nacho's Supreme* *7 Layer Bean Dip* *Oklahoma Bean Dip* *Crockpot® Fajitas* *Mexican Black Beans* *Mexican 5-Bean Soup* |
| _____ | 1-2 | **Potato chips** **Baked Lays®** | **Snacking** **Sandwiches** **Soups** |
| _____ | 0-1 | *Fig Newtons®* **regular or fat-free** | **Snacking** **Desserts** **Lunchbox treat** |

| Restock | Par Stock | Item and size | For use in ... |
|---------|-----------|---------------|----------------|
| _____ | 0-1 | **Gingersnaps** | **Snacking** **Desserts** **"Ice cream" sandwiches** **Lunchbox treat** |
| _____ | 0-12 | **Fortune cookies** (only 30 calories each, fat-free and fun) | **Stir-fry dinners** |
| _____ | 1 | **Saltines, whole-wheat** | **Snacking** **Soups** |
| _____ | 1-2 | *Triscuits®*, **reduced-fat** | **Snacking** **1-Minute Mini-Meals** |
| _____ | 1 | **Graham crackers, low-fat** | **Snacking** **Desserts** **"Ice cream" sandwiches** |
| _____ | 1-2 | **Popcorn, microwave** *Orville Redenbacher® Smart Pop® or Pop Secret® by Request* | **Snacking** **Soups** |

## Margarine or butter?

For information see page 151.

## Light cream cheese and sour cream vs. fat-free

I find that many people do not like the taste of fat-free cream cheese but love the taste of light cream cheese. Likewise, while some recipes taste fine using fat-free sour cream, others do not. To keep everything tasty and shopping simple, all recipes call for light cream cheese and light sour cream. I have carefully calculated and used the amounts that still allow the overall recipe to meet the recommended guidelines. Again, you are welcome to substitute fat-free if you wish, and you will save more fat grams if you do.

*Lickety-Split Meals*

## Should we give eggs a break?

Egg yolks certainly do have a lot of cholesterol (a full day's allowance in just 1) AND 5 grams of fat. Egg whites, on the other hand are fat and cholesterol free. The recommendation is to consume fewer than 4 egg yolks a week and fewer (or none) if you have high cholesterol.

I choose to limit egg yolks by diluting them with egg whites, as called for in these recipes. I find this convenient and economical. This provides some of the color and texture of eggs, while staying within the weekly recommendation. However, to completely omit egg yolks from your diet, replace each egg yolk with 2 whites. You can also use egg substitutes: 1/4 cup replaces 1 egg.

# Grocery List

| Restock | Par Stock | Item and size | For use in ... |
|---|---|---|---|

## Eggs & Dairy

| Restock | Par Stock | Item and size | For use in ... |
|---|---|---|---|
| _____ | 2 | Dozen eggs (or egg substitute) | Various uses |
| _____ | 1-2 | Skim or ½ % milk (gal) | Various uses |
| _____ | 2 | Soy milk, optional | Pancakes<br>Baking<br>Cereals<br>*Scrumptious Swiss ...* |
| _____ | 1 | Margarine, light (tub) | Used in one recipe only:<br>*Chocolate No-Bakes* |
| _____ | 1 | Spray butter, *I Can't Believe It's Not Butter*® | Variety of uses |
| _____ | 1 | Sour cream, light (16 oz) fat-free if you prefer | *Creamy Chicken Enchiladas*<br>*Chicken and Bean...*<br>*Chicken Paprikash*<br>*Simple Baked Chicken...*<br>*Creamy Chicken Dijon*<br>*Chicken Dijon Stuffed...*<br>*Guiltless Nachos Supreme*<br>*Beef Stroganoff*<br>*"Appeteasers"*<br>*Spinach Dip*<br>*South of the Border Roll-ups* |

| Restock | Par Stock | Item and size | For use in ... |
|---|---|---|---|
| _____ | 1 | Cream cheese, light (8 oz) fat-free if you prefer | *"Appeteasers"*<br>*Turkey and Hot Mustard...*<br>*South of the Border...*<br>*Chocolate-Amaretto...*<br>*Carrot Cake*<br>*Brownie Banana Split*<br>*Oatmeal Cookies* |
| _____ | 1 | Cottage cheese, light or non-fat (16 oz) | *1-Minute Mini-Meals* |
| _____ | 1 | Ricotta cheese, light (15 oz) buy 2 for double batch | *LaZonya* |
| _____ | 1 | String cheese, part-skim mozzarella | *1-Minute Mini-Meals* |
| _____ | 1 | Non-fat plain yogurt (16 oz) | Baking<br>Mixing with *Miracle Whip*®<br>  Light 50-50<br>*Smoothies* |
| _____ | 6 | Non-fat fruited yogurts (8 oz) optional | Snacking<br>Breakfasts<br>Lunches |

## How does cheese fit into a healthy diet?

I would really miss cheese if I had to give it up, wouldn't you? And thanks to so many low-fat and fat-free cheeses on the market, we don't have to!

The ideal is to use fat-free cheese. But what about taste? There are great tasting low-fat cheeses available, but they run 6-7 grams of fat per ounce, which is TOO MUCH. So, when it comes to shredded cheese, why not mix fat-free with reduced-fat for a great compromise? I recommend *Sharp 2% Milk by Kraft®* and I mix it 50-50 with the fat-free cheese by *Kraft®*

or *Healthy Choice®*. This produces a wonderful, tasty, and evenly melting cheese for only 3 grams of fat per ounce. I do this with both cheddar and mozzarella. This is the "reduced-fat shredded cheese" I am referring to in all recipes. If you prefer to use the fat-free exclusively, please do!

The next trick is to keep your portion to 1 ounce only (equal to ¼ cup of shredded cheese). This actually goes a long way melted across a serving of broccoli, pizza or nachos! Enjoy!

### Parmesan cheese

Parmesan cheese *is* high in fat. However, the amounts called for in this book do not add unreasonable amounts of fat. I therefore suggest using regular Parmesan cheese and have calculated the recipes accordingly. If you would like to use fat-free instead, please do. (I personally have had great results mixing regular and fat-free, 50-50.)

*Lickety-Split Meals*

# Grocery List

| Restock | Par Stock | Item and size | For use in ... |
|---------|-----------|---------------|----------------|

## Eggs & Dairy (continued)

| Restock | Par Stock | Item and size | For use in ... |
|---------|-----------|---------------|----------------|
| _____ | 1 | Parmesan cheese, regular or fat-free | **Numerous entrées** |
| _____ | 1 | Mozzarella, shredded, fat-free, *Kraft®* or *Healthy Choice®* | **Numerous entrées** |
| _____ | 1 | Mozzarella, shredded part-skim | **Numerous entrées** |
| _____ | 2 | Cheddar cheese, shredded fat-free, *Kraft®* or *Healthy Choice®* | **Numerous entrées** |
| _____ | 2 | Cheddar cheese, sharp shredded, *2% Milk by Kraft®* | **Numerous entrées** |

*Make your own reduced fat yet still delicious cheese, by mixing the two white cheeses and two cheddar cheeses together. Do this when putting groceries away so you don't forget. Freezes well!*

## Convenience Meat

| Restock | Par Stock | Item and size | For use in ... |
|---------|-----------|---------------|----------------|
| _____ | 1-2 | Smoked turkey breast slices (lb) | **Sandwiches** *Turkey Roll-ups with Lavash* |
| _____ | 1 | Ham, 98% fat-free chunk or slices (lb) | **Pizza topping** *Split Pea Soup* *Breakfast Casserole* *Scrambled Omelette* |

*(When putting groceries away, chop and divide ham into 8- 2 oz portions. Freeze in air-tight bags).*

| Restock | Par Stock | Item and size | For use in ... |
|---------|-----------|---------------|----------------|
| _____ | optional | **Canadian bacon** | |

## Seafood

| Restock | Par Stock | Item and size | For use in ... |
|---------|-----------|---------------|----------------|
| _____ | | Orange Roughy, fresh or frozen filets (lg bag) | *Broiled Orange Roughy* |
| _____ | | Trout, fresh (2 lbs) | *Delicate Baked Trout* |
| _____ | | Shrimp, frozen, cooked ready to eat (12 oz bag) | *Shrimp Pizza* *Pasta Primavera* |

**What about pork?**

See page 134 for good news about today's pork!

## Red meat. Where do you draw the line?

All you have to do is follow these 3 guidelines, and you can enjoy red meat up to 3 times per week!

**#1 Choose lean.** NOT prime rib, but tenderloin or filet mignon; NOT hamburger but ground sirloin. Whatever you do, don't worry about it costing more, because guideline #3 will offset the cost. Besides, you either pay now…or you pay later!

**#2 Trim well.** Trim all meats *meticulously*.

**#3 Think small.** Keep your portion to 4 ounces. (This looks like the size of a deck of cards.) Fill the plate up with lots of vegetables and a big baked potato. Of course slicing the meat up for stir-fry or pepper steak works great. Try it!

# Grocery List

## Poultry • Beef • Pork

| Restock | Par Stock | Item and size | For use in ... |
|---|---|---|---|
| ____ | | **Chicken breasts, skinless, boneless (4 lbs)** Buy individually frozen or, to save on sodium, buy fresh and freeze each breast half individually | *Marinated Sesame...* *Creamy Chicken Dijon* *Skillet Chicken &...* *Chicken Marsala* *Chicken Paprikash* *Southwest Chicken Pizza* *Chicken Chutney Pizza* *Saucy Almond Chicken...* *Sweet & Sour Stir-fry* *Kickin' Chicken* *Chicken & Vegetables...* *Creamy Chicken Enchiladas* *Crockpot® Fajitas* *Chicken Cacciatore* *Sweet & Sour Chicken* |
| ____ | 1 | **Chicken leg quarters** optional (thigh and drumsticks, pkg. of 4) | **To accompany** *Oven Fries and Ratatouille* |
| ____ | 4 | **Turkey, extra-lean ground breast (1 lb. pkgs.)** | *Unstuffed Peppers* *Veggie Sghetti* *Tantalizing Turkey-Loaf* *3-Bean Chili* *Turkey Joes* |

| Restock | Par Stock | Item and size | For use in ... |
|---|---|---|---|
| ____ | 1 | **Turkey tenderloin boneless (1 lb.)** | *Turkey Vegetable Stew* |
| ____ | 1 | **Turkey tenderloin boneless, slices or cutlets (1 lb.)** | *Parmesan Turkey Cutlets...* |
| ____ | 1 - 2 | **Lean sirloin or flank steak (1 ± 2 lbs.)** | *Easy Pepper Steak Stir-Fry* *Beef Barley Soup* *Beef Stroganoff* |
| ____ | | **Pork tenderloin (2 lbs.)** | *Cranberry Pork Roast* *Optional in Sweet & Sour...* *Gypsy Stew* *Crockpot® Fajitas* |

## Alcohol for Cooking

*Purchase small bottles.*

| Restock | Par Stock | Item and size | For use in ... |
|---|---|---|---|
| ____ | 1 | **White wine** | *Chicken and Vegetables...* *Oven-Baked Lentils and Rice* |
| ____ | 1 | **Amaretto** | *Chocolate Amaretto ...* |
| ____ | 1 | **Banana liqueur** | *Flaming Bananas Foster* |
| ____ | 1 | **White Rum** Frozen or Bottled Juices | *Flaming Bananas Foster* |

# Tip

## Will I need to buy a deep freezer?

It's definitely a plus to own a deep freezer. But if you don't have one, simply plan on extra strict cleaning and organizing to optimize capacity. Either way, be sure to reserve a separate area for vegetables, meats, juices, etc. so you can keep things rotated (first in, first out) and find things FAST.

**Remember:**

- Use your fresh produce early in the week and frozen later in the week.

- A full variety of frozen vegetables is nice to have on hand.

- A one pound bag of vegetables should serve 3-4, not 5-6.

- Frozen fruits are a delicious snack eaten frozen or just partially thawed.

- Try chocolate syrup drizzled over frozen cherries for "healthy" chocolate covered cherries!

# Grocery List

Photo-copy permission granted
for personal shopping use only.

| Restock | Par Stock | Item and size | For use in ... |
|---|---|---|---|

## Frozen Veggies

*Yes, I do suggest having all these on hand, in addition to having a full drawer of fresh. Use the fresh early in the week and the frozen later in the week.*

| Restock | Par Stock | Item and size | For use in ... |
|---|---|---|---|
| _____ | 1 | Corn (16 oz) | **Various entrées** |
| _____ | 1 | Peas (16 oz) | **Various entrées** |
| _____ | 1 | Lima beans (16 oz) | **Various entrées** |
| _____ | 1 | Mixed vegetables (16 oz) | **Various entrées** |
| _____ | 1 | Cut green beans (16 oz) | **Various entrées** |
| _____ | 1 | Whole green beans (16 oz) | **Various entrées** |
| _____ | 1 | California blend (16 oz) broccoli, cauliflower and carrots | |
| _____ | 1 | Mixed stir-fry vegetables (16 oz) *Freshlike®* Broccoli Stirfry (with onions & water chestnuts) | *Easiest Stir-Fry Ever* |
| _____ | 4 | Spinach, chopped (10 oz) | *Veggie Sghetti* *Unstuffed Peppers* *Gypsy Stew* *Spinach Dip* |

| Restock | Par Stock | Item and size | For use in ... |
|---|---|---|---|
| _____ | 1 | Peas pods or snow peas (10 oz) | **Various entrées** |
| _____ | 1 | Carrots, crinkle cut (10 oz) | **Various entrées** |
| _____ | 1 | Asparagus (10 oz) use fresh if you prefer | *Chicken Dijon Stuffed…* *Creamy Chicken Dijon* |
| _____ | 1 | Hash browns with onions and peppers, *Ore Ida®* O'Brien Potatoes | *Breakfast Casserole* *Scrambled Omelette* *Cheesy Potato Skillet* *Cheesy Scrambled Tofu* |
| _____ | 1 | Potato Wedges with skins *Ore Ida®* | *Kickin' Chicken w/Fries* |

## Frozen or Bottled Juices

| Restock | Par Stock | Item and size | For use in ... |
|---|---|---|---|
| _____ | 4 | Orange juice concentrate (cans) | Snacks |
| _____ | 1 | *V-8®* juice, low-sodium (1 qt. jar) | *Miracle Soup* *3 Bean Chili* |
| _____ | 1 | *V-8®* juice, low-sodium (6 pack of 6 ounce cans) | Snacks |
| _____ | 4 | 100% fruit juice, your choice of flavors, *Dole®* | Snacks |

# Grocery Store Checkout
# One Minute Stress Buster

Whew! Aren't you glad you're done? Now for the tortuous checkout. While waiting there (instead of musing about the slow line, reading tabloids, or drooling over the chocolate bars), refresh your body by doing some deep breathing, stretching, and strengthening exercises.

1. Lift your hands straight up over your head and stretch. Take a deep breath in. Exhale. (Care not what others think of you!) Repeat twice.

2. Raise up on your toes, hold, and lower (calf-raises). Once you get good, stand on one foot at a time and work each calf separately.

3. Looking first, lift your leg straight out behind you. Feel the muscle in your buttocks contract. Alternate legs.

4. Standing with feet shoulder-width apart, curl your foot up to almost kick your behind. Feel the muscle in the back of your leg contract. Alternate feet back and forth.

Before you know it, it will be time to start unloading your cart, and you will hardly have noticed that the line was slow, or that the candy bars were a temptation.

**P.S. No matter what you've been doing all day, chained to your computer, running errands, chasing children, or flying from airport to airport, give these 1 minute stress busters a try!**

# Grocery List

Photo-copy permission granted
for personal shopping use only.

| Restock | Par Stock | Item and size | For use in ... |
|---|---|---|---|

## Frozen Fruit

| | 1 | **Strawberries** (12 oz bag) | **Snacks** *Smoothies* |
| | 1 | **Blueberries (12 oz bag)** | **Snacks** *Smoothies* *Blueberry Buckle* |
| | 1 | **Cherries (12 oz bag)** | **Snacks** |

## Frozen Miscellaneous

| | 1 | **Honey-wheat bread dough (pkg. of 3)** | *Glazed Cinnamon Nut Buns* |
| | 1 | **Cheese ravioli (25 oz bag)** | *Ravioli Stew* |

*Choose 1 or 2 of the following:*

| | 1 | **Vanilla ice cream or frozen yogurt low-fat or fat-free, *Edy's*® or *Healthy Choice*®** | *Blueberry Buckle* *Flaming Bananas Foster* *Applesauce Dumplings* |
| | optional | **Lemon or Raspberry Sorbet** | **Dessert** |
| | optional | **Fudgesicles** | **Dessert** |
| | optional | **Frozen yogurt bars** | **Dessert** |

| Restock | Item and size |
|---|---|

## Cleaning Supplies

____  _____
____  _____
____  _____

____  _____

## Personal Hygiene

____  _____
____  _____
____  _____

____  _____

## Paper Goods

____  _____
____  _____
____  _____

____  _____

| Restock | Item and size |
|---|---|

## Laundry Supplies

____  _____
____  _____
____  _____

____  _____

## Pet Supplies

____  _____
____  _____
____  _____

____  _____

## Optional Items

____  _____
____  _____
____  _____

____  _____

*Lickety-Split Meals*

Frozen Fruit / Frozen Miscellaneous / Personal Items

# Index

# INDEX Recipes by Topic

# INDEX Recipes by Topic

# INDEX Recipes Alphabetically

# INDEX Tips

# INDEX Tips

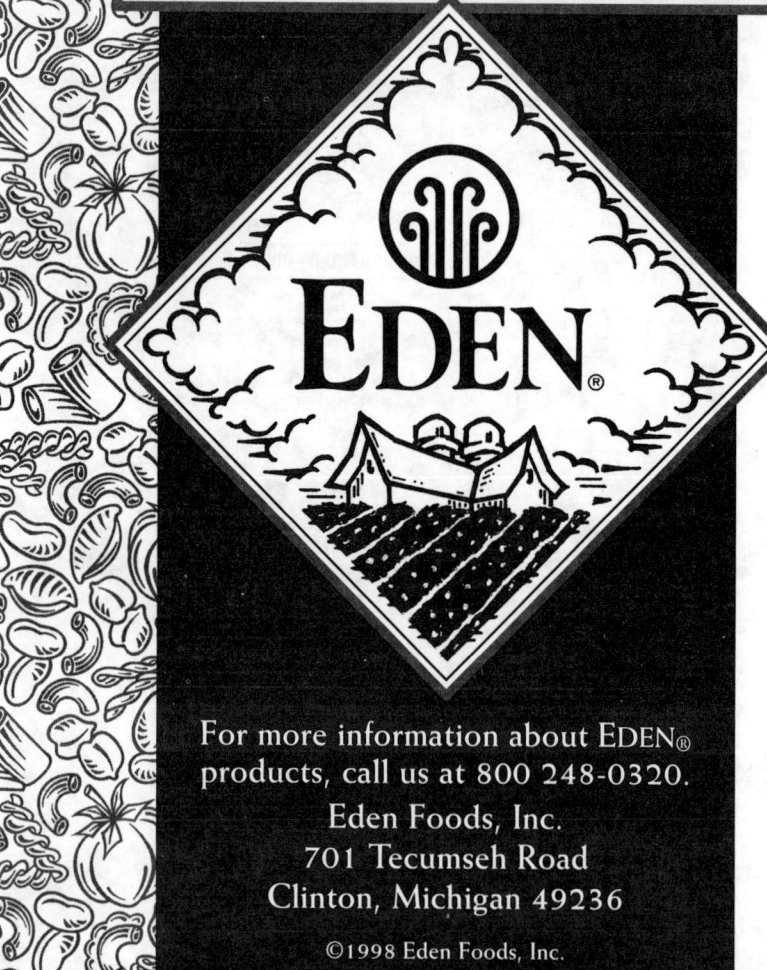

# ORDER FORM
## Give the Gift of *Lickety-Split Meals!*

### PRICING

| Quantity | Price | Shipping |
|----------|-------|----------|
| 1 book | $ 23.95 each | FREE |
| 3 books | $ 22.95 each | FREE |
| 5 books | $ 21.95 each | FREE |
| **10 books** | **$ 19.95 each** | **FREE** |

**Buy in quantity and save!**

### ORDER FORM

Qty. _____ x Price $ _____ = Total $ _____

(x .06) 6% Sales Tax (MI only) _____

Shipping _____ FREE _____

TOTAL DUE $ _____

**Happy *Lickety-Split* cooking!**

*Thank you for your order!*

### ALSO AVAILABLE

✓ **Reusable Pocket-Size Grocery Guide**

✓ **Wipe Erase Weekly Menu Board**

✓ **Lickety-Split Apron**

✓ **Video & Audio Programs**

*Call for more information and a complete catalog!*

---

## Plan ahead! Buy now! Save time & money!

- Birthdays
- Mother's Day
- Father's Day
- Christmas
- Weddings
- Showers
- Anniversaries
- Employee Wellness
- House Warmings
- Graduations
- Thank Yous

### Choose from 3 ways to order:

**1** **Mail** your order to ➠ (Check or credit card orders)

**Zonya Health International
PO Box 275
Walled Lake, MI 48390-0275**

**2** **Call** anytime, **toll-free** ➠ **1-888-884-LEAN**
(Credit card orders)
*If you get our voice mail, it's very trustworthy!*

**3** **Fax** your order, anytime ➠ **248-960-8157**
(Credit card orders)

**Make checks payable to:** Zonya Health International

Credit Cards: ☐ Visa ☐ Mastercard Exp. Date _____

Credit Card Number: _____

Signature _____

Name (please print) _____

Your phone number _____

Today's date _____

Ship to _____

_____

_____

_____

---

## ORDER FORM — The perfect gift for all occasions !

# ORDER FORM
## Give the Gift of *Lickety-Split Meals!*

---

### PRICING

| Quantity | Price | Shipping |
|----------|-------|----------|
| 1 book | $ 23.95 each | FREE |
| 3 books | $ 22.95 each | FREE |
| 5 books | $ 21.95 each | FREE |
| **10 books** | **$ 19.95 each** | **FREE** |

*Buy in quantity and save !*

### ORDER FORM

Qty. _____ x Price $ _____ = Total $ _____

(x .06) 6% Sales Tax (MI only) _____

*Happy Lickety-Split cooking!*

Shipping _____FREE_____

TOTAL DUE $ _____

*Thank you for your order!*

### ALSO AVAILABLE

✓ **Reusable Pocket-Size Grocery Guide**
✓ **Wipe Erase Weekly Menu Board**
✓ **Lickety-Split Apron**
✓ **Video & Audio Programs**

*Call for more information and a complete catalog!*

---

### Plan ahead! Buy now! Save time & money!

- Birthdays
- Mother's Day
- Father's Day
- Christmas
- Weddings
- Showers
- Anniversaries
- Employee Wellness
- House Warmings
- Graduations
- Thank Yous

### Choose from 3 ways to order:

**1** **Mail** your order to ➠ **Zonya Health International**
(Check or credit card orders) **PO Box 275**
**Walled Lake, MI 48390-0275**

**2** **Call** anytime, **toll-free** ➠ **1-888-884-LEAN**
(Credit card orders)
*If you get our voice mail, it's very trustworthy!*

**3** **Fax** your order, anytime ➠ **248-960-8157**
(Credit card orders)

**Make checks payable to:** Zonya Health International

Credit Cards: ☐ Visa ☐ Mastercard Exp. Date _____

Credit Card Number: _____

Signature _____

Name (please print) _____

Your phone number _____

Today's date _____

Ship to _____

_____

_____

_____

---

## ORDER FORM — The perfect gift for all occasions !

## What do you think of Lickety-Split Meals?

It would be just the best, if you could take a moment to share your opinions about this book. It is my life's work to update and improve it with every reprint. All responses will be acknowledged!

**In advance, I Thank YOU!!!**

**Fax to:** (248) 960-8157
**Email to:** zonya@tir.com
**Mail to:** ZHI Publishing
P.O. Box 275
Walled Lake, MI 48390

Your name, address, phone and email:

_____

_____

_____

_____

|  | Poor | | | | Great! |
|---|---|---|---|---|---|
| **The recipe layout** | 1 | 2 | 3 | 4 | 5 |

Comments: _____

| **The grocery list/guide** | 1 | 2 | 3 | 4 | 5 |
|---|---|---|---|---|---|

Comments: _____

| **Page by page health and fitness tips** | 1 | 2 | 3 | 4 | 5 |
|---|---|---|---|---|---|

Comments: _____

| **The flip-chart design, easel back & page numbering system** | 1 | 2 | 3 | 4 | 5 |
|---|---|---|---|---|---|

Comments: _____

| **The graphic design & cartoon-like illustrations** | 1 | 2 | 3 | 4 | 5 |
|---|---|---|---|---|---|

Comments: _____

**Has this book helped you to lose weight? Lower your cholesterol? Save you time?**
If so, please explain!

_____

_____

_____

**Recipes I'd like to see added:** (If you have a recipe you'd like to submit, please send it on!) _____

_____

**Recipes I'd like to see changed:**

_____

_____